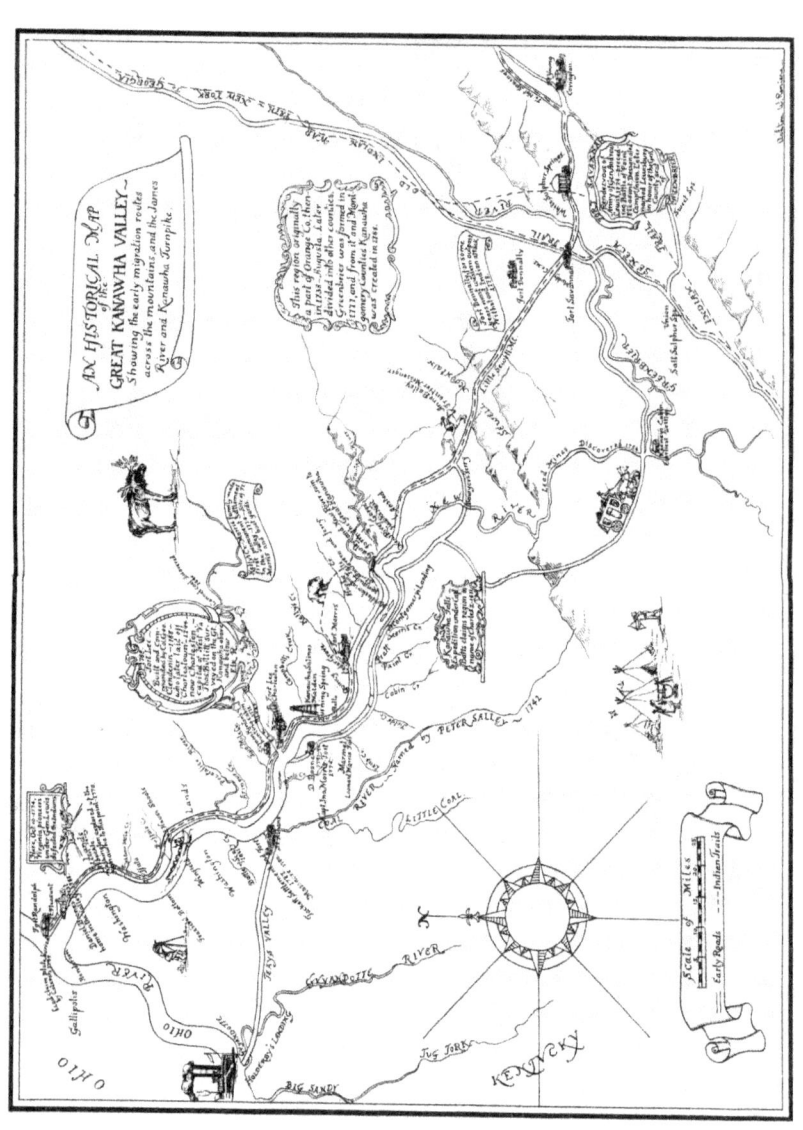

Pioneers and Their Homes on Upper Kanawha

by

Ruth Woods Dayton

Drawings by
Naomi S. Hosterman

Map by
Ashton Woodman Reniers

HERITAGE BOOKS
2012

HERITAGE BOOKS
AN IMPRINT OF HERITAGE BOOKS, INC.

Books, CDs, and more—Worldwide

For our listing of thousands of titles see our website
at
www.HeritageBooks.com

A Facsimile Reprint
Published 2012 by
HERITAGE BOOKS, INC.
Publishing Division
100 Railroad Ave. #104
Westminster, Maryland 21157

Copyright © 1947 Ruth Woods Dayton

— Publisher's Notice —
In reprints such as this, it is often not possible to remove blemishes from the original. We feel the contents of this book warrant its reissue despite these blemishes and hope you will agree and read it with pleasure.

International Standard Book Numbers
Paperbound: 978-1-55613-516-3
Clothbound: 978-0-7884-9439-0

Pioneers and Their Homes on Upper Kanawha

By

RUTH WOODS DAYTON

WEST VIRGINIA PUBLISHING COMPANY
CHARLESTON, WEST VIRGINIA
1947

Copyright, 1947

By

RUTH WOODS DAYTON

Facsimile Reprint

Published 1991 By
HERITAGE BOOKS, INC.
1540 Pointer Ridge Place, Bowie, Maryland 20716
(301)-390-7709

ISBN 1-55613-516-5

- Notice -

The foxing, or discoloration with age, characteristic of old books, sometimes shows through to some extent in reprints such as this, especially when the foxing is very severe in the original book. We feel that the contents of this book warrant its reissue despite these blemishes, and hope you will agree and read it with pleasure.

Printed and Bound in the U. S. A.

To
A. S. D.

Foreword

Having spent three or more years assembling material and writing a volume of some several hundred pages, one would imagine all there was to say, had been said—an exceedingly erroneous conception. However obvious and tiresome explanations may seem, they nevertheless appear to be a necessary accompaniment, and a "Foreword," the author's clothesline on which to hang his (or her) excuses, is as inevitable as washday itself. When that most unlovely-sounding creature, a "housewife," attempts to write a book, particularly one involving research and endless note-taking, much correspondence, many time-consuming, and generally fruitless, interviews, interspersed with motor jaunts hither and yon, she is embarking on an obstacle-strewn journey. Furthermore, if she has been so unwise as to commence it in a war era of maidless households and transportation problems, and to end it in a year interrupted by major surgery and two months of hospitalization, she is either endowed with an undue amount of unrealistic optimism or an equally superfluous supply of persistence, a quality which, if too pronounced, might be designated by a less polite word and called "stubbornness."

Be that as it may, the author is a little surprised that she has not succumbed to old age and decrepitude before its completion. Her chief desire, now that publication has irrevocably recorded the hundreds of dates, names, and family relationships with which she has struggled, is that she might flee to some remote isle until the error-finders have grown weary and ceased to impart their doleful news. Knowing full well that errors have a glaring way of confronting writers when it is too late, she can only say she has made a sincere attempt to clarify discrepancies, and to verify, in so far as possible, data obtained from various sources. Genealogical information secured from descendants has, when compared with deeds, wills, and other documentary evidence, often proved incorrect, and explains certain changes which may not otherwise be understood.

She regrets the necessity of numerous dull repetitions, but with the many intermarriages and business associations among the early families, a constant overlapping of identifying material is unavoidable.

This is not a county history, but concerns chiefly the valley of the Great Kanawha River from its beginning at Gauley Bridge to its tributary, Davis Creek. I hope to follow with a later volume dealing with the lower section to the mouth of the Kanawha at Point Pleasant. It is the story of some of those settlers whose century-old houses still remain, and of a few whose homes no longer exist. Seldom architecturally impressive, these dwellings for the most part are plain and substantial structures of simple design. Such houses are part of the background of the pioneer of western Virginia, who, first of all, was a woodsman and hunter, a man of dauntless courage and unconquerable tenacity, whatever else he may later have become of wealthy landowner, salt-maker, and statesman.

It is impossible to enumerate all those persons who have been helpful in the preparation of this book. Those who have lent me their treasures of records, clippings, books, and pictures; those who have replied to my letters, and answered my inquiries; others who have aided me in securing much needed information, and who are found in Pratt, Montgomery, Cedar Grove, Belle, Malden, Charleston, St. Albans, and other towns on the upper Kanawha—to all of these go my sincerest thanks.

Especially am I grateful to Dr. Roy Bird Cook, who has generously given me access to his valuable collection of historical material, and to whom I have appealed for solution of many puzzling questions.

To Naomi Hosterman, who has not only made the drawings, but who has contributed unflagging interest and cooperation under many trying conditions, I am greatly indebted; and to Ashton Reniers, whose interesting map of the Kanawha River is an important addition to this book, I also owe my appreciation.

The work of typing and retyping the manuscript, with its confused mass of changes, erasures, and substitutions, and its series of clipped-on notes marked "Insert A" and "Insert B," was both a tedious and monotonous task. For a business woman whose hours are more than filled, this undertaking has meant the sacrifice of many Sundays, evenings, and lunch hours, and for this invaluable assistance, and many kindnesses, I am deeply grateful to Carrie W. Davis.

R. W. D.

August, 1947.

CONTENTS

	Page
Early Territorial Claims and Indian Warfare	1
Simon Kenton, Hunter on the Elk, 1771	9
First Permanent Settlement, 1774	14
Houses of Leonard Morris and Samuel Hensley	23
The Revolution Begins	28
Fort Lee and the Clendenins, 1788	31
Anne Bailey, Frontier Messenger	38
County of "Kenhawa," 1788-1789	46
Daniel Boone, County Lieutenant, 1791	50
The Cobb Homestead	59
"The Town at the Mouth of Elk," 1794	66
Fort Lee Ends with Militia System, 1795	71
First House on Paint Creek	73
John Harriman House	75
"The Old Riggs Place"	78
Benjamin Morris House	81
Harmony Hill	83
Three Homes of the Hansfords	86
The Montgomerys	93
The Ruffner Family	95
Holly Grove Mansion	103
Rosedale	110
Augustus Ruffner House	114
The Salines	118
"Kanawha Court House," 1801	134
Shrewsburys and Dickinsons	140
Anne Royall, Early Charleston Resident	161

"Cedar Grove" and Virginia's Chapel	176
"The White House" Tavern	185
Levi Welch House	190
Kanawha Salines Church	197
Colonel Wood House	203
Dr. Richard Ellis Putney House	206
Colonel Donnally House	209
Charleston, 1820-1840	219
The Elms	222
Dr. Patrick House	225
Miller House	228
Rogers Pharmacy	232
The Quarrier Family	237
Elm Grove—the Craik House	242
Rand House	248
MacFarland House and the Rubys	257
Littlepage Mansion	264
The Lovells and the Breams	269
Glenwood	275
Appendix	287
Bibliography	309
Index	313

APPENDIX—TABLE OF CONTENTS

	Page
Kanawha Valley	287
Officers and Rangers Who Built and Garrisoned Fort Lee	289
Organization of Kanawha County	290
First Trustees of "Charlestown"	290
Morris Family Outline	291
First Will Recorded in Kanawha	297
Family of Samuel Shrewsbury, Sr.	298
Family of John Shrewsbury, Sr.	299
Family of Joel Shrewsbury, Sr.	299
Family of Colonel Andrew Donnally, Jr.	301
Family of Colonel Alexander Quarrier	304
Partial List of Pre-Civil War Salt-Makers	305
Roster of Kanawha Riflemen	306
Charleston Streets Named for Early Kanawha Settlers	308

DRAWINGS

	Facing Page
Leonard Morris House and Stockade, Marmet	16
Hansford House, Pratt	32
Salt Well on the Kanawha, Malden	48
Rosedale, Charleston	64
Harmony Hill, Pratt	80
Holly Grove Mansion, Charleston	96
"The Stone House," Belle	112
"The Frame House," Quincy	128
"The Brick House," Belle	144
"Cedar Grove," Cedar Grove	160
Virginia's Chapel, Cedar Grove	176
Welch House, Malden	192
Kanawha Salines Church, Malden	196
Colonel Wood House, South Malden	204
Putney House, Malden	208
Colonel Donnally, Jr. House, Charleston	224
Rogers Pharmacy, Charleston	228
The Elms, Charleston	236
Elm Grove, Charleston	240
Rand House, Charleston	256
Littlepage Mansion, Kanawha Two-Mile Creek	260
Glenwood, Charleston	268

Early Territorial Claims and Indian Warfare

KANAWHA is a word synonymous in West Virginia today with wealth, power, and politics—the name of one of the State's largest rivers and counties, heart of the southern coal, oil, and gas fields, center of great chemical industries, and the home of the State Capitol.

Its origin so obscure as to be almost forgotten, the name, spelled in a variety of ways, beginning with C or K, and ending in S or Y, first appeared on the early maps of explorers as that of the most important river encountered in their travels through the region. It is said to have been the tribal name of a band of Indian hunters who long ago followed the stream in search of game, but whose identity faded into oblivion when conquered by roving tribes of the strong Indian Confederacy of the Six Nations. The small Coh-no-was tribe became merged with those of its captors, who, claiming conquest of all the territory lying between the Allegheny Mountains and the Great Lakes, confidently returned to their villages in northern New York.

Thus began years of struggle for a vast region of which the area now embraced in Kanawha County constituted only an insignificant part, a contest not only between Indian tribes, but between the two rival nations of Great Britain and France. Each had coveted the fertile valleys bordering on the Ohio River ever since 1669, when La Salle, following his discovery and exploration of the Ohio, returned to France bringing glowing tales of their richness, tales quickly borne across the English Channel.*

Taking no account of Indian claims, and relying upon the Common Law of Nations that gave to the nation discovering the mouth of a river all the land drained by it, France felt her title secure. Her chief interest was the continuation of her long established and flourishing fur trade, and the undisturbed maintenance of her numerous trading stations. Making no attempts to colonize, France lost her golden opportunity to grasp the prize within her hand, and perhaps to write a different American history.

While France was basking in her supposed security, Great Britain was making plans. In 1671 the Virginia colonist, Captain Thomas Batts, and his exploring party, commissioned by Major Abraham Wood "For the finding out the ebbing and flowing of ye waters on ye other side the Mountains, in Order to the Discovery of ye South Sea," had come as far westward as the Falls of the Kanawha River—a short distance below the juncture of the New and the Gauley rivers. Naming the beautiful stream Wood River in honor of their sponsor, whose illness prevented his accompanying them and who died during their absence, the explorers took formal possession in the name of Charles II. There was little use for a name, as the course of the river was unknown and the region through which it flowed was unexplored. Nevertheless, it appeared on early maps, meandering in all sorts of directions, under an assortment of names, the most exhausting of which was the Indian title of

---

*See Kanawha Valley in Appendix.

Chinodashichetha. Some cartographers, becoming hopelessly confused, frequently used several names or called it simply "New" river. After the river became more fully explored these difficulties were finally resolved by retaining the name of "New River" for the upper section from the source to the Gauley, and giving the name "Kanawha" to the hundred-mile section from that point to its mouth at the Ohio.

Following the Batts expedition nothing further was done, however, to disturb French possession for many years, except for the gradual infiltration into the territory of more and more English traders.

A revival of interest in the region resulted from the travels of John Peter Salley and a group of men commissioned by the Governor of Virginia to conduct an expedition of discovery, with a grant of land as a reward. They set out from Augusta County in 1742 and, crossing the Alleghenies, located and named various water courses, but their most distinctive discovery was that of coal along the stream to which they gave the name "Coal River." They followed the Kanawha to its junction with the Ohio, at a spot long called The Point, later to become historically significant as the site of the Battle of Point Pleasant. Passing The Point, they continued some distance down the Ohio before turning back on their long homeward journey.

As a result of this exploration, Great Britain two years later secured from the Six Nations for the sum of four hundred pounds, their title to lands lying between the Allegheny Mountains and the Ohio River, which embraced the Kanawha Valley. This and the area extending to the Mississippi and beyond had already been claimed by Great Britain as a part of her Virginia colony, and designated by the General Assembly in 1738 as within the boundaries of its enormous County of Augusta, although the latter was not organized as such until 1745.

Marquis de la Galissoniere, Governor of Canada and Commander General of New France, soon learned of these unwelcome activities and determined to assert more vigorously his country's claims to the territory. Accordingly, in 1749 he dispatched from La Chine, Canada, a detachment under Captain Celoron de Bienville, consisting of fourteen officers and cadets, twenty soldiers, one hundred and eighty Canadians, and a band of Indians, carrying six possessively inscribed leaden plates, with instructions to bury them at the mouth of each of the Ohio's principal tributaries, and thus forever to settle the matter of ownership.

Starting on June 15 in twenty-three birch-bark canoes, the journey proved a tedious one. Conditions of travel were hard, and involved long portages. The weather was none too good, with much rain and severe summer heat. After the expedition reached the Allegheny River, there arose a feeling of uneasiness due to the unfriendly attitude of the Indians along the route. The Canadian Governor had sent letters to these Indians, calling upon them as "his children" to be loyal to their parent and oust the evil British traders from their midst without delay. Captain de Bienville read the letters to the Indians at each of his stopping places, but however eloquently he voiced his appeal, there was no responsiveness worthy of the name, and he knew the British had already secured the Indian commitments. At some places the attitude was one of threats and hostility. The situation was upsetting to the nerves of the travelers, and with a number of his men ill, provisions running low, and his own Indians somewhat out of hand from being humored by too much liquor, de Bienville, his task of depositing the tablets finally accomplished, sealed the ceremonies in a pouring rain, with a somewhat perfunctory toast to Louis XV, and happily turned his back on this unfriendly land and his face toward New France.

The whole affair would seem to have been a futile gesture, for the floods came and the plates were soon lost in mud and silt, the one at the mouth of Kanawha not being discovered until 1846, while some of them lie buried to this day. Even had they remained visible, there was no one to read the inscriptions nor to be impressed by their assertions, for the British were too busy colonizing.

The Virginians, realizing the Indian title to the Kanawha Valley was disputable, had taken the added precaution of securing from the newly organized Ohio Land Company a grant for 200,000 acres located west of the Alleghenies, and had at once begun its occupation. Such was in compliance with the grant which specified that a fort be built, and one hundred families settled in the area within seven years, with the added agreement that upon fulfillment of this condition, the company should have an additional 300,000 acres, provided it settled three hundred more families within the following seven years. To accomplish such an undertaking was a feat too staggering for today's generation to comprehend. Although an occasional explorer and adventurer had made crude and incorrect maps of streams and mountains, recording his travels as well as his discomforts and ailments, and other land companies were being formed and surveying parties sent out, the greater part of this region had never been seen by white men. A land of extremes in topography and climate, its wild and rugged terrain provided shelter for all sorts of game.

Shut in by foothills, the lowlands along the river valleys were sultry and humid, filled with a jungle of undergrowth and debris left by the driftwood and uprooted trees of many floods, while to the east the mountains, covered with massive hardwood trees, rose to cool and wind-swept heights.

For long years it had been the great hunting ground of the Indian. Each spring bands of Indian hunters forsook their tepees in Ohio, and crossing the Ohio River at the mouth of the Kanawha, disappeared for months into its wilderness. Finding the trail left by the migrating buffalo, they followed it for more than a hundred miles, leisurely lying in wait at the water holes and salt licks for elk, deer, bear, and other wild game.

In the wake of surveying parties of 1750, the explorations of Dr. Thomas Walker and others, and through reports of hunters from the Shenandoah Valley who scaled the mountains, to return with irresistible tales of a land untouched, small settlements began to group themselves on the western slope of the Alleghenies. They clustered around the mineral springs and along the waters of the Greenbrier River and the beautiful surrounding mountain plateau called by the Indians a savannah.

Busy clearing lands and building homes, the newcomers were hardy woodsmen, not psychologists nor students of human relations. They spent no time wondering what reaction the Indian might have to their presence, nor in trying to understand his viewpoint; neither did they consider it necessary that he be given any explanations. They simply ignored him. But the Indian was watching, and thinking, and forming his own conclusions, and one thing became quite clear to him. In this land long regarded as his own, where he had hunted and fished all his life unhindered, usurpers had come, and now he was no longer alone and free. Smelling wood smoke rising from a stone chimney, hearing the bark of a dog, the sound of an axe in the woods, or finding the footprints of the white man on the game trails, anger flamed in his heart, and he recognized an enemy with whom he determined to deal in the Indian way.

The lack of understanding on both sides, stupid and unexplained mistakes, broken promises, treachery, even though frequently unintentional and committed through ignorance, could have but one result. Soon the flames of burning cabins reddened the night sky, massacres occurred, white women and children were taken away captive to the distant villages of the savages, their meager belongings destroyed or divided among their captors. Pioneering virtually ceased as the French and Indian War grew more ominous, and many of the more remote settlers left their cabins and moved nearer the few small forts that were built in the savannah.

In 1753 Governor Dinwiddie, of Virginia, hopefully sent Major George Washington to the French Commander on the Allegheny River, protesting against its possession by the French, but the mission proved unsuccessful. The following year, when the French were reported as extending the construction of forts to include one on the Greenbrier River, in addition to those on the Ohio and Monongahela, the Governor realized the time for protests had passed and that war was inevitable. Hoping not only to secure an army, but at the same time to safeguard the British claim to the territory by insuring further settlements after the war, he offered a bounty of free lands, over and above their pay, to those Virginians who volunteered in His Majesty's service against the French and Indians.

The French had taken full advantage of the Indian resentment against the settlers, and had cemented alliances with many tribes. Ten years of war followed. For the pioneer, they were years of terror, hardships, and a constant struggle to hold on—planting corn with a gun slung across one shoulder, remembering never to allow a child to go alone to the spring, listening for the snap of a dry twig under a stealthy moccasin, longing for the deep winter snows when anxiety lessened and there was a blessed interlude before the renewal of fear that came with the first sign of spring.

Although the French and Indian War was terminated by treaty in November, 1762, the French defeated, the Ohio Indians forced to relinquish many captives, and although by the treaty of Fort Stanwix in 1768 western Virginia had been ceded to the British, Indian depredations did not cease, nor did pioneer vigilance. Scouts and woodsmen, disguised as Indians, silently and alone roamed the forests, spying on the whereabouts and activities of the savages. Absent from their homes for weeks at a time, these men constituted for the settlers their greatest bulwark of safety.

Simon Kenton, Hunter on the Elk 1771

SURROUNDED by the glow of excitement and danger, the names of such scouts as Arbuckle, Young, Morris, Cobb, and countless others, still enliven the pages of Kanawha frontier history. The fame of two others, Simon Kenton and Daniel Boone, spread far beyond this locality, yet each lived for a time in the Valley, and for this reason one may be pardoned for repeating the familiar story of their lives.

Born in Fauquier County, Virginia, in 1755, Simon Kenton roamed the woods as a boy, the forest his only school. When but sixteen he had a fight with a man whom he thought he had killed in the encounter. Panic-stricken, he ran away from home, continuing his flight without hat, coat, or weapon, until hunger drove him to ask for food at a cabin. He hit upon a clever and effective scheme of inquiring at each stopping place the name of the settler whose home he would next reach. When he arrived there he would announce that his name was Jones, Smith, Morris, or whatever happened to be the name of his would-be host. Surprised exclamations were forthcoming and in no time at all, following the well-accepted Virginia tradition, they were "cousins," and Simon was welcome to linger indefinitely. This procedure was repeated many times, until Simon reached a man named Butler, where he became Simon "Butler," and remained long enough to earn a gun.

By that time his panic had subsided, and feeling more independent with a gun in his hand, he abandoned his cabin-to-cabin existence, joined hunting parties, and sold his pelts for such meager necessities as he required. Still fearful that his true name might bring recognition, he retained the name of Butler for several years. During this time he traveled down the Ohio by dugout canoe, visited Fort Pitt, and there met John Yeager and George Strader. Yeager had been a captive of the Indians for a number of years, knew their languages, and had accompanied them on hunting trips to Kentucky. Having later made his escape, he was now eager to return to the rich hunting grounds he had visited, and easily persuaded Simon to join him and his friend. They built a canoe, accumulated blankets and other supplies, and started. Seventy miles below Fort Pitt they hid their canoe, went inland, and stayed at an Indian village for a time. Resuming their travels, they floated past the mouth of Muskingum, where de Bienville had sunk one of his leaden French plates in 1749, and the site of the present Marietta, Ohio, passing many villages of the Indians.

As they journeyed, Yeager talked and young Kenton listened, absorbing from the older man all his store of valued experiences and his knowledge of the Indian, his methods of fighting, and his way of thinking. Kenton learned all the skill of his woodcraft—how to stalk a brush-strewn path and make no sound, how to stand against a tree, unmoving, and remain unseen in the camouflage of the woods, how to distinguish slight sounds, and to observe the smallest detail that might reveal the presence of an enemy. Thus was laid the foundation of the later skill of perhaps the greatest Indian fighter of his day.

The hunters, after a long and difficult journey, finally reached the wilderness of Kentucky, but it had taken longer than anticipated, and, short of supplies, they barely got back to more familiar territory before the winter began. Returning to the mouth of the Kanawha, they followed the old and beaten buffalo trail about a mile and a half above the mouth of Elk River, and there in 1771 built a cabin and settled down for a winter of trapping and hunting. Well satisfied with their success, the following spring they took their pelts down river to a trading post on the Ohio. Exchanging them for clothes, ammunition, and other articles, the hunters returned to their cabin.

In March of the next year, 1773, the two younger men visited their traps as usual one cold, rainy day, and in addition to their pelts, brought back a wild turkey to roast for their evening meal. Wrapping their wet guns carefully in blankets to prevent rust, they stacked them in the shelter of the cabin. While Yeager stood by turning the turkey on its spit, they removed their wet leggings and moccasins and sat down to steam them slowly dry by the fire. A slight movement and the men looked up to find several Indians a few yards away with guns leveled. Yeager, a perfect target, silhouetted against the flames, was shot. The two younger men scrambled to their feet and, murmuring the location of a meeting place, dashed into the darkness of the woods in different directions. Later in the night they met at their appointed place and started their barefoot journey to the Ohio, sixty miles away. The evening of the fifth day, exhausted and famished, they stumbled into a cabin about six miles above the mouth of the Kanawha, and were there fed and clothed from the scanty supply of its owners. A party of surveyors, under Joel Reese, had also arrived shortly before by canoe, and the following day Kenton joined them as hunter, and accompanied them back up the Kanawha, remaining with them until he had once more earned a gun.

In May the gun was his, and when another party composed of about fourteen men, under Dr. John Wood, appeared, Kenton joined them on their journey down the Kanawha. This group had expected to meet a party led by Thomas Bullitt then inspecting lands in Ohio, but upon arrival at the designated spot, they found only an abandoned camp. Dr. Wood feared the Bullitt party had been captured by Indians, and apprehensive that his own men might fall into a trap, decided to abandon his canoes and return overland to Virginia—the first such trip attempted from that point. Kenton, only eighteen at the time, agreed to act as guide, and in spite of the sickness, hunger, and weariness of its members, he brought the party in safety to Greenbrier — quite a feat for a boy of his age.

Fearful to be so near his home and the scene of his supposed crime, Kenton departed at once for Kentucky, and spent the winter trapping on the Big Sandy. Remaining in Kentucky, he next became associated with George Rogers Clark, acting as a spy. Having made a name for himself with Clark, he was later engaged by Lord Dunmore in the same capacity, and it was he who carried messages from Dunmore to General Lewis on the eve of the Battle of Point Pleasant.

After that battle, Kenton's life became more and more colorful. Learning that the man whom he thought he had killed years before was alive, Kenton resumed his own name in 1779. A mature man, he now began acquiring lands in Kentucky, married, and settled there on Quick's Run. In 1783 he made a journey back to Virginia and persuaded all but two of his family to join him there, his aged father dying on the journey. Kenton maintained a station with trained men on duty; was a Major under General Anthony Wayne, with a company of one hundred spies, and brought in scores of prisoners, doubtless killing equally as many. The value of his services was inestimable. A friend of Daniel Boone, the two had many adventures together, as well as narrow escapes, and Kenton is known to have saved Boone's life from the Indians on at least one occasion.

As Kenton grew older he increased his land holdings to include vast tracts in Missouri and Ohio, as well as in Kentucky, and became the owner of a large brick mansion in Kentucky. There he served lavish meals to all comers, kept perpetual open house, owned many slaves, horses and farm animals, and maintained all the equipment of a wealthy man's establishment. The house burned, however, and his wife's death shortly afterward marked the beginning of another era in the life of this unusual man. Marrying a second time, Kenton moved to Ohio and thereafter gravitated between the three states where his lands were located. Unable to read or write—although he had learned to trace his name—Kenton, rightly or wrongly, began to feel that he was being taken advantage of by his associate and those with whom he had dealings, and brought suit against his business partner, Colonel Ward. Complications and money troubles became more and more serious, and he was imprisoned for debt and taxes more than once. By 1832 little remained of his extensive land holdings or his money, and after a life of great service to his country, filled with dangers, exploration, poverty, wealth, once the owner of many thousands of acres of rich land, he came to the end in 1836 engulfed in debt, at the lowest ebb of his fortune.

First Permanent Settlement
1774

IN 1774, when General Lewis and his army left Fort Savannah on the long journey which was to end in the Battle of Point Pleasant, there lay ahead of them tortuous mountain ranges whose altitude exceeded thirty-four hundred feet. These densely forested and steep barriers the troops circumvented whenever possible by following the circuitous course of the various creeks that wound around the mountains; otherwise the route traveled was largely that of today's well-known east and west U. S. Highway No. 60—the Midland Trail, a modern road based on the ancient route followed first by migrating buffalo, then by the Indians, and finally by white men.

Beyond nine-mile-long Gauley, last of the mountains, the valley of the Kanawha began, and, in it, twenty miles east of Elk River and the present city of Charleston, a little stream called Kelly's Creek, pushing its way down the ravines between the northern hills, empties into the Kanawha at the site of the small village now called Cedar Grove. This spot is historically significant as the location of the first permanent settlement in the Kanawha Valley—that of William Morris, Sr., and his sons, who had arrived during the spring and summer of 1774, and were busily engaged in completing their cabins and clearing their lands when the Lewis army passed the head of Kelly's Creek. Although every man was needed to speed the work of settlement before the winter began, William Morris, Jr., the twenty-eight-year-old eldest son, and five of his brothers—Henry, Leonard, Joshua, Levi, and John—accepted their burden of military duty, and joined the troops as they journeyed on toward Point Pleasant.

His ancestors, natives of Scotland originally who had moved later to England, William Morris, Sr. (1722-1792), was the patriarch of the Morris family in America, although he had seemed anything but a patriarch when he stepped ashore in this country. Instead, his arrival was that of a somewhat bewildered boy of twelve, minus parents, funds, or belongings, as his departure from home had been entirely accidental—or had it? At any rate, he had gone aboard ship in England to see some relatives off for America, and when the ship sailed, he was still engrossed in the proceedings, and still on board. Landing in Philadelphia, he was befriended by a merchant until he was twenty-two years old. Education was apparently not a part of the befriending, which accounts, no doubt, for the fact that William Morris could neither read nor write.

Mr. Morris was married in Orange County, Virginia, about 1745 to Elizabeth Stipps (1729-1795), and they were the parents of ten children—eight sons and two daughters: William, Jr., Henry, Leonard, Joshua, Levi, John, Achilles (Carrol), Benjamin, Elizabeth, and Frances. The Morris family resided in Culpeper County, Virginia, for a time, but, about 1765, journeyed to Greenbrier County, where they lived for nearly ten years on Muddy Creek before crossing the mountains to the Kanawha in the spring of 1774.

A man no longer young, the majority of whose children were adults and some of them married, William

Morris, Sr., exhibited youthful spirit and courage in leaving the more populated section of the country to settle in a completely uninhabited wilderness, seventy-five miles beyond Donnally's Fort near Lewisburg, which was then the western frontier. He obviously had no more fear of ghosts than of visible dangers, and might almost be said to have flaunted himself in the face of both with equal casualness, for with thousands of acres around him, he coolly chose the very site where tragedy had come to his predecessor, Walter Kelly, only a few months before.

Kelly had erected the first cabin in the Valley in 1773. Located at the mouth of the small creek that yet bears his name, he had lived there but a short time when he was discovered and slain by the Indians. Warning from Fort Donnally that Indians were coming had been received in time for his wife and children to reach the fort, but Kelly, driven to seek this lonely spot because of some dark page in his not-too-distant past, feared to be seen in the settlement, and chose to remain behind. Knowing these facts, Mr. Morris may have philosophically looked upon the death of Kelly as nothing more than an example of retribution for sin, and ghosts, if any, being entirely unauthorized, were to be disregarded. Be that as it may, in Mr. Morris as in other pioneers of his time the quality of perseverance was strongly developed, and once embarked on a course, there was no turning back because of obstacles, imaginary or otherwise, in the path.

Whether all the Morris family arrived together is uncertain. Some writers say the sons Leonard and John came first, preceding their father; others say it was Leonard and William, Jr. Some even assert these men were not sons of William Morris, Sr., but were his

Leonard Morris House and Stockade

brothers. Neither do all accounts agree as to the date of the settlement. John Young, early scout and pioneer, applying for a pension in his old age, testified that he first arrived in the Kanawha in 1783 in company with Leonard and John Morris, Michael See, and others "who had come out in advance of their families to raise a crop," and such as had families moved them out that fall. This may have been the result of a faulty memory or an error in copying the record, and the year may have been intended as 1773, instead of 1783. The deposition of Leonard Morris taken in 1815 in a land suit states that he was living in the Valley in 1774, and that surveyors, whom he names, stopped at his cabin and obtained two men as helpers, and his statement is verified by the surveyors. Most historians have accepted the date of 1774 as correct, and all agree that the Morris family and its several groups were unquestionably the first permanent settlers in the valley of the Kanawha, and it appears altogether likely they were assembled and established during the year 1774.

Although the Morris family had no neighbors, its members at least had the advantage of living on the trail which all travelers, however few in number, followed. Thus, on occasions, news could be obtained from the settlements to the east. The travelers, too, welcomed an opportunity for companionship and conversation in this lonely land. But the location had its disadvantage also, for Indian parties frequented the same trail and sooner or later were certain to discover the new cabins. This danger was realized more keenly after the Lewis troops had passed down the Valley. A feeling of apprehension descended on the waiting settlement, as it recognized the utter hopelessness of its position should the Virginians be defeated, and the aroused Indians, left free, take the trail to wreak vengeance on the first in their path.

Anxiety and waiting finally came to an end with the appearance of the first company of returning soldiers sighted through the trees. Although William Morris, Jr., had been wounded in the battle, he was recovering from his injuries, and as the Morris family, reunited, listened thankfully to the tale of victory, they relaxed in the realization that winter could be faced with a new and comforting sense of security. The winter, however, proved but a brief interlude in the long years of Indian warfare that lay ahead before peace came permanently.

The spring following the Battle of Point Pleasant, various surveying parties appeared in the Valley, some on their way to the lands of Ohio and Kentucky, others to survey along the Kanawha. It was one such group under Samuel Lewis, previously referred to in the testimony of Leonard Morris, that stopped at the Morris settlement and procured two persons as chain bearers to assist in the survey for George Washington and Andrew Lewis of two hundred and fifty acres surrounding and including the Burning Springs, the joint patent for which was later issued in 1780 by Thomas Jefferson, then Governor of Virginia.

Colonel Thomas Bullitt had recently inspected lands in this region, and his surveyors were also engaged in making several surveys. One survey of one thousand and forty acres embraced an area lying between the hills and the northern side of the Kanawha River, with Elk River the western boundary; and a second survey, somewhat larger, beginning on the opposite side of Elk River and extending westward to Two Mile Creek. The two covered all of the business section and a great part of the residential area of the present city of Charleston. Additional surveys were made farther west along Coal River and along smaller streams, as well as in the wide valleys nearer Point Pleasant and the Ohio, where many thousand acres were already owned by Colonel George Washington.

The Morris family, however, except for Joshua and John who later obtained lands below Charleston, were content with the upper end of the Valley, and increased their holdings to include surveys on both sides of the river from the Falls down to Campbells Creek (a few miles above Charleston), the various sons settling on these tracts. William Morris, Sr., lived on the north side of the river, later moving a few miles above Kelly's Creek to the mouth of Hughes Creek, where he is said to have died and been buried. William, Jr., remained at Kelly's Creek. Henry and Benjamin also resided on the north side, and Leonard, John, and Levi lived on the south side.

Scattered as they were, at least three of the family built their homes to serve as forts by erecting stockades around them—Leonard at Lens Creek (Marmet), John a little farther west opposite the mouth of Campbells Creek, and William at Kelly's Creek, where in 1780 the Virginia Council, recognizing the importance of the Morris station as a link in the weak chain of its frontier defense, ordered a new fort built and garrisoned. Later, in 1788, after the building of Fort Lee twenty miles farther west, these two forts divided the valley between them for the length of the river, the Morris rangers scouting in the upper half, and the Fort Lee soldiers covering the lower section.

The matter of supplying food for these men was simple so far as meat was concerned, since game was plentiful, but obtaining meal and flour was a real problem. The difficulty was greatly relieved when William Morris erected a small grist mill on Kelly's Creek. At Cedar Grove the cone-shaped buhrstone of this early and crude mill now lies at the base of an historic roadside marker designating the site of the Morris settlement.

When George Rogers Clark received official sanction to undertake his daring and ambitious expedition against the western forts of Illinois, directions were given that rangers stationed at the Morris fort supply as many dugout canoes as might be required. Local interest being thus aroused, it is not surprising that this region supplied not only boats, but the greater number of the men that made up the small and carefully selected group, of whom John Morris was one, to undertake a mission so hazardous as to seem nothing short of fantastic. Fearless and hardened woodsmen, they were well chosen to execute so dangerous an undertaking as its brilliant accomplishment so amply proved. The far-reaching result of Clark's exploits extended into western Virginia, where it produced a very quieting effect upon the Indians, who had undoubtedly received a great psychological setback when they discovered the British were not, after all, invincible.

Beginning with the construction of the Clark canoes, the mouth of Kelly's Creek early became an important location, where boat building grew into a large-scale business that continued over a long period of time, and which was the terminal point for overland travel. It was many years before an adequate road existed beyond this spot. Fortunately the river here widened and became navigable the rest of its length, making journeys westward much more easily and quickly continued by boat. Dugout canoes could be hired for the trip, but if the supply happened to be low, it was not uncommon for travelers to wait several days for others to be built. Soon this busy place was known as "The Boat Yards"—Daniel Boone, as County Lieutenant, referring to it as such in his reports to the General Assembly in the seventeen nineties. Still later many barges and flatboats were constructed for the salt-makers farther down the river, and as the salt industry flourished until the beginning of the Civil War, the Boat Yards enjoyed equal activity for a similar period.

The first eighteen years in the life of a settlement begun in a wilderness is not long, but it was all that William Morris, Sr., saw of the development of his venture in pioneering, as his death occurred three years after the formation of Kanawha County. His will, recorded on January 3, 1793, was the first in the county record book.

A man, vigorous mentally and of recognized worth, though without formal education, Mr. Morris, with Henry Banks, was chosen as a delegate to the General Assembly for the session of 1792, sitting from October 1 to October 28. This was the third session since Kanawha's formation. In the first session in 1790 the county was represented by Colonel George Clendenin, Commander of Fort Lee, and Colonel Andrew Donnally, and in the second, in 1791, by Clendenin and Daniel Boone.

When he arrived in Richmond, Mr. Morris laid aside his hunting clothes and moccasins, and outfitted himself in fashionable broadcloth and boots. Even so, handicapped by his inability to read and write, his more cultured surroundings made him very conscious of his deficiency, and he was forced to go to some lengths to conceal the fact as adroitly as possible. While attending the Assembly he received a note from the Governor which he opened and threw on the floor, saying loudly for the benefit of bystanders, "I'll support no such law!" One of the members, seeing the Governor's signature, picked up the note and said: "Why, Mr. Morris, you are mistaken. This is an invitation from the Governor for you to dine with him tomorrow." "Is it?" exclaimed Mr. Morris, feeling in his pockets as if searching for spectacles (which he did not possess). "Is it indeed? I thought it was a note from Mr. ———— to get me to vote for his bill now before the House, which he knew very well I wouldn't do, and as I left my spectacles in my room, I could not read it"—which was getting out of a tight spot very neatly.

Descendants of William Morris are still numerous in the Valley, many persons with names other than Morris tracing their ancestry to this worthy pioneer. His name is perpetuated in one of the residential streets of Charleston, and also in the name of the William Morris Chapter of the Daughters of the American Revolution. This organization has placed on the outer wall of Virginia's Chapel at Cedar Grove a memorial tablet to him and his wife, and another to his son, Major William Morris, Jr.

Because of the importance and size of the Morris family, the frequent references to its various members, and the descriptions of several of their homes, it seems necessary to give the outline found in the appendix. Each branch of this large family carried on the same names through succeeding generations until one must be something of a genealogist to arrive at any accurate idea of the different relationships. This writer makes no claim to such qualifications, and has stumbled upon numerous discrepancies in her attempt to evolve even a simple sketch, the accuracy of which she does not guarantee.

Houses of Leonard Morris and Samuel Hensley

LEONARD, third son of William Morris, was grown and married when the Morris family settled in the Kanawha Valley in 1774. He and his married brothers chose home sites each to his own liking, Leonard selecting a spot on the south side of the river at the mouth of Slaughters Creek. He apparently did not remain there long, but moved farther down the river to the mouth of another stream which, emptying into the Kanawha about eight miles above Charleston, still bears his name, Lens Creek. Here the present highway forks, one road following the river bank east and west, and the other, following the creek, turns directly south toward Boone County. Mr. Morris built his two-story log house with its back to the river, the trees on the bank screening it from any passing Indians. The bank was rather high, and the land, sloping downward in front of the house, was cleared in a large area and entirely surrounded by a stockade. Following the contour of the land, it rambled up and down, and enclosed granary and other farm buildings, and also provided ample space for horses, cows and other animals, with a second barrier nearer the house. The dwelling had a good vantage point, and from it an occupant could overlook the stockade and still remain out of gun-range.

On their trips to and from the mountains, the Indians usually kept the river between them and the garrison at

Fort Lee by following the south bank west of the Paint Creek ford. Consequently, with their frequent passages through the neighborhood, the Leonard Morris stockade was no perfunctory gesture of defiance, but a very necessary means of protection, and proved its worth on many occasions. More than once members of the family barely reached its safety, with bullets thudding into the logs behind them. When cattle and pigs strayed far from the enclosure they were frequently found slaughtered in the woods, and in the spring of 1793 a Negro slave of Mr. Morris' was captured and carried away.

This pioneer home evidently stood for a great many years, as the drawing of it in this book is not imaginary, but made from a faded picture in possession of Morris descendants. It is the only picture of a pioneer log house, with its actual stockade still standing, that the writer has ever encountered, and she is most thankful for its preservation.

It was necessary for Mr. Morris to make long journeys at intervals to the eastern Greenbrier settlements to obtain supplies for his large family and it is said Mrs. Morris on several occasions defended her home and children from the Indians in decisive and business-like fashion, earning several notches on the stock of her gun while her husband was absent. These trips were important events in the lives of those left behind—the adults eagerly awaiting news of their friends and former neighbors beyond the mountains and the children filled with anticipation as to what their father might bring back with him. There was one never-to-be-forgotten day when he brought a dog and cat—the first such pets to arrive in the Valley.

The Morris cabin, having two stories, was really a very commodious dwelling for the time, with large stone chimneys at each end, a small window in each of its four rooms, and a little porch in front. In spite of all these commendable features, however, with a family of sixteen children under its roof, one can readily see why early marriages were not frowned upon. Apparently it was the only remedy to relieve the housing problems of the seventeen hundreds.

The first name by which this locality was known was Lens Creek Post Office. When Mr. Charles Brown (1770-1849) arrived in 1808, purchased a farm of several hundred acres, and began operation of a salt furnace, the name was changed to Brownstown. Mr. Brown married Elizabeth, daughter of Reuben Slaughter and Mary Donnally Slaughter, and was a man of means. Some of the deepest salt borings on the Kanawha were in this vicinity, one of which was operated by Mr. Luke Wilcox, whose well was on the east side of Lens Creek.

Mr. Brown was a resident until 1849. After the Civil War, and the decline of the salt industry, coal production began, and in 1900 the name of this small community was again changed to its present name of Marmet, for William and Edwin Marmet, operators of a coal mine.

While every vestige of the Leonard Morris house disappeared years ago, another log house remains in the locality that was its contemporary, at least for a time— the home of his daughter, Cynthia. One of the younger children of her father's second marriage, Cynthia married Samuel Hensley, presumably about 1819. She and her husband were given a portion of land by her father, and upon it Hensley built their home. Little is known of Samuel Hensley. His name appears among soldiers engaged in the Battle of Point Pleasant, and early county records show that he served as constable at various times.

He is also said to have operated a salt furnace on Lens Creek for Luke Wilcox. About three miles south of Marmet on Route 119, the Hensley house faces the road and creek, beyond which the steep, tree-covered hillside rises sharply. It stands in an open space near a ravine that divides the hill behind it. In the face of the hill is a rock cliff that doubtless furnished the stone for the enormous chimneys at each end of the house. Very wide at the bottom, they narrow toward the top and represent a laborious undertaking, as each stone is carefully cut into huge blocks put together with "cement" made from a mixture of clay and gravel procured from the creek.

The old house, weary and sway-backed with age, is two stories in height. The great notched logs of the walls are amazing and reveal the huge size of the Valley's virgin timber. Flat on the outside, they are eighteen inches wide and four inches thick, of yellow poplar, one of the softest of the hard woods, easy to work, immune to decay under almost any weather conditions. Then obtainable in all sizes, it was the first choice of the pioneer as a material for his cabin.

The ceilings are extremely low, not more than six and a half feet high. Standing on the floor one can easily touch the hand-grooved beams overhead. These are of pine, while all the other wood used, including the joists, is of yellow poplar. The original floors remain, though those of the first floor have been overlaid in recent years. There is no hallway, the two rooms on each floor having connecting doors. The stairway is in one corner, and is a very narrow, steep and hazardous affair, with a small door at the bottom—probably to stop those who fall from the top. The small windows with their sash cut into tiny squares still have the early glass panes. A rather feeble-looking porch shelters the entrance door, and while it may not have been built when the house was erected, it apparently has been there a long, long time.

The usual frame addition of a room or two has been added in the rear, but, looking at this primitive dwelling directly in the front, it appears surprisingly untouched.

The age of this house is uncertain, but it seems reasonable to assume it was built shortly after the Hensley marriage, which would make it approximately one hundred and twenty-seven years old, this in spite of attributed dates from various persons, who glibly place the house many years before any settlers were in the Kanawha Valley. The present owner of this pioneer cabin is Mr. Garner Williams, of Kayford, West Virginia, and his tenants, the William Price family, have occupied it for the last twenty-five years.

The Revolution Begins

WITH the Indians pushed beyond the Ohio and the boundaries of their territory clearly defined following the Battle of Point Pleasant, the settlers for the first time enjoyed an interlude of relief from tension and fear. Proving but a two-year respite, it fortunately occurred at a time of most value, for it enabled the colonists to leave their homes and enlist in the Continental Army, to perfect an intelligence system of spies and scouts that was efficient and valuable, to accomplish the construction of a number of badly needed forts, and otherwise to contribute toward a strong defense at the beginning of the war with Great Britain.

By the end of these first two years of the Revolution, Great Britain had convinced the Indians that the colonists were all bad and the British all good, and that the good could prevail much more quickly with the aid of the Indians. Equipped with arms, and paid for their services, the Indians in their new role of allies, with the Revolution as a cover, were again on the warpath against the settlers, filled with renewed grievances and desire for vengeance. In present West Virginia many forts were attacked, many burned, and countless atrocities committed. In 1778 the Shawnees, making an unsuccessful attack on the fort at The Point, swept through the valley of the Kanawha to attack Fort Donnally, the western outpost of the Greenbrier settlements, stealing horses, cows and pigs, and burning cabins as they went. Warned by scouts of the Indian approach, many of the settlers had reached the fort, and with the aid of a company of volunteers from Fort Savannah, about ten miles distant, after a harrowing siege, were successful in driving away the savages, who lost many more men in the encounter than did the whites.

    The incident, though one of many in this time of horror and bloodshed on the defenseless boundary of western Virginia, served to draw the attention of the Virginia Council to the vulnerability of its western frontier. After the Battle of Point Pleasant the first two temporary forts at that place had been replaced in 1776 by a more substantial one called Fort Randolph. Constructed under the supervision of Captain Matthew Arbuckle, it was also garrisoned and commanded by him until 1778. Captain William McKee was next in command, with a body of State troops enlisted under the new system at Continental expense. For some reason the garrison was withdrawn in 1779, and, its abandonment discovered by the Indians, the fort was promptly burned. This serious situation brought immediate action, and the Virginia authorities in 1780 ordered Fort Randolph rebuilt, and also directed that a fort be constructed at the Morris settlement on Kelly's Creek, and a garrison of twenty-six rangers be installed there. It was thought the Morris fort would serve a useful purpose as a loading base for food, tools, and other necessities to be sent down river for the construction of the other fort. Later, this location at the mouth of Kelly's Creek came to be the shipping and starting point for all river travel to Ohio and Kentucky, and was called "The Boat Yards."

    Fort Morris and Fort Randolph being eighty miles apart, there was little hope of settlers who lived in the wilderness between the two taking much comfort from the fact that they existed, except for the knowledge that scouts were on duty. In 1781 those who had been forced to flee from their new cabins in the Kanawha Valley and return to the more settled sections of Greenbrier because of the constant fear of Indians, petitioned the Assembly for a fort at the mouth of Elk, twenty miles west of the Morris settlement. No action was taken at that time, although the request may have influenced subsequent developments.

Fort Lee and the Clendenins
1788

DURING the turbulent period of the Revolution and for several years afterward, the danger to the western Virginia settlers was repeatedly brought to the attention of the Assembly by various landowners. One of those most interested was George Clendenin. Born in Scotland in 1746, he was the eldest son of Charles Clendenin, who had moved from the Shenandoah Valley to the Greenbrier region about 1761, and who had three other sons, Robert, William, and Alexander, and a daughter, Mary Ellen, all born in the 1750's. George and William became prominent in county affairs, particularly George who, as a veteran of the Battle of Point Pleasant and as a member of the Virginia Assembly in 1781, was in a position to voice an effective appeal for a more active defense of the frontier, and as a means to that end, to propose the opening of a road from Lewisburg westward at least as far as the Gauley River.

The matter of the road brought differences of opinion concerning the more desirable of two suggested routes. Local controversies arose and delays ensued. Henry Banks of Richmond, a member of the Assembly and owner of extensive land patents in western Virginia, having a personal interest in its development, made a journey to Greenbrier to ascertain the real situation. Finally in 1786 "Koontz's New Road" was opened from Lewisburg to The Boat Yards on the Kanawha at the mouth of Kelly's Creek, and a year later was ordered carried from Kanawha Falls to Kentucky. In the meantime Mr. Banks had reported to Governor Randolph in February, 1787, that the pleas of Clendenin were justified, and concurred in his demand that more consideration and protection be given the families who had previously settled along the Kanawha. Acting upon this report, the Assembly appointed a committee to ascertain the number of additional forts needed, the number of rangers required to construct and garrison them, and the probable cost.

George Clendenin, practical and farsighted, grasped an opportunity which presented itself while he was in Richmond attending the Assembly. Encountering Cuthbert Bullitt, then owner of the Kanawha Valley surveys of his deceased brother, Thomas Bullitt, Clendenin found him agreeable to a sale, and purchased from him, on December 28, 1787, the 1,040-acre tract lying along the northern side of the Kanawha River and extending to the mouth of Elk. This accomplished, and his decision made to settle upon the tract, Clendenin saw no reason why he should not benefit from State assistance, if possible, and having agreed to undertake a contract to furnish supplies for defense of the frontier, at once fixed upon his own lands at the mouth of Elk as a desirable location for one of the proposed forts. As Greenbrier County Lieutenant, he was directed by the Governor to proceed with the enlistment of a company of rangers, and the construction of a fort at the best place for the defense of his region. At this time there were perhaps not more than four small settlements in the Valley, one at Point Pleasant; Tackett's at the mouth of Coal River; the John Morris, twenty miles above it on the south side of the Kanawha; and the William Morris

Hansford House

settlement on Kelly's Creek, with about ten persons living at each place.

After the adjournment of the Assembly on January 30, 1788, Clendenin hastened back to Greenbrier, and by April 1, had assembled and organized a company of rangers under command of his brother William as Captain. Other officers were George Shaw, Lieutenant, Francis Watkins, Ensign, Shadrack Harriman and Reuben Slaughter, Sergeants. There were about twenty privates, with perhaps a few others who joined the company on its way down the Valley. This was a selected group of men particularly fitted for the work ahead, experienced woodsmen, carpenters and joiners, as well as frontier scouts and fighters.

Laden with sufficient food and supplies to maintain themselves—necessary cooking utensils, tools, ammunition, and other equipment strapped upon the backs of pack horses—the party reached its destination at the mouth of Elk on the fifth of April. Accompanying Colonel Clendenin were his wife, Jemimah, their children, and his father, brothers, and sister. He also brought six or more slaves, eight cows, and several horses. Upon their arrival two scouts were immediately dispatched to the fort at Point Pleasant to learn how matters fared there, and whether any Indian parties were in the vicinity. Clendenin wished no surprises, hoping to construct the fort before the Indians learned of his presence.

The ground was gone over carefully in order to choose the most advantageous location for the fort. The final selection, two miles above the Elk, was a site near the Kanawha at a point where a jutting curve in the high bank gave a good view up and down the river, and where a near-by stream, twisting through the bottom land from the distant hills, found its way to the river, and provided what might be termed a small and well-concealed harbor for canoes—a spot later known as Brooks Landing.

Soon the rangers were at work felling trees, splitting and hewing logs, whipsawing rafters, fashioning wooden pins and pegs, making clapboards for the roof, and collecting field stone for the chimneys. The building itself was not actually a fort, but merely an unusually strong two-story log house, thirty-six feet long and eighteen feet wide, with a large stone chimney at each end. Supplied with puncheon floors, and small windows front and back, the first floor had two rooms and a small hallway, while a ladder led to a similar arrangement on the second floor. Around the building was then erected a heavy stockade, made of large logs placed close together in an upright position in a deep trench, which was then filled in and tamped down. All crevices between the logs were carefully filled to make it bullet and arrowproof. There were two large gates placed opposite each other in the front and rear walls, and at intervals platforms were erected inside the walls in order that guards might view the surrounding area, which had been cleared of all timber and underbrush.

The stockade measured two hundred and fifty feet long by one hundred and seventy-five feet wide, and within the enclosure were built several rough sheds for supplies and a few small cabins for use of the rangers. These were erected in such a way that the rear walls formed a section of the stockade. They had the disadvantage of being within reach of firebrands hurled from the outside, but precautions were taken by making the roofs slope in one direction only, and that away from the wall, making it possible for a man to lie on the roof and extinguish a fire without being observed from the outside. It was thought wise also to build a small blockhouse as a lookout post, about a mile farther east along the river bank, and there Captain William Clendenin and his family made their home.

The rangers worked hard and under difficulties, for spring rains turned to floods, with the Kanawha and Elk rivers out of bounds. Signs of Indians in the neighborhood furnished an incentive to complete the fort as speedily as possible. No doubt the floods were more of a benefit than otherwise, for had it not been for the high waters, there would doubtless have been a larger number of Indians in the region. By May the last log was in place, and this, the first structure on the site of what was later to become Charleston, the capital city of West Virginia, stood upon a location identified today as just above the northeast corner of Brooks Street and the Kanawha Boulevard.

At first the fort was referred to as "the fort at the mouth of Elk," "Clendenin's station," or simply as "Clendenin's," and since Colonel Clendenin and his family occupied it as their residence, travelers who stayed there usually wrote in their journals of being entertained at Colonel Clendenin's "mansion house." When Henry Lee, the famed "Light Horse Harry," of Washington's Continental Army, and distinguished father of General Robert E. Lee, became Governor of Virginia in 1792, the fort was given its official name of "Fort Lee" in his honor. It was he who, during a second Congressional term at the time of Washington's death, paid him the well-known tribute of "First in war, First in peace, and First in the hearts of his countrymen," sometimes erroneously attributed to John Marshall, who offered upon the floor of Congress the memorial resolution, of which Lee was the actual author, that contained these words.

The fort completed, Colonel Clendenin went to Richmond in June to make a report to Governor Edmund Randolph. This report included not only the construction details, but described conditions in general on the frontier—the continued Indian attacks, the number of persons killed and captured, of others who were wounded and made narrow escapes, and of the great loss to the settlers in the large number of stolen horses. He stressed the great difficulty of securing supplies and ammunition, the need of funds with which to pay the rangers, and the indifference with which the Assembly treated the matter. This was the first of many such reports and pleas over a period of years, to most of which the Assembly turned, if not a deaf ear, certainly one in which the hearing was considerably dulled.

Clendenin's fort, larger and better built than many, had cost more than the usual amount expended for such structures, and the State Auditor and other authorities, safely ensconced in Richmond, were inclined to be critical of the constant financial drain necessary to maintain these distant frontier defenses, and determined to curtail it. In the latter part of August, a little more than a year after the construction of Fort Lee, a messenger was sent to Clendenin directing the reduction of the garrison to twelve rangers and two sergeants. This news, coming upon the heels of a summer of severe drought, with scarcity of provisions and scanty crops, was added cause for concern, particularly so, as Indians had frequently been near the settlements, and during the summer one man had been killed, a boy and a slave were captured and about thirty horses stolen. By the following summer (1790) there was even more cause for alarm, as refugees fleeing from the Tackett settlement, fourteen miles west, had reached Fort Lee with the terrifying news that Indians had destroyed the recently erected fort of Lewis Tackett on Coal River, and burned all the cabins. Several persons were killed and Hannah Tackett and others of the family were taken prisoners.

Some time previously, George Washington wrote to Colonel Clendenin requesting that he take over the management and settlement of Washington's several surveys along the Kanawha and Ohio rivers, two of which were less than fifteen miles from the mouth of Elk. Coming, however, at a time when Clendenin was particularly concerned with border problems, it is not surprising that he had no inclination to assume additional duties and apparently made no effort to comply with Washington's request.

Anne Bailey, Frontier Messenger

THE history of Fort Lee is incomplete that does not recount the doings of courageous Anne Bailey, colorful figure in the annals of border warfare. Her life story needs none of the fantastic embellishments contributed by some writers. The untrimmed facts are thrilling enough. On the other hand, there are those scribes who have made of Anne almost a parlor ornament, with never a "dram" nor a "cuss word."

As a matter of fact, Anne was obviously not ornamental, and certainly cared nothing for accepted standards of lady-like behavior. Had she done so, there would have been nothing to tell, just as there is nothing to tell of the lives of countless other heroic women of the frontier whose quiet endurance of hardship, privation, and danger was the accepted routine of their daily lives, and therefore unrecorded—all that went down in the history books being some such casual statement as that a certain Mary Smith was the wife of John Smith, and became the mother of eleven children!

But when Anne Bailey deliberately chose to depart from the usual pattern, and take her dangers far from home and alone on the Indian trails, her story brightened the pages of history in all its romantic appeal.

Anne Hennis was born in Liverpool, England, in 1742. Blessed with unusual strength and vigor, unhampered by fear of the new and unknown, and full of cockney assurance, she landed in America in 1761, and found her way to Staunton, Virginia—then a small settlement which had been laid off in lots in 1748. There, she lived for a time in the home of a family named Bell. Four years later she married a soldier, Richard Trotter, and their home was a crude cabin near the present Covington, Virginia, where a son, William Trotter, was born in 1767. Her husband was killed in the Battle of Point Pleasant in 1774, and it was afterward that Anne, leaving her child with a neighbor, Mrs. Moses Mann, embarked upon her unconventional career.

Short, heavily built, unfeminine, and coarse in appearance, she donned masculine apparel and led the life of the men of the frontier, asking and receiving no quarter. She always carried a hunting knife, a small axe, and a gun, and was fully able and equipped to take care of herself under all circumstances. When she needed a canoe she chopped down a tree, hollowed out the trunk, and made one; if she found herself in the woods at night she slept in a cave or under an overhanging rock on a mountain side. On a hill below Charleston, near the mouth of Thirteen Mile Creek, there is a shelving rock, long known by old settlers as "Anne Bailey's Cave," where she frequently spent a night on her way between Fort Lee and Point Pleasant. Sometimes a hollow log sufficed. She shot game and cooked it on a stick, eating her solitary meal many miles from any habitation. Winter and summer she rode the trails on a black horse called "Liverpool" that became as well known on the border as its rider, who soon was referred to as "Mad Ann." She was certainly not mad, however nonconforming. Others who had not seen her, but had heard strange tales of her mysterious comings and goings, declared her a phantom. Such instances as the following lent credence to the belief.

Anne was once returning to Charleston from Point

Pleasant and was in the vicinity of the present Winfield, when she was seen by a party of roving Indians who started in pursuit. Fearful of capture, Anne dismounted, and running into the underbrush, concealed herself. After a long search the Indians gave up the hunt, and failing to find her, took her horse and departed. Anne had no intention of losing her good horse, and remained in her hiding place till dusk, when she cautiously emerged and trailed the Indians to their camping place for the night. Waiting until it was dark and the Indians asleep, she crept near, and untying his tether, mounted "Liverpool," and with a defiant and piercing scream, delivered in true blood-curdling phantom style, galloped off into the darkness.

On November 3, 1785, Anne again married a soldier, John Bailey, member of a ranger company and veteran of the Battle of Point Pleasant in which her first husband had lost his life. The marriage was performed in Lewisburg by the Presbyterian minister, the Reverend John McCue. Bailey may have continued his connection with the Eastern Virginia forts for a time, but at least by 1792 he was in Kanawha County, and his name appears on the ranger payroll of Fort Morris on Kelly's Creek. He also worked out of Fort Lee, and later was a member of Captain Caperton's company. He died in October, 1794, and was buried on the Joseph Carrol farm near Kelly's Creek, a region in which he is said to have acquired lands.

Anne's remarriage seems in no way to have altered the independence of her existence, which one might say was that of a ranger "without portfolio." Rangers were not always so numerous as their commanders could have wished. Scattered here and there in small groups among the little settlements, and off in the woods on scouting duty, they were not always available, nor could they be spared to go on long journeys to the distant forts with messages. Anne's services for such duties were freely offered and gladly accepted. At times she may have carried ammunition, and very likely did. In none of the official letters nor reports of Colonel Clendenin does he mention Anne's name, nor a siege of Fort Lee. Nevertheless some of the more imaginative accounts of her exploits picture Anne flying over the mountains laden with ammunition, "Liverpool" leaping from crag to crag with the grace of a gazelle, and arriving amid plaudits of assembled throngs just in the nick of time to save the "besieged" garrison of Fort Lee from complete annihilation. According to some accounts of the date of her birth this feat would have occurred when Anne was ninety years old and "Liverpool" long in his grave.

All embellishments to the contrary, Anne was unquestionably a very real, a very capable, and a thoroughly dependable and useful messenger and scout. Completely fearless, the Indians could not understand her, and influenced by her purposely implanted assertions that she was endowed with supernatural powers, they came to believe it. She told them if they harmed her their whole tribe would be wiped out in punishment. The idea was a good one, and her unpredictable behavior and action bearing out the belief that she was indeed possessed of unusual qualities, worked surprisingly well. For that reason or through sheer good fortune there is no record of Anne suffering any injury at the hands of the Indians.

There is a story told which, if it does not actually prove the "tongue is mightier than the sword," at least proves its effectiveness in certain circumstances. Anne, once caught in a snowstorm in the mountains, crept into a hollow log for protection, and to keep her faithful "Liverpool" from also straying in search of shelter, she looped his halter around her foot. A passing Indian saw the horse, but not Anne, and thinking himself blessed by Providence, began to tug at the snow-buried halter. Whereupon, Anne came backing out of her burrow, and confronting the amazed Indian, gave him such a cockney tongue-lashing, that he was only too glad to leave the horse and stumble away into the snow before the heavens fell upon him—which she assured him was an imminent possibility.

Anne had no squeamish scruples and was as free in the use of weapons as in the use of her tongue. She knew there was more finality in the bark of a gun than in the echo of a spoken word, and it was her frequent boast that she had once killed two Indians with the same bullet.

With the close of Indian hostilities, Anne, deprived of "official" duties, hit upon a new scheme that would give her somewhat the same kind of life to which she had become thoroughly accustomed, and which she had no thought of abandoning. She organized herself into a sort of private express company, operating along the Kanawha Valley, into the Greenbrier region and beyond, and in the opposite direction below Fort Lee along the Ohio to Gallipolis. In this thinly populated valley, with no store within a hundred miles, where a needle and thread, medicine, a small package of tea, a bit of nutmeg, or a new farm tool were coveted luxuries, Anne must have been regarded by many a needy housewife as a gift from heaven, for it was for such things that Anne traveled hundreds of miles. Laden down with all her horse could carry, she often walked and led him much of the way. There were times when she drove pigs, sheep, or poultry, and is even credited with bringing along with her other cargo, the first copper "worm still" to cross the mountains. If so, it must have been the pioneer ancestor of West Virginia's moonshine stills which, newspaper and magazine publicity to the contrary, are not found behind every clump of bushes!

Anne was very meticulous in her handling of money, and in spite of her conglomerate assortment of commissions, and the different sums of money given her for their purchase, she never became confused nor careless, but brought back to each customer the article desired, together with the proper change, and spared herself no effort to fill every order entrusted to her.

It is said that after the Clendenins had left the Valley and Captain William Clendenin had settled below Point Pleasant, he commissioned Anne to bring him some tame geese from Greenbrier. A meticulous person, he specified the number should be exactly twenty—no more, no less—and if otherwise, the bargain was off, and he would not be obligated to pay for them. Anne agreed, and departed for Greenbrier. By this time there was a road of sorts—poor sorts—across the mountain, and Anne, her twenty geese collected, set out for home, driving them before her. All went well until she neared Charleston, when one of the geese succumbed to the rigors of the journey, and died. This was indeed a serious moment, and one requiring concentration and deep thought. However, Anne's usual resourcefulness stood her in good stead, and after a slight delay, her problem solved, she resumed her journey, and at last arrived at Captain Clendenin's doorstep with her geese quacking about her.

Captain Clendenin, much pleased, methodically counted the geese, but somewhat crestfallen, finding there were only nineteen, told her she had not fulfilled her bargain, and consequently there was no sale. Anne turned away, and going to her horse hitched by the fence, untied a sack which she brought back and opened. Dumping its contents out on the ground, she said, "There's your twenty," and the dead bird lay at his feet. The bill was promptly paid.

Anne's son, William Trotter, had somehow, somewhere, lived and grown to manhood, and in 1800 married Mary, daughter of a well-known pioneer, Captain Leonard Cooper, owner of a blockhouse on Cooper's Creek, nine miles above Point Pleasant. A few years later, 1814, Trotter bought a farm on the south side of the Kanawha above Point Pleasant, and his mother lived there with him for a short time. She was now seventy-two years of age, and, known to everyone, her time was spent in visiting friends and neighbors, recalling and retelling the exciting tales of her adventures, and hopefully anticipating the proffer of a sociable "dram," which had no doubt become more and more a means of escape from the rebellion she must have felt at the enforced limitations of a body growing old. In spirit Anne still longed to be free and untrammeled of any restraint or binding ties.

When her son sold his farm in 1818 and moved to Gallia County, Ohio, she wished none of it, and betook herself to Harrison Township, four miles below Gallipolis, where she managed to build a rough shelter of rails with her own hands, and prepared to stay. Her son arrived and, with great difficulty, finally persuaded her to accompany him home, but she agreed only on condition that he build on his premises a cabin for her where she might live alone. This he did, and there she spent the rest of her life. Still strong enough to pole a canoe up the river, and occasionally to walk the nine miles to Gallipolis, she knew no debilitating and wasting illness, but on November 22, 1828, at the age of eighty-six, she died in her sleep, alone in her own cabin, except for two small grandchildren—a fitting end to so individual a life.

County of "Kenhawa"
1788-1789

THE year in which Fort Lee was built was not only one of serious responsibilities for Colonel Clendenin, but it and the ensuing year were ones in which occurred important events in the history of the nation. The first United States Congress had met and George Washington had taken his place as the first President. Colonel Clendenin was a member of the Virginia convention that ratified the Constitution of the United States. During the summer recess of this Convention he was active in a movement which developed to form a new county from the western section of Greenbrier and Montgomery counties. A bill to that effect was introduced in the Assembly, and was passed on November 14, 1788, but specified the new county "known by the name of KENHAWA," with the county seat the yet unnamed settlement at Fort Lee, was not to be organized until the following year—October 1, 1789.

The suggestions of Clendenin and Andrew Donnally, Sr., as to the appointment of certain men as "gentlemen justices" for the new county were forwarded to Richmond and the appointments made accordingly. The first week in October, 1789, the new justices met at the fort, which served as a temporary courthouse, and there formed their county government with the help of a lawyer from Greenbrier who came to open the record books which Colonel

Clendenin had provided. This man, William Cavendish, was named the first county clerk, but as he was there merely in the capacity of instructor, his work was soon completed, and he turned the office over to the deputy clerk, Francis Watkins. Others present were Thomas Lewis, Charles McClung, Benjamin Strother, William Clendenin, David Robinson, George Alderson, Leonard Morris, James Van Bibber, and Robert Clendenin.

Colonel Thomas Lewis, the eldest member of the court, was legally entitled to the commission of High Sheriff and was duly designated as such by the Governor, serving until 1792, when he was succeeded by Captain William Clendenin. The county surveyors of Virginia received their appointments through the president and professors of William and Mary College, usually upon the recommendation of the county court, and Reuben Slaughter was chosen surveyor for Kanawha County. It is interesting to note that the first survey entered by Reuben Slaughter comprised one thousand acres near the mouth of Coal River for Phineas Taylor, grandfather of the great circus owner and showman, Phineas Taylor Barnum. The commissioners of revenue were Benjamin Strother, John Van Bibber, and David Robinson, and the two coroners were William Droddy and William Rogers. The first order of the court was that public buildings be erected as near the mouth of Elk as possible.

These matters disposed of, the next meeting of the justices, occurring on October 6, was for the purpose of forming the county military organization which became a part of the militia system of Virginia, under Colonel John Steele, United States Inspector of Western Defenses. Kanawha County was in Division Three, Brigade Thirteen, and had ten companies, two of which were composed of riflemen. George Clendenin was recommended for the same post he occupied in Greenbrier County—that of County Lieutenant—and as such, ranking military officer for the county. For Colonel, Thomas Lewis, eldest brother of General Andrew Lewis; Lieutenant Colonel, Daniel Boone, who was not present; Major, William Clendenin; Captains, John Morris and Leonard Cooper; Lieutenants, John Young and James Van Bibber; Ensigns, William Owens and Alexander Clendenin. The commissions of all of these officers were recorded at the spring term of court in 1791.

The destruction of the Tackett fort on Coal River aroused Colonel Clendenin anew to the need for more rangers and scouts, and on January 1, 1791, he was again in Richmond, once more urging a stronger defense of the frontier. For the next three years this ritual was repeated with varying degrees of success. At times there were a reasonable number of rangers in service, at other times very few. During the winter months the Indians seldom molested the settlers, and the majority of the rangers were dismissed. In the spring they were recalled to duty.

The ranger captains varied from time to time, John Morris and William Clendenin serving perhaps longer than any others. Morris, son of the pioneer settler of Kelly's Creek, kept his headquarters there at the Morris fort, where he was occupied in operating a much needed grist mill, erected by the Morris family about 1792, which supplied most of the meal and flour used by the militia. Captain Morris at one time had as many as eighty-five men under his command, most of whom he dispersed in small groups among the scattered inhabitants above and below his fort, roughly dividing the valley territory with Captain William Clendenin,

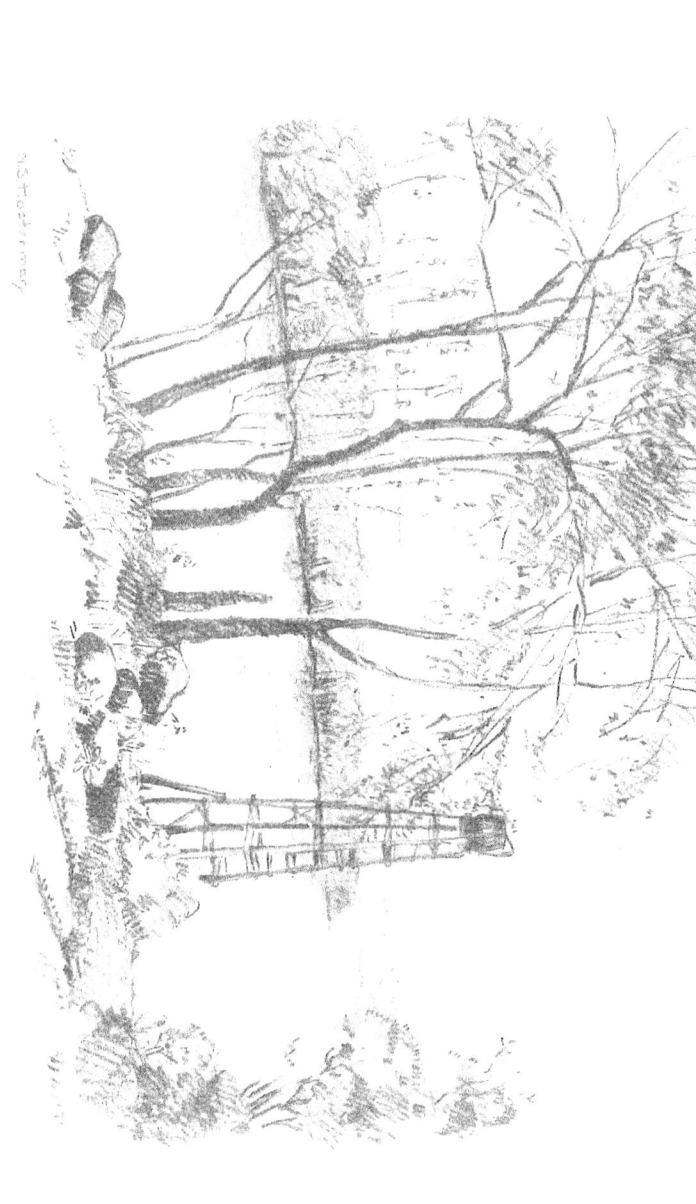
Salt Well On The Kanawha

brother of Colonel George Clendenin who maintained his station twenty miles below at Fort Lee and operated between that point and Fort Randolph, sixty miles farther west at the mouth of the Kanawha.

A controversy arose in the matter of distribution of ammunition and supplies, the posts on the Kanawha complaining that those on the Monongahela received more than their share, while the Kanawha militia had less than its quota. One complaint led to another, and due to overlapping military authority and other causes, partly political, Colonel Clendenin and a later commissioned ranger captain became involved in a feud. Military charges resulted against the captain, and a lengthy and wearisome trial was held in Lewisburg, with many witnesses and a great deal of mud-slinging, during which some of the charges were sustained, others not. Justly or unjustly, the prestige of Clendenin in the Assembly appeared to suffer after this happening.

Daniel Boone, County Lieutenant 1791

NEAR the Route 60 highway, on the eastern limits of Charleston, there is a plot of ground lying along the Kanawha River bank that is maintained for recreational purposes. It is called the "Daniel Boone Roadside Park," and a stone marker is placed to indicate the location on the opposite side of the river where Daniel Boone once lived. His log house stood on the Donnally farm near the upper end of Kanawha Avenue, in that part of Charleston known as Kanawha City. It was a good location, with a view of a slight bend in the river and the mouth of Campbell's Creek on the opposite side, where old "Thorofare Gap" marked the well-beaten buffalo trail to the Salt Licks. The area in which the house was situated is now occupied by manufacturing buildings and residences, but there remains an old cemetery where broken stones bear the names of later generations of the pioneer family of Colonel Andrew Donnally, Sr., upon whose lands the Boones resided. The two families were connected by marriage, Colonel Donnally's son, Andrew, Jr., marrying Marjorie Van Bibber, sister to the wife of Daniel Boone's son, Jesse.

The story of Daniel Boone, rich in drama and outstanding in achievement, has been told and retold, but it still remains a thrilling tale. A few years younger than George Washington, Boone, one of seven brothers, was born in 1734. When he was fifteen his father moved to western North Carolina. There, Daniel grew to manhood, married Rebecca Bryan, and they became the parents of a family of nine children. The two eldest, James, born 1757, and Israel, born two years later, were slain by Indians before they were grown. The four daughters, Susannah, Jemima, Lavinia, and Rebecca, all married and lived in Kentucky. The three younger sons, Daniel Morgan, born 1769, Jesse, 1773, and Nathan, 1780, eventually settled in Missouri.

Shortly before the Revolution, Boone moved to Kentucky, where he was active in acquiring lands, making surveys, and in establishing the settlement of Boonsborough. Unlike Simon Kenton, he was educated to the extent of reading and writing—though one could hardly include spelling, for his was often quite unique—and was also qualified as a surveyor. His great love, however, was hunting and trapping, and he was more at home in the woods than at a platting table. Traveling hundreds of miles, absent from his family for months at a time, spying on the Indians and familiar with their language and habits, his knowledge, experience, and judgment were of the greatest value on the frontier, and he was the first man thought of by Governor Dunmore for service as a messenger to warn scattered surveying parties of the approaching war. On this one mission he covered eight hundred miles of Kentucky wilderness. Made a captain, he commanded various forts on the frontier. He knew and came in contact with Kenton and all the great scouts and Indian fighters of his time, one of whom, Kit Carson, hero of the West, was a cousin. None surpassed Boone in coolness and in steady and accurate judgment.

His experiences with the Indians were numerous and exciting, as well as heartbreaking and bitter in the death of his own two sons. He had many narrow escapes, rescued many white captives, and was himself taken prisoner. Upon one occasion he was held prisoner for many months. The Indians admired his courage, his superior skill and woodcraft, and his ability as a hunter, and, considering him worthy to be one of them, took him into their tribe. During his captivity he influenced them to turn aside from an attack on Boonsborough, but months later they refused to be dissuaded, and were determined to carry out their plans. Five hundred Indians against the unsuspecting settlement in which his own family lived, meant only one thing to Boone—he must escape at whatever cost and warn them. The savages intended to take him with them, and were watching him closely, but somehow he managed to elude them. His absence detected almost at once, he was immediately pursued, but utilizing to the utmost his knowledge of their methods, he dodged, back-tracked, swam, and kept going without food or rest, his only meal a wild turkey which he risked killing when he felt far enough away to be temporarily safe. In five days he had covered one hundred and sixty-five miles and had reached Boonsborough in an emaciated and exhausted condition, only to find his family had long since given him up for dead, and had returned to their former home in North Carolina. Disappointed at their absence, but relieved as to their safety, he prepared the inhabitants for an attack. Finding the fort in bad condition, he at once saw to its repair, and in ten days the work was finished and the fort stocked with supplies and ammunition.

Indians, true to type, were thrown off balance by the unexpected, and after Boone had escaped, and they learned of his arrival at the fort, became uncertain what to do, and delaying for several weeks, lost the advantage of attacking an unprepared fort. Realizing they would now have Boone's leadership against them, they made still more elaborate preparations, and when the attack finally took place it lasted for nine days, the most prolonged siege on record, but even so, it was unsuccessful, and the Indians were forced to abandon it. Following this defense of the fort, Boone was advanced in rank to that of Major. After again restocking and reinforcing the fort, he departed to join his wife and children in North Carolina, later bringing them back to Boonsborough.

Boone's land holdings were extensive and valuable, but misfortune descended upon him when court decisions against a land company rendered his title void. Many other persons were caught in the same net, and on behalf of his neighbors and friends, Major Boone gathered together such money as he could and went to Richmond in an unsuccessful attempt to redeem their lands. The Virginia Legislature voted to give him a thousand acres free, which was negligible when weighed against his valuable military service on the frontier.

The Boones left Boonsborough and moved a few miles away, where they built a new home and stockade, called Boone's Station. Indian warfare was still a dreaded reality and they had lost their second son at the hands of the savages. Kentucky was being overrun by settlers and land speculators. Over twelve thousand people had arrived in 1783 and 1784. The courts were filled with litigants trying to unravel the technicalities of good and bad land claims, and again Boone was confronted with lawsuits and worthless titles. Appealing to the Legislature for redress proved a futile gesture and brought no reply, and after the final suit was ended, the debacle was complete, and he emerged a disheartened man with not an acre of ground that was his own. Though temporarily embittered, Daniel Boone was not one long to succumb to depression, and at once adopted his never-failing remedy by embarking on a strenuous season of hunting and trapping. The family coffers somewhat replenished as a result, he and his family departed on a visiting trip to Pennsylvania and Virginia, and in the fall of 1788 they reached Point Pleasant at the mouth of the Kanawha.

The Virginia frontier was not unfamiliar territory to Boone, for in his hunting and trapping trips he had followed the game trails wherever they led, and they had frequently led into that region. He had visited the mouth of Elk, inspected the salt licks, the Burning Springs, and other landmarks of the Valley, and by the same token was known to settlers and trappers everywhere. At Point Pleasant, renewing acquaintance with the Van Bibber, Lewis, and other families, some of whom he had met in other states, Boone decided to remain, and settled down in a log house on Crooked Creek, now within the town's eastern limits. Leaving his family in their new home, he was soon off on a hunting trip of several months that took him up the Big Sandy and along the Monongahela rivers and which may have accounted for his absence at the time of his appointment on October 6, 1789, as Lieutenant Colonel for the new County of Kanawha. He did not appear at Fort Lee to qualify as such until the April term of court in 1791.

While at Point Pleasant, Daniel Boone's seventeen-year-old son, Jesse, fell in love with Chloe Van Bibber, and a date was set for the wedding. Securing a license was an arduous procedure entailing a journey of sixty miles up river, either by canoe or by trail, to the county clerk at Fort Lee, with Indians likely to be encountered enroute. Eager to make an occasion of it, nine of Jesse's friends, including several of the Van Bibber boys, decided to accompany him, and August (1790) found them embarking in their canoes. They stopped for the night at Fort Tackett on Coal River, and the next day reached Fort Lee, only fourteen miles away, early enough to obtain the license and be off for home in short order. The return trip, aided by the down current, was made quickly and uneventfully—while unknown to them, a party of Indians was even then waiting to destroy Fort Tackett, and before the month ended had accomplished their purpose.

Daniel Boone moved from Point Pleasant to the location on the south side of the Kanawha River above Fort Lee shortly after this incident and assumed his duties of Lieutenant Colonel, as well as those of delegate to the General Assembly to which he, with George Clendenin, had been elected in April, 1791. It is said Boone, unassuming as usual, followed his customary mode of travel and went on foot to Richmond, and not as one embarking on an official journey, culminating in his formal seating in the newly completed and impressive capitol building.

Placed on a committee on "Propositions and Licenses," Colonel Boone submitted a recommendation to the Assembly specifying the number of spies and rangers needed on the Kanawha, and at what stations. He was given the contract to supply ammunition to the forts on the Monongahela and the Kanawha, the carrying out of which brought in its train many complaints from certain of the recipients. The long distances involved and the unavoidable delays in receiving personally carried requisitions and messages may have accounted for much of this dissatisfaction. There was never enough of anything in the nature of supplies—either food or ammunition—so complaints were routine at every military outpost.

In spite of other duties Colonel Boone engaged in making several surveys in the Kanawha region. The original plat of one of them, made in 1791 for ten acres on Crooked Creek, is preserved in the West Virginia State Museum. He also carried on his successful hunting and trapping business—sometimes alone and frequently with members of the Van Bibber family, brothers and relatives of his daughter-in-law. Buffalo, deer, and bear trails led up and down the valley and beyond, and hides brought good prices in the eastern market. Furs were also in demand, and Boone trapped many beavers in the Long Shoals of the Kanawha, accompanied at times by young Paddy Huddleston, whose father, Daniel Huddleston, lived near Kanawha Falls. The beaver trap they used may be seen in the Museum at the State Capitol.

The Huddlestons came to the Kanawha shortly before the arrival of the Clendenins, and about 1785 had built their two-story log house some miles east of the site of Fort Lee. They kept an ordinary, a welcome shelter for travelers who never failed to stay the night under its roof and to partake heartily of the excellent brandy made by their host. Although the log house was destroyed by fire, the chimney of this early hostelry still stands near the highway of Route 60, and bears a commemorative marker.

Indian hostilities at an end, and military duties terminated, Colonel and Mrs. Boone, with their youngest son Nathan, determined to leave the Kanawha Valley and return to Kentucky, and in the early summer of 1795 neighbors and friends gathered at the boat landing in front of Fort Lee, to assist in loading their few possessions on flatboats and to bid them farewell. Several persons accompanied them, one being Matthias Van Bibber who joined the party at Point Pleasant. They finally reached a point near Millersburg, Bourbon County, Kentucky, and locating there, were joined in the fall of 1797 by Jesse Boone and his family. Colonel Boone's life on the trails had unfitted him for contentment in a permanent abode. It was not long before the Colonel once more said good-by to Kentucky, and the Boones made their last move to join their son, Daniel Morgan Boone, in Missouri. There Mrs. Boone died in 1813.

In Missouri, Daniel Boone became a magistrate, in which capacity he served with dignity and fairness for several years. But difficult days lay ahead, as he again became embroiled in the red tape of land title trouble, the United States purchase of the Louisiana territory having rendered uncertain the validity of Spanish land grants. Although his Spanish grant was finally confirmed by Congress, such was several years later, and Boone in the meantime, impoverished by this final unfortunate land experience, had resorted once more to his long-tried panacea for heartache and financial ills, and taken to the game trails. This time it was with a new incentive. He longed and determined to be free of all financial obligation. His hunting trip was lengthy and strenuous, and extremely successful, and at last, with his earnings in hand, he made a final trip to Kentucky in 1810, and there, seeking out every creditor, paid all his debts in full. Relieved and satisfied, he traveled back to Missouri, happy and penniless.

Vigorous and active, Boone lived to be eighty-six, dying in 1820, after a three-day illness, at the comfortable stone house of his youngest son, Nathan. In all his extensive and varied travels covering thousands of miles and leading him from the Mississippi to the Yellowstone, Daniel Boone was a man whose poise and dignity earned him great respect and courtesy. His strong quietness and his thoughtful and kindly manner impressed all with whom he came in contact, and wherever he went, crowds traveled long distances to see and speak to him.

Audubon, the famous naturalist, wrote of Daniel Boone: "His countenance gave indication of his great courage, enterprise and perseverance; and when he spoke the very motion of his lips brought the impression that whatever he uttered was true." This comment was based upon personal association, as Boone, on several expeditions, had acted as Audubon's guide.

The Cobb Homestead

IN a day when being a frontiersman required, as a matter of course, skill with a gun, knowledge of the woods comparable, and frequently superior, to that of an Indian, and strength and stamina that could withstand all manner of hardship and danger, Fleming Cobb, or Cobbs, as his name was often spelled, was outstanding. One of the early scouts and settlers of the Kanawha Valley, certain of his exploits are still retained in the annals of West Virginia.

Though tales of frontier heroes are numerous, and grow a little more inspired with each repetition, none has reached more impressive heights than those involving Fleming Cobb. While mathematically-minded persons may compute distances with obviously lifted eyebrows, the fact remains that his marksmanship and his skill as a canoeman, coupled with his great physical endurance, were exceptional.

Born in Albemarle County, December 23, 1767, Cobb was twenty-two, the right age to respond when the appeal of the exciting life of the frontier brought him to the Kanawha in October of 1789, the year after the building of Fort Lee. Remaining through the winter, he determined to settle permanently in the Valley. Before doing so, he went back to eastern Virginia, the first of the following August for a visit to his uncle, Thomas Upton, probably persuading his relative to return with him in October. At any rate, the Upton family moved to the Kanawha that year, 1790, and Mr. Upton at once acquired two hundred and forty-one acres of land five miles below Fort Lee, on the south side of the river on, and below, Davis Creek, where he erected a cabin on a smaller stream, still known as Upton's Creek. Davis Creek got its name from Thomas Davis, to whom Upton sold a part of his acreage.

During the time of Cobb's visit to Albemarle a serious and disturbing tragedy had occurred only nine miles below Davis Creek. The Indians had attacked and destroyed the Tackett fort and settlement on Coal River. The boldness of this outrage made it dangerous for the Uptons to live on their farm, and Mr. Upton secured land in the Clendenin holdings, where his wife and children could be near Fort Lee, while he cleared his first acquired land and continued to go back and forth looking after his farm. In Colonel Clendenin's report to the Assembly in 1792, regarding the settlers on the Kanawha, he mentions Upton as "making a crop at his place" down the river.

Thomas Upton, Jr., served as one of the rangers at Fort Lee, where his cousin, Fleming Cobb, was also on the roll. Years later, in Cobb's application for a pension, he states that he served as a scout two hundred and sixty-one days that year, part of the time being on duty with John Young, another important figure of the frontier.

It was in course of his earlier services at Fort Lee, (1790), that Cobb is said to have performed one of his amazing accomplishments. The story, for the accuracy of which the author does not vouch, runs as follows: That year the Indians were much in evidence, and Colonel Clendenin, apprehensive of a possible attack on Fort Lee, had no intention of being caught without adequate means of defense. Choosing Fleming Cobb, the expert canoeman, as the ranger best qualified to undertake a speedy and perhaps hazardous mission, Colonel Clendenin sent Cobb down the river by canoe to bring back a load of ammunition from Fort Randolph, at Point Pleasant.

Atkinson's history says Cobb traveled under cover of darkness and floated down the river at night, while in the daytime he pulled his canoe ashore, concealed himself, and slept. When about ten miles from Fort Randolph, he counted a party of twenty Indians on the opposite bank traveling in the direction from which he had come. As soon as they were out of sight he pushed his canoe out of the bushes and hastened on to his destination. His canoe soon loaded with ammunition, he could only wait for darkness to begin his return journey, knowing the futility of starting by daylight and thus making of himself a perfect target for so large an Indian party.

In spite of his precautions, however, the sharp ears of the Indians detected the sound of his canoe in the stillness of the night, and the savages followed him along the bank, shooting at intervals. Cobb gave them little chance for accurate aim by poling constantly, keeping in the shadows of the opposite shore, and out of range as much as possible. Occasionally firing a shot himself just to let them know he was still able-bodied and to be reckoned with, he killed one Indian. His chief concern, however, was not to kill Indians, but to elude them before daybreak, and to carry his load of shot and powder safely to Fort Lee before the Indians could discover what the canoe contained, as he no doubt feared they were on their way to attack Fort Lee. As daylight came, and he drew nearer the settlement, his pursuers abandoned the chase, and at ten o'clock in the morning Cobb landed his canoe at the fort—a journey of sixty miles or more, upstream, without rest or food, in fourteen hours time. Long afterward, his son and grandson related the incident in a family sketch prepared for Hardesty's *Encyclopedia* (1883), but made no mention of the Indian encounter.

No doubt weary of hearing this tale of ancestral prowess, Hiram Cobb, another grandson, by way of demonstrating there were yet good fish in the pond, is said years later to have duplicated his grandfather's canoe trip from Point Pleasant to Charleston, between sunrise and sunset, minus Indian pursuers, and with nothing more at stake than the winning of a wager, the reward being a gallon of peach brandy, which, after all, may have been a somewhat more tangible incentive than posthumous fame and glory!

Fleming Cobb is credited with killing the last Indian slain in Kanawha County, and the doing of it was in the usual extraordinary Cobb fashion. The savage had come up the Kanawha in a canoe and landed at Wilson Island, a small island just below Blaine Island, opposite the present South Charleston. Cobb,* who lived in that locality, saw him, and firing from the south bank of the river, a distance of two hundred or more yards, killed him instantly.

In 1793, the year before the little town of Charleston was officially established, Mr. Cobb purchased what was later designated in the town plat as Lot Number Three, adjoining that owned by his friend, John Young, and no doubt expected to live there. However, a legacy from his uncle, Thomas Upton, whose death occurred the following year, 1794, determined the location of Cobb's

---

*The hickory wood powder flask of this pioneer marksman may be seen in the Museum at the West Virginia State Capitol.

future residence which was on part of the Davis Creek lands, left to him by his uncle.

Cobb married on January 16, 1796, Sarah (Sally) Morris, daughter of Leonard Morris, who lived on the south side of the Kanawha above Fort Lee, in a home pictured in this book. The Cobb homestead, probably constructed within a year or so after his marriage, is situated a few miles below Charleston, on the south side of the river to the left of the present entrance to the Kanawha Country Club grounds. This old house is one of the earliest of the pioneer dwellings in this region, and was still habitable when purchased in 1945 by the Carbide and Carbon Chemicals Corporation.

At the mouth of Davis Creek, on the hard clay of its eastern bank, the house stood through the years as solidly as when it was erected. Its log walls chinked with the rock-like clay, which is characteristic of this site, remained strong and substantial. It was weatherboarded at an early date, and other rooms added on one side. Although the newer section does not have log walls, the details of its weatherboard construction show it to have been of a very early period. The house is small and low, the whipsawed ceiling beams within reach of one's hand. The side walls, sealed with wide boards, in later years were covered by countless layers of wallpaper. Of yellow poplar throughout, some of the ceiling boards measure twenty-three inches in width, the virgin forest permitting a lavish use of only the largest and finest trees. Few nails were used, everything being carefully pegged and mortised together. The low sloping roof extends from the ridge in unbroken line to the eaves of the porch across the front of the house, where the solid, square-cut posts are mortised into the crossbeams above.

There is evidence of an outside stairway that led to

the upper rooms, which constituted little more than a loft. A small kitchen wing, with large chimney and Dutch oven, extends in the rear. The chimneys and hearths are of stone, and in the cellar the native stone is exposed. The small window panes still retain their original glass, its wavy characteristic plainly visible.

A large log barn, removed within the last two years, stood in the bottom land some distance away, as well as a poultry house whose frame construction and material appeared to be contemporary with the house. Century-old elms were spaced on each side of the house, and the yard also contained walnut and other trees. It is a tradition that the first fruit trees growing in the Kanawha Valley were two apple and two pear trees, brought across the mountains in leather bags by Fleming Cobb. The former were planted on this farm, where as late as 1945 gnarled apple trees still stood in the strip of low land between the house and the barn. The pear trees were said to have been planted on near-by (Wilson) Blaine Island, where Cobb planted certain of his crops.

When the old James River and Kanawha Turnpike was built about 1824, it crossed the river by ferry at Charleston from the present Goshorn Street, and followed the south bank down the Valley, cutting through the Cobb farm in front of the house. Such liberties were not to be taken lightly by Mr. Cobb, who appeared before the court in 1830 to protest and seek damages. While this section of the early narrow road is still in usable condition, it has long since been supplanted by a relocated highway much nearer the river. Today the old route is here paralleled by the high roadbed of the Chesapeake and Ohio Railroad, leaving the small house forlornly lost in an isolated spot where it is not seen except by one searching for it.

Rosedale

Remarkable as it seems, the Cobb property remained in possession of members of the family until the sale in 1945. Here Fleming Cobb died on January 10, 1846, at seventy-nine years of age, and was buried in the family cemetery which is now on the property of the Kanawha Country Club. His widow lived to be eighty-one. He was also survived by his son and namesake, Fleming Cobb, Jr. (b. 1813), who, twice married, had a family of nine children, and they, as well as many other descendants of their grandfather, lived at least a part of their lives in this early homestead.

"The Town at the Mouth of the Elk"
1794

ALTHOUGH Colonel Clendenin did not know he stood on one of the nation's great undiscovered treasuries of natural resources, he did see more in the Kanawha Valley than an advantageous site for a fort. Lying directly across the pathway to Ohio and Kentucky and the fabulous western lands beyond, the mecca of so many settlers, he visualized the valley at the mouth of Elk as a desirable location for a growing town. With that thought in mind he began dividing parcels of his lands into lots, and in 1794 procured Alexander Welch, surveyor of Greenbrier County, to make the plat of a town.

He selected forty acres of the section of his survey lying below the enclosure around the fort and extending almost to Elk River (approximately Capitol to Clendenin streets). There were two streets running parallel with the Kanawha—that nearest the river was called Front Street, now Kanawha Boulevard, and the other was called Main or Back Street, now Virginia Street. There were six blocks on each street, those on Front divided into four lots to a block, while the blocks on Main contained only two lots. The cross streets beginning at the eastern end were numbered 1, 2, 3, 4, and 5, no numbers being given to the boundary streets. The lots bore numbers beginning with number 1 on the eastern limit of Front

Street and running to 24 on its western end, while those on Main Street began with 25 and ran through 36.

A few cabins had already been erected and crops harvested on parts of the area before the survey was made, one of which belonged to Lewis Tackett, builder of Fort Tackett on Coal River, destroyed by the Indians in 1790. He had escaped to Fort Lee and was grantee in a deed for Lot Number 1 on Front and Sixth streets which evidently covered his previous holding. Lot Number 2 was purchased by his son-in-law, John Young, well-known scout and ranger who, with his wife and her day-old child, had also escaped the massacre and reached Fort Lee after a sensational trip by canoe from the burning fort on Coal River. Lot Number 3 was acquired by Fleming Cobb, another scout, and a friend of Young.

George Alderson purchased Lot Number 4, and Dr. Jesse Bennett, a physician and surgeon who attained national recognition, and who later settled near the mouth of the Kanawha, secured a lot in 1796. Numerous other purchasers acquired town lots, including Colonel Andrew Donnally, former resident of Greenbrier County and builder of Donnally's Fort. In fact, the town at that time had a population of sixty people. There were a number of inhabitants in the vicinity, however, who owned and lived on larger acreages. Among these were Alexander Clendenin, youngest brother of Colonel Clendenin who had purchased two hundred and seven acres, and the other brother, William Clendenin, who had bought land above the fort upon which the small blockhouse stood, and there made his home.

The county officers were in no haste to build a courthouse in the new town, as the fort served the purpose adequately. The first need seems to have been that of a jail, and one was erected in 1792 on the river bank between the lots of Lewis Tackett and John Young. It consisted of a small two-story building, twelve feet square, with ceilings seven feet high. The lower room was largely under ground. Built by Lewis Tackett, it was pronounced unsatisfactory by William Clendenin, who was sheriff at the time. It was doubtless used, however, until a later one was built.

A public lot was finally acquired from George Alderson in settlement of an unpaid balance of about one hundred dollars which Alderson owed the county through a former purchase. There, in 1796, the first courthouse was erected—a small one-story log structure, forty by thirty feet, with two jury rooms fourteen feet square, a building which left ample room for the customary large public green surrounding it. This lot on Front Street was on the original town plat, and is the same upon which the present courthouse stands, the green having been long since absorbed by buildings.

A second jail was subsequently erected on this lot. Nearby also stood the pillory and stocks, and later there extended along the river in front of the courthouse a large covered public market house, which was burned prior to 1850 during a severe epidemic of cholera. The next county building was the clerk's office erected in 1802, and, though small, it was a much more permanent structure than any of its predecessors. Built of stone, it was located some distance from the other public buildings on the site now occupied by the Ruffner Hotel.

When Colonel Clendenin went to Richmond in 1794 to attend the Assembly, he felt it was high time his town received official title and recognition. He accordingly introduced a bill to that end. On December 19 it was favorably acted upon, and the town at the mouth of Elk was given the name of "Charlestown," honoring Charles

Clendenin, father of the founder, whose death in 1790 was the first to occur in the little settlement, and who was buried inside the stockade of Fort Lee. The grave is thought to be located in what is now the grass plot between the sidewalk and street at or near number 1204 Kanawha Boulevard. The trustees appointed by the Assembly for "Charlestown" were Reuben Slaughter, Andrew Donnally, Sr., Captain William Clendenin, John Morris, Sr., Leonard Morris, George Alderson, Abraham Baker, John Young, and William Morris.

The name of "Charlestown" was used for a time, but gradually became shortened to Charleston, and on January 19, 1818, the shorter name was officially adopted, although, strangely enough, the post office, designated "Kanawha Courthouse" in 1801, was not changed to conform to the name of the town until long afterward —1879.

Although hostile Indians still occasionally visited the valley, their depredations were on a gradually diminishing scale, and 1795 marked the last year of the existence of Fort Lee as a unit of the Virginia militia system. After the official order from Richmond directing the dismissal of all ranger companies had been received and complied with, a messenger arrived at Fort Lee asking help for the settlers farther west who were alarmed by the information that about twenty-five Indians had crossed the Ohio and it was feared were headed for the settlements on the Elk and Kanawha. Colonel Clendenin, having no rangers, ordered six of his former scouts on duty. The Indians, as a matter of fact, did not molest the settlements, but certainly Colonel Clendenin could not deny the appeal for help. However, the authorities in Richmond thought otherwise and directed him to discharge the scouts at once. They also informed him very curtly that in the future such matters would be handled by Colonel Thomas Lewis of Point Pleasant.

Colonel Clendenin took the rather broad hint, and returning his commission to Governor Robert Brooke, tendered his resignation, along with a few pertinent farewell words: "* * * it is an office that I never solicited, and have found it both unthankful and unprofitable, having never received a single Farthing from the public coffers, but on the contrary, have for the protection and support of my country, expended many hundred pounds, which the public have shewed very little or no disposition to refund."

The Indian wars at an end, and his military career behind him, Colonel Clendenin, feeling none too kindly toward the Assembly for the treatment he had received at its hands, was no doubt glad to dispose of his Kanawha land holdings when opportunity offered. After selling the residue of his tract along the river, in the latter part of August, 1796, to Joseph Ruffner, Colonel Clendenin departed for a visit to his daughter, Mrs. John Meigs, in Marietta, Ohio, perhaps with some idea of acquiring lands and removing his family to Ohio. Whatever his plans may have been, Colonel Clendenin, used to a life of action and warfare, had little opportunity to accustom himself to the quiet of peaceful pursuits, since he did not live to the vigorous old age of many pioneers, but died at the home of his daughter the following April (1797), when but fifty-one years of age. Captain William Clendenin sold his lands also to Joseph Ruffner, and with his family removed to the Point Pleasant region where he later died.

Fort Lee Ends with Militia System 1795

THE old Fort Lee building passed through many hands and today no vestige of it remains. A stone marker on Kanawha Boulevard, just above Brooks Street, denotes its location.

After the fort was vacated by the Clendenins it was occupied by the Ruffner family—first Joseph Ruffner and then his son, David, who lived there about ten years, selling the property to James Wilson in 1814. The stockade was removed about that time. Mr. Wilson sold the property in 1830 to Isaac Noyes, Bradford Noyes, and Frederick Brooks, the latter residing in a two-story frame house on the corner of a street next to the Fort, which was given his name of Brooks. The property became involved in litigation, and the next owner, John A. Truslow, acquired it through a court decree in 1861.

Mr. Truslow "modernized" the house by weatherboarding and plastering it, and may have added a porch. After this it ceased to be known as the fort and began to be spoken of as the Truslow house. The fort area meanwhile was divided into lots, and the building and certain of the lots were sold by Mr. Truslow in the summer of 1870 to Dr. John P. Hale who conveyed the fort site two years later (1872) to Charles Cameron Lewis, Sr. The deed stipulated that Hale remove the buildings then on the lot, which were the Brooks house and the fort. This he did, moving the Brooks house back to the northeast corner of what is now Brooks and Virginia streets, and the log fort back to a location now occupied by a residence numbered 1209 Virginia Street.

The fort house had by this time undergone many changes. The old stone chimneys had been replaced by new ones of brick, and a stairway, extra rooms, and porches had been added. Dr. Hale sold it to Mordecai Levi, father of a present Charleston resident, Mr. Noyes Rand (Plus) Levi, who lived there as a child. Mr. Levi in turn sold the fort house to its last owner, Mr. Thomas E. Jefferies for $2,500, which then was considered a very high price. Mr. Jefferies and his family occupied the property until April 1, 1891, when it was completely destroyed by fire—an unworthy end to this staunch century-old monument to the founders of West Virginia's capital city.

First House on Paint Creek

THE Paint Creek region has a special interest, its aboriginal inhabitants having been an unknown people who left curious stone enclosures on the top of the steep hillsides, their purpose still unknown. The first Indians in the Valley found them, but knew nothing of their origin or meaning, expressing complete ignorance to the questions of the early white settlers. Partially fallen into rubble, portions of these strange walls still stand as a mute monument to a vanished and mysterious race—whether related to the builders of the numerous burial mounds found throughout the Valley or preceding them, has never been determined.

The Delawares gave the name of Ot-to-we, "deer creek," to the stream that flows through three counties to enter the Kanawha from the south bank about twenty-two miles east of Charleston. Here was one of the early fording places used by the Indians, and here was found the ocherous clay that gave the stream its modern name and with which the savages blazed the trees along the trails of the short route to the upper New River. Indications are that it was a much frequented place, burial grounds, pottery, beads, and many stone implements being found in the vicinity.

White men were also attracted to this locality. Arriving upon the heels of the last departing Indians, they quickly changed the name Ot-to-we to Paint Creek, and at once began a settlement upon the former Indian thoroughfare. The earliest settler was John Jones. Born in Culpeper, Virginia, in 1755, he first came to the Valley with the army of General Lewis. Wounded in the Battle of Point Pleasant, he nevertheless continued in service throughout the Revolution. After the war he returned to the Kanawha, and having married Frances, youngest of the children of William Morris, Sr., immediately began acquiring lands, and by 1797 had secured patents for nearly a thousand acres on the upper Kanawha, as well as four hundred acres in Teays Valley below Coal River.

Selecting a site a short distance above the mouth of Paint Creek, Mr. Jones built his home high on the bank and facing the river. A substantial man of quiet, though positive, temperament, he lived there until his death in 1838. The Jones house is no longer in existence, but near its site stands the attractive brick dwelling built by Dickinson Morris on land out of the original Jones tract.

John Harriman House

ONE of the company of rangers that accompanied Colonel Clendenin to the Kanawha Valley in 1788, and who helped to build and garrison Fort Lee, was Shadrack Harriman. He first lived inside the fort, but later built a cabin just below Charleston's present Capitol Street. In the latter part of the year 1790 he and his wife, Susanna Pryor, daughter of William Pryor, large landowner in the Paint Creek region, removed to a new cabin on the south side of the Kanawha opposite Fort Lee and a mile or so above it.

Located on a plot of ground previously cultivated by Harriman, the cabin stood near the mouth of Venable Branch, now Union Mission Hollow, and on land for many years a part of the Colonel Andrew Donnally, Sr., farm. This was not a safe location, as Indians frequently passed up and down the south side of the Kanawha, avoiding contact with the rangers stationed at Fort Lee. On March 7, 1791, while Harriman was at work on his land, he was attacked and killed by a party of savages. His family made their escape across the river to the small blockhouse which served as an outpost of Fort Lee, and as a residence for Captain William Clendenin. It stood near the site of the present Executive Mansion.

Many accounts of this event credit Harriman with being the last man killed by Indians in the Kanawha Valley, and give the date as 1794. Such is entirely incorrect as shown in *The Annals of Fort Lee,* by Dr.

Roy Bird Cook, who states that court records on April 5, 1791, show that Mrs. Harriman, her brother, William Pryor, Joseph Carroll, and John Young were appointed appraisers of Harriman's estate.

There were later instances of Indian attacks in the Valley, one of which occurred soon after the death of Harriman, when James Hale was killed in October of the same year. His death also occurred on the south side of the river, almost opposite Fort Lee, where a little stream flowing into the Kanawha is still called Hale's Branch.

Mrs. Harriman, no doubt still a young woman, was married in 1794 to David Milburn, and in 1804 she deeded to John Harriman, a son of her first marriage, lands near Paint Creek which had been given to her by her father. This tract was an original grant to William Pryor I, dated 1787, and was described in the usual vague terms employed in early grants, as "all the bottom land and the front of the hill." It probably adjoined the Morris surveys.

It is thought a house of logs was first built upon this tract, on a site now occupied by a brick dwelling. Mrs. D. W. Taylor, granddaughter of John Harriman, believes him to have been the builder of the brick structure, but is uncertain of the date. His death occurred about 1845, so it appears the house is well over a hundred years old.

The wife of John Harriman was Nancy Morris, daughter of Joshua Morris, fourth son of William Morris, Sr., and the house later was owned and occupied by her distant relative, Fenton Morris, son of Sarah (b. 1792, daughter of Major John Hansford) and William Morris. After this ownership the property went out of the hands of the Harriman-Morris clan, and is now owned by Mrs. C. H. Matics, its present occupant.

This house is located in East Bank, near what was first called Harriman's Branch, and now known as Buck's Hollow. On the lower side and close by the public road, it conforms to the usual pattern of the 1820's, with oblong facade and wing in the rear. The roof is very low, having no space between the stone lintels above the five shutter-trimmed windows of the second floor and the hand-carved wood cornice which ornaments the front and ends of the house. There may once have been a small portico covering the central doorway, but in course of time it disappeared, and as the long-porch era arrived, was supplanted by one of the newer style. Even so, the change is not unduly disfiguring, and is easily forgotten, while one enjoys the picture made by distant hills beyond the river as they rise to make a pleasing background against which the old red house smiles cheerfully with the afternoon sun in its face.

"The Old Riggs Place"

LEVI MORRIS, fifth son of the pioneer William Morris, Sr., of Kelly's Creek, was, according to a roadside marker, the first settler on the site of the present town of Montgomery, having come there by mule from Alexandria, Virginia, about 1770. Laidley's *History of Kanawha County* devotes much space to this family, and states that Levi Morris was not born until 1768, and that his father and brothers did not reach the Valley until 1774. If such be true, Levi must certainly have been a precocious child. Taking up land, and riding a mule alone across the mountains at the tender age of two, would seem to have been a somewhat ambitious undertaking, even in that day of physical giants. Where and how this story originated no one seems to know, and yet it is frequently encountered, and the mule is always present. The writer has seen the same account used in connection with the name of a much later settler, Henry Montgomery. That mule apparently had as long a life as Anne Bailey's octogenarian horse "Liverpool."

In the section of the *West Virginia History* magazine called "West Virginia in the Revolution," where data is based on pension applications and other definite records, sketches are given of several of the Morris sons, and the birth date of Levi varies greatly from that given by Mr. Laidley. It appears as 1753, which would make his pioneering activities seem a bit more reasonable. Even so, seventeen is still a rather youthful age for such venturing, particularly as his parents and brothers did not come until four years later, and the region was uninhabited. He and the mule must not have had a very chatty time!

Discrepancies to the contrary, certain it is that Levi Morris was living twenty-four miles east of Charleston on the south side of the river at the time of his father's death in 1792, and no doubt can be safely considered the first settler within the area of the present town of Montgomery. His log house was erected in the western section above the mouth of a stream that is still called Morris Creek. This land was a part of the extensive Morris holdings, and in the settlement of his father's estate, was allotted to Levi with a large surrounding acreage.

Twice married, Levi Morris had a family of eight children, and his descendants have continued to be identified with this locality, particularly the children of his son James, whose daughter, Susan, married Dickinson Morris, builder of "Harmony Hill," elsewhere described. Her sister, Emma, married as her second husband, William Riggs. Their home, the earliest house now standing in Montgomery, is spoken of as "The Old Riggs Place."

Successor to the first log dwelling of Levi Morris, the Riggs house is near the same site, the date of its construction being uncertain, possibly in the 1820's. Said to have been built by Levi Morris, the house is more identified with later members of the family, as Levi died in 1834. His brother, Benjamin, built a brick house on the opposite side of the river in 1824, which Levi purchased, and may have moved there and have been living in it at the time of his death.

"The Old Riggs Place" still retains a family association and is now owned by a Morris descendant, Mrs. B.

H. Early, of Pratt, and is rented and occupied by her relatives, Mr. and Mrs. W. T. L. Crocker.

The house, facing First Avenue, stands high on the bank above the river, with enormous maple trees and a border of flowers on each side of the steep grassy path leading from the street below. Constructed of brick, the simple dwelling is not large. Oblong in shape, with a one-story rear wing, it is built low upon the ground, with a fairly shallow slanting roof. A typical mark of early houses is found in the stone lintels, which are above the shuttered windows that flank the square double portico covering the entrance. Firestones of the first log house serve as steps. Exhibiting no unusual details, this house, like many others mentioned in this book, is chiefly interesting because of its association, rather than its architecture.

Harmony Hill

Benjamin Morris House

BENJAMIN MORRIS, youngest of the sons of William Morris, Sr., was born in 1770, four years before the family settled in Kanawha Valley. In 1788 he and three other brothers, William, Henry, and Levi, joined the company of rangers recruited by Colonel Clendenin to build and garrison Fort Lee at the mouth of Elk. Benjamin had a reputation as a great hunter, and it is actually stated that he once killed one hundred and thirty-three bears in one day. Although bears were plentiful, this appears to be carrying things to an extreme, as even a few bears would seem a fair day's work.

Benjamin Morris married Nancy Jarrett, and they were the parents of seven children, several of whom lived in other states. A daughter, Celia, married Captain John Harvey, and their son, Morris Harvey, became well known in West Virginia, where his name is perpetuated in that of Morris Harvey College in Charleston.

Benjamin Morris built, in 1824, a large and substantial brick house upon the north side of the Kanawha a little below the bridge to Montgomery, where it is plainly visible from the opposite side of the river. While its once red brick walls, later painted white, are now grown a dingy gray, the good lines of the house are still satisfying, and with reasonable restoration it could emerge into a surprisingly attractive place. Oblong in shape, it is two stories high, with inside chimneys piercing the low slanting roof at each end. The pleasing entrance doorway, with glass side panels and curved glass above, leads into a central hall from which open large square rooms.

The house is below and well back from the highway, in a tree-shaded lawn that slopes gradually down to the water's edge. The land was part of the Morris surveys that extended for miles on both sides of the river. When his father's estate was settled in 1793, Benjamin was apportioned an acreage on the opposite side of the river, possibly adjoining that of his brother Levi. Oddly enough, they kept the river between them, although they apparently exchanged sides—for Benjamin sold his new home to Levi, and took up his residence on the south side, while Levi shifted over to the opposite bank to become the occupant of the brick house.

Harmony Hill

DICKINSON MORRIS, a son of the second marriage of his father Leonard Morris, married Susan, daughter of James Morris and granddaughter of Levi Morris, an uncle of Dickinson himself. Her father was one of the first to acquire land above Paint Creek. The oldest house in Handley, now a hotel called "The Morris House," was his home. His lands extended for some distance up the river, and when the village was laid out, the only buildings on the site were two houses and the Morris slave cabins.

"Harmony Hill," erected in 1840-41 of brick burned on the site, is a well-preserved and good-looking building. High on the bank above the public road the hill rises steeply behind the house and furnishes a green coolness on summer days. Large trees shade the side yard, and in front are several old cedars. The house is two stories in height, with a three-room wing added in 1861. Inside chimneys at each end pierce the slanting roof. There was no skimping of brick in the construction, the deep window sills and partition walls measuring eighteen inches in thickness.

The windows are unusually large and very attractive, some having twelve panes of glass in the upper sash and eight in the lower, and others having eight in each. Of the five windows across the front on the second floor, the central one is trimmed with additional "side lights," corresponding to those on each side of the heavy paneled front door below. Originally, a one-story portico covered the entrance, and likely had a rail trim around the top, giving a reason for the extra window lights above, as they suggest a doorway onto the roof. This portico, later removed, was replaced by the present porch extending the length of the house.

The stairway against the right wall crosses to the left at the rear of the central hallway, and its round handrail is supported by two square spindles on each step. The original floors remain in several of the large rooms opening from the hall. The unusually high mantels, the wide grooved window casings with panels below, the sturdy paneled doors, and all other interior woodwork were made by hand. The hewn window shutters were made by a man named Johnson, to whom the owner gave a plot of land. The milk house was built into the conveniently near hill, while the other farm buildings and slave cabins were scattered along in the low lands. The wellhouse still stands near the kitchen doorway.

At the time of the Civil War, Harmony Hill was used as headquarters by Federal officers, and during this occupancy a man committed suicide in one of the upper rooms—whether friend or foe, or for what reason, is now a forgotten "military secret."

Today Harmony Hill is the home of Mr. and Mrs. Herndon V. Frazer and Mr. Roland C. Frazer, descendants of the well-known proprietor of Frazer's Tavern in Lewisburg, an early and famous hostelry catering to the prominent judges who sat in the various courts of Virginia held there before the Civil War. The Frazer home in Greenbrier County was called "Harmony Hill," and with Frazer ownership of the Dickinson Morris house, the same name was adopted.

Along Paint Creek are several small neighboring towns whose names and post offices have been changed so frequently that one hesitates to say definitely where a house is located. At the moment, "Harmony Hill" is in Pratt. It used to be in Dego (an appalling inspiration of post office authorities), and previously it was in Clifton, so named from the sheer cliffs on the face of the mountain that rises above the town. This name, by far the most suitable, was chosen and specified by Dickinson Morris in 1851, when he laid off a portion of his lands for a town, deeding it to Samuel Hanna, Morris Hansford, and Mathew P. Wyatt, trustees. The name of Clifton was used for a time, but abandoned later because of confusion with another town of the same name in Mason County. It was then it lost its distinction and became "Dego." Years later when the Charles Pratt Coal Company made large purchases and began operations on Paint Creek, the town was named "Pratt" and incorporated as such in 1905.

Three Homes of the Hansfords

Major John Hansford

MAJOR John Hansford (1765-1850) of Orange County, Virginia, married Jane (1770-1854), eldest child of Major William Morris about 1787, and they were the parents of a large family of sons and one daughter. The Hansfords first lived near her parents on Kelly's Creek, but in 1798 moved to the south side of the river to lands which her father had given them. There Major Hansford spent that year and the next building a home which was so much finer than any others in the Valley that it was nothing short of sensational. It stood below the mouth of Paint Creek at Crown Hill.

Although the house is long since gone, it has been frequently described. A small picture owned by descendants shows it standing on the slope of the hillside surrounded by tall cedars and other trees. The chief innovation was its frame construction, which is said to have been the Valley's first departure from the use of logs. The outside chimneys were of brick imported from England, wide at the base and narrowing toward the top. Supported by a stone foundation, the house was two stories in height with a one-story wing on the right. It contained six rooms—a feature then so unusual that it no doubt aroused much speculation as to what in the world the Hansfords would do with all of those rooms! However, Major Hansford did not stop with this magnificence, but finished the interior in paneled cherry and walnut. In all respects it was an excellently built and comfortable home, whose owner was obviously a person of discriminating taste.

Major Hansford is described as a handsome man, well dressed in blue broadcloth and silk hat, an agreeable and hospitable host. A man of prominence, he represented Kanawha in the Virginia Assembly from 1811 to 1818. He served as a Magistrate and as Captain of the County Militia, and was active in other public duties, as well as in operating two salt furnaces and in farming his large estate. Owner of thirty slaves, he was noted for his kindness to them. A religious man, he nevertheless was famous for his good brandy, which he served unstintingly to his guests and to the militia company following the regular Muster Day drill which was held near his home.

Felix G. Hansford

ONE of the sons, Felix G. Hansford, who was born in 1795, built an interesting house which is now the oldest remaining in this locality. Immediately below the mouth of Paint Creek, it is placed with its back to the river, facing the early public road that passed its door. Today it must look at the roadbed of the main line of the Chesapeake and Ohio Railroad, the highway being relocated and paralleling the railroad on the opposite side.

Constructed in 1825 of bricks burned on the bank of the Creek, and now painted dark red, this house is in splendid condition and is a rarity in that it is architecturally unchanged. Few early houses exist that have not undergone at least some alterations, and it is a sad fact, but indubitably true, that they are usually deplorable ones. The first thing to go is always the little square entrance portico, but in this house it remains unaltered, and stands staunchly supported by white columns—plain, simple, and harmonious. Although the house is two stories in height, its rather flat roof makes it appear lower. A story and a half wing extending in the back is actually a small house in itself, but is connected with the main building by a breezeway enclosed on the windward side by heavy doors fastened by rod locks. It is said the small house was built first and used for living quarters until the house proper was completed.

The interior is in original condition, with wide pine floor boards, rather plain mantels with curved tops and grooved sides, and low wainscot around the first floor rooms. In the central hallway the wainscot is paneled horizontally, with boards twenty inches wide. An interesting detail is the wooden strip around the wall with pegs for hanging hats and coats. The stairway is fairly narrow and steep, curving sharply, as the hallway is small. A pair of long French entrance doors have an inside iron bar slanting across their width—a surprising feature—the single door at the rear of the hall being also barred in the same way. One wonders if this was a Civil War precaution. Both doors still have their large English-made box locks, marked with the British coat-of-arms.

The windows retain their original wavy glass—one of the most costly and most difficult to secure of all the items needed in early house construction. Both upper and lower sash are cut into twelve panes, and the usual hand-hewn shutters trim the windows. A small frame building stands in the side yard and was used by Mr. Hansford as his office. Here he reckoned his accounts and looked after the affairs of his farm.

Mr. Hansford attended school in Lewisburg at the early Academy, and while a student there, married Sarah

Herndon Frazer (b. 1795) of Greenbrier County, in 1821. An intelligent and well-read woman, she also possessed unusual physical vigor and lived to the extreme age of ninety-four. She is buried with others of her family in the Hansford cemetery on the near-by hill.

The Hansfords had six children:

(1) James, who married Annie Noyes;

(2) Martha Jane, who married John S. F. Smith, of Charleston, South Carolina;

(3) Sally, who married Phillip Doddridge;

(4) Felix G., who married Louella Hamilton, of Kentucky;

(5) Bettie, who married James Middleton;

(6) Philadelphia, who married William Hobson, of Virginia.

Descendants of these families are numerous in the Kanawha Valley. Mrs. Dennis (Eleanor Baillie) Brennen, granddaughter of Mr. and Mrs. Phillip Doddridge, is the present occupant of the Hansford house. There numerous pieces of "heirloom" furniture are still happily at home, particularly a heavily carved and massive poster bed that stood in the same second floor room for a hundred years before it was removed to the first floor. A special treasure is a two-part dining table with serpentine ends and reeded legs. It is of Mount Vernon association, as it came through the Parks family. Milton Hansford (b. 1811), brother of Felix G., married Mary, daughter of Andrew Parks, whose mother was a niece of George Washington.

After the death of Washington in 1799, a life interest in Mount Vernon passed to his widow, by whose will the majority of the household effects were divided among her four grandchildren. In this way the original furnishings of the mansion became scattered.

Dr. Marshall Hansford

ONE of the most attractive houses in the Paint Creek region is located in Pratt, at the eastern terminus of Washington Street. Built in 1856 by Dr. Marshall Hansford, who was born in 1807, it is of a considerably later period than the Paint Creek home of his brother, Felix G. Hansford, who was twelve years his senior. With a strip of green lawn sloping gradually to the river's edge, and a pair of enormous trees flanking the entrance and throwing their shadows across the doorway, the original setting of this home must have added greatly to its appearance of spacious dignity. Today the house seems crowded, as a street has been laid out in front of it, with small dwellings scattered along on the other side. The two great trees now stand outside of an iron fence, and being directly in the path of any potential sidewalk, one shudders to think of their possible fate, since a hundred-year-old tree is only a problem to sidewalk-layers, whose admiration seems to center chiefly on an uninterrupted expanse of concrete.

Substantially constructed, the brick walls of this house are supported by a foundation of large blocks of cut stone. Oblong in shape, with a rear wing on a slightly lower level, the plan is the usual one of large rooms opening from a wide central hall extending the depth of the building. When built, a square double portico obviously covered the front entrance, the upper portion of which is still intact. It extends to the roof line, and the hand-carved cornice across the front of the house is continued around it. Enclosed by a balustrade in diamond design, the portico is supported by interesting handmade columns of narrow vertical strips of wood. The corresponding portico for the first floor was evidently removed later, and substituted by a long porch extending the width of the house. The columns for this porch, while the same size as those above, are of the usual mill construction. The entrance door, which still retains its early square box lock, is wide and paneled, with square panes of glass above it and on each side to light the wide hallway. The windows are large, and instead of the twelve and eight panes of glass found in earlier houses, the panels have here grown in size, and each sash contains but six. Green shutters contrast pleasantly with red brick and white woodwork. The small brick office used by Dr. Hansford still stands in the yard, and faces a side street.

After about twenty years of occupancy, Dr. Hansford sold his home to Oscar A. Veazey, husband of his greatniece, Mattie B. Smith, daughter of J. S. F. and Martha J. Hansford Smith. Oscar Alfonso Veazey (b. 1851), who became a well-known civil and mining engineer, was the son of James A. and Eliza Stockton Veazey. He was born at Kanawha Falls, home of his mother's father, Aaron Stockton, one of the best known and most popular of the early tavern-keepers along the James River and Kanawha Turnpike. Mr. Stockton's secretary still serves a useful purpose, and now stands in one of the rooms of the Veazey house. The Stockton tavern, today known as Glen Ferris Inn, is the large whitecolumned and much altered building close by the highway on the north side of the Kanawha at Glen Ferris.

After the death of his parents, Oscar Veazey continued to reside with his grandparents during his schooling. In 1877 Mr. Veazey married Mattie Smith, and they were the parents of five children: Verna, who married J. A. B. Holt; Victor S., who married Marguerite Beirne; Kathleen, who married Bradford Coleman, and two other sons, Edward and Louis A. Veazey. After the death of his wife in 1906, Mr. Veazey married Miss Maude C. Perry, and they were the parents of three children. Mrs. Veazey and her daughters still own and occupy this pleasant house.

The Montgomerys

THE town of Montgomery on the south side of the Kanawha, twenty-four miles east of Charleston, was first known as Montgomery's Landing, and was much used for many years by southern counties as a shipping point for river traffic. The old landing was just above the present bridge over the Kanawha, and the home site of the Montgomery family stood a short distance above the landing.

Major Henry Montgomery was an adventurous young Indian fighter who could be found wherever there was action. Commissioned a Major in the Virginia Militia, he participated in many battles with the savages, and for his military services was awarded numerous tracts of land on both sides of the river. His wife was Nancy Keeney, great-niece of General Andrew Lewis, and they were the parents of eleven children.

In 1809 Major Montgomery built his home near the Kanawha Falls. Being exceptionally well and carefully constructed of walnut logs, the house stood for a hundred years. It was used as a slave house under the later ownership of James, one of the sons of Major Montgomery, who was a man of means and political interests, and who served as a member of the Virginia Assembly. He was an ardent secessionist, and when the Kanawha Valley was occupied by Federal forces, took his family farther south for safety. He suffered the loss of a son in the war, as well as property, money, and slaves, and when he returned to the Kanawha, found his home and equipment all destroyed, with only the old house built by his father, remaining. He thankfully occupied it until he could restore his farm, and when this old building was torn down in 1908 each of Major Montgomery's grandchildren was given one of the handmade locust pins used in its construction.

One granddaughter was Ann, daughter of Michael Montgomery, operator of the first ferry near the Falls, and which he sold later to Aaron Stockton, who continued its operation. In 1869 Ann was married to Benjamin, son of Levi Morris, thus joining the two pioneer families of Morris and Montgomery.

Early homes of the Montgomery family are long since gone, but descendants are still residents and property owners in the town which bears their name, and has grown into a busy medical and educational center. The buildings crowd into the narrow strip of land between river and hills and extend for some distance east and west, the upper portion of the town now lying in Fayette County. The brick buildings of the excellent school, West Virginia Institute of Technology, are located here. Montgomery is also the home of Laird Memorial Hospital, a uniquely conceived and successfully executed experiment, proving that beauty and order can go hand in hand with high professional skill, and efficient business management, and still maintain an extensive and unobtrusive program of charitable work. The hospital and its founder and chief surgeon, Dr. William Laird, enjoy a deserved national, and even international, reputation.

The Ruffner Family

THE origin of the Ruffner family in this country began long ago, when Peter Ruffner, a nineteen-year-old lad, third son, it is said, of a German Baron, left school, without the knowledge of his parents, and accompanied by an only sister, sailed away in 1732 on a pioneering venture to the little known land that was America. Their home having been either in Germany or near the German border of Switzerland, the Ruffners no sooner landed in America than they made their way to a settlement of German Lutherans in Lancaster County, Pennsylvania, whose religion, language, and customs were familiar to them.

In 1739, Peter married Mary Steinman, daughter of a wealthy and established German farmer, who gave them a large tract of land in what was then Orange, now Page, County, Virginia, which included the present town of Luray. The newly married couple, taking with them Peter's sister, moved to Virginia, and upon this land built a home in a grove of locust trees at the juncture of Big and Little Hawksbill creeks, which they named "Locust Row."

Soon the sister married Abraham Strickler, a young man who had come from his home in Switzerland some years previously, first settling in Pennsylvania, and later in Page County. There he acquired patent for one thousand acres of land which he called "Egypt," land even yet known by that name and where still stand several of the homes built by his sons—large, well-proportioned stone houses with the unusual and characteristic feature of vaulted-roof "fort" cellars. Descendants may be found living upon portions of this land today, and often occupying these early homes.

The Stricklers and Ruffners had much in common, and were friends as well as relatives. Peter Ruffner qualified in 1746 as administrator of the estate of Abraham Strickler, and years later, in 1772 when Peter Ruffner's will was probated, the name of his "friend Benjamin Strickler" appeared as one of the executors, and that of Jacob Strickler as one of the witnesses.

Abraham Strickler and Peter Ruffner had large families and became men of mark and influence in the locality. Industrious and thrifty, they added other lands to their estates and were able to give to their children, upon marriage, plantations upon which to establish homes. Mr. Ruffner's eldest son, Joseph, was given lands on Hawksbill Creek, where he and his wife, Anne Heistand Ruffner, lived for a number of years. After the death of his father, Joseph, with his family, returned to the home of his mother and assumed the responsibility of farming her lands and operating her grist and sawmills for a period of several years.

Joseph had studied agriculture in his native country and was at heart a farmer, with an innate love for the land. A man of stalwart physique and strong character, he also inherited his father's pioneering spirit. He was drawn irresistibly by the stories of returning hunters, scouts, and explorers who told of the rich lands to be had in the river valleys beyond the sparsely inhabited western mountains. Learning of the Great Buffalo Salt Licks along the Kanawha River, he was attracted by the thought of the future commercial development of salt drilling, and in 1794, he purchased, sight unseen, from

Colonel John Dickinson, of Virginia, a survey of five hundred and two acres located near Campbell's Creek, six miles east of Fort Lee. The survey included the ancient Salt Licks which, though much frequented by wild game and long patronized by Indians, had never been utilized by white men.

In the spring of 1795 Mr. Ruffner, eager to inspect his new lands, and scorning all thought of danger from roving Indians or from possible accident, set out alone on horseback on his three-hundred-mile journey, the most hazardous feature of which proved to be the crossing of Gauley River. The state militia system now abandoned, there were no longer rangers stationed at the ford to assist travelers in crossing. The Gauley was notoriously treacherous even when on its good behavior, and now it was in flood stage, with heavy drift running.

Paddy Huddleston, keeper of the small log tavern five miles below Kanawha Falls, happened to be standing on the opposite side of the river bank and was a witness to Joseph's original methods of procedure, which he described as follows: "* * * I had got about seven miles from the mouth of Gauley when I saw a man on the opposite side leading his horse down a steep place to the bank of the river. There was no trail to this point, and I didn't know how he got there, but he looked as if he meant to cross the river, but I couldn't think he would be fool enough to try to ford it, or to swim it with all the load he had. I couldn't imagine what he was going to do, but presently he took a short handed axe from his saddle and went to work on a dry chestnut tree that had fallen against the cliff. The trunk he cut into lengths and split. He then took a rope and tied them to his horse's tail and dragged them to a place to suit him. Then he took from his saddlebag some wrought iron nails, and made a raft which he put in the water and loaded his things on it. He tied the raft to the horse's tail and pushed him into the river and started over. He guided the horse by speaking to him and got safely over. Then he knocked the raft to pieces, put the nails back in the saddle bags, and came home with me for the night." Of course, Joseph could have made camp and waited until the flood abated, but he was not the kind to wait for obstacles to disappear, but dealt with each one as he encountered it.

The small sturdy tavern, built by Paddy Huddleston's father, Daniel Huddleston, was a well-known stopping place, and as previously mentioned, had been visited by Daniel Boone when trapping and hunting in that region. Its accommodations, while certainly meager so far as comfort was concerned, were all that were expected, and the rates, fixed by the courts, brought no complaints. The cost of "a warm diet dinner" was 16-2/3 cents, and lodging in "a good bed and clean sheets," 8-1/3 cents. If that seemed a bit expensive one could economize by having a "cold diet dinner" at 10½ cents, and by dispensing with such fripperies as sheets, and the luxury of having a bed to oneself. By sharing a bed with one or more fellow travelers, the tariff dropped to 5½ cents. If one wished to eliminate all expenditure, advantage could be taken of Paddy's religiously motivated generosity. It was only necessary to arrive on Sunday and stay entirely free of cost, as Paddy made no charges on the Sabbath day. Another of Paddy's unusual characteristics was his antipathy toward liquor. Despite his reputation as a brandy maker par excellence, the liquor was used solely by the patrons, and entirely untouched by him and his sons.

After a night's rest at Paddy's ordinary, Mr. Ruffner

was again on his way, and a few hours later had reached his journey's end. After inspecting his lands, he was even more enthusiastic about his purchase than previously, and decided while in the vicinity to extend his explorations a few miles farther west and pay a visit to Fort Lee.

The fort, no longer under military control, was now used solely as the residence of Colonel George Clendenin, and, together with the six log houses of the little town of Charleston, plus a few scattered cabins in the neighborhood, represented an established settlement that looked new and promising to Mr. Ruffner. Colonel Clendenin, after seven years of the hardships of border warfare, culminating in the curt treatment he had received from the Assembly, with its thankless acceptance of his long services, was doubtless in an ideal mood to welcome a purchaser for his property. Fate obliged in the person of Joseph Ruffner whose visit resulted in the purchase of all the Clendenin holdings, including the small acreages of the two brothers, William and Alexander. The property, embracing more than a thousand acres of bottom land on the Kanawha River, extended north to the hill at the line of the later Kanawha and Michigan Railroad, with Elk River as its western boundary. The only exclusions were the few town lots previously sold by Mr. Clendenin.

His transactions completed, Mr. Ruffner returned to the Shenandoah. He sold his property there, and in the autumn (1795), accompanied by his wife and six of their children, the youngest of whom was then fourteen, with about twenty slaves, a number of horses, cows, and other farm animals, turned his face toward the mountains. Lead by a six-horse wagon covered with bearskins, this imposing caravan started for the Kanawha. Arriving without incident, the family was soon settled in the fort, which, with its abandoned ranger cabins, furnished excellent quarters until a more permanent home could be erected.

By the following spring Mr. Ruffner had selected the site for his home. About a mile east of the town, it faced the river, near the little blockhouse formerly occupied by William Clendenin. With the labor of numerous servants, soon a substantial two-story log house was completed, and the Ruffner family comfortably installed. Slave quarters, barn, and other necessary buildings followed.

A year later David Ruffner, eldest son of Joseph, arrived from the Shenandoah with his wife and children, and taking up his abode in the now vacant fort building, completed the family circle of Mr. and Mrs. Joseph Ruffner, the names of whose children were:

Esther—born 1765, died at eighteen before her parents came to Kanawha;

David—born 1767, died 1843, married Anne Brumbach 1788;

Joseph, Jr.—born 1769, married Margaret _____, moved to Ohio;

Tobias—born 1770, married Mary Muzzleman. He died, Kanawha, 1834;

Samuel—born 1773, married Catherine Daggs, moved to Ohio;

Eve—born 1777, married Nehemiah Wood(s), moved to Ohio;

Daniel—born 1779, died 1869, married (1) Elizabeth Painter, (2) Elizabeth Singleton;

Abraham—born 1781, married Martha Ross; moved to Ohio.

Joseph Ruffner was constantly occupied in the development of his plantation. With the assistance of his sons he was busy clearing land, planting his fields, and erecting and operating grist and sawmills along the creeks that twisted through his property. Like his father before him, Mr. Ruffner grew prosperous. Farseeing and capable, he acquired large additional tracts of land in near-by counties, as well as in the fertile Ohio Valley, which later became the home of four of his children.

Mr. Ruffner, for all his vigor and strength, did not live to see the fulfillment of all his plans and hopes, but died in 1803 at the age of sixty-three, barely eight years after his arrival in Kanawha.

About a month before his death Mr. Ruffner made his will and divided his property among his children. He separated the Kanawha lands into three sections. The central section containing the log homestead was given to the wife, Anne, for her lifetime, and then to their son, Daniel; the lower, toward Elk River, which included the town site and the Fort Lee building where he then lived, went to the son, David, while the upper lands, including the Dickinson tract, were given jointly to David, Joseph, Jr., and Tobias.

Mrs. Ruffner survived her husband twenty years, and their tombs may be seen today in the little park in the center of the fifteen hundred block of Kanawha Boulevard. This plot of ground has had a rather turbulent history. Some years after his father's death, Daniel Ruffner deeded the adjoining section to the town of Charleston as a public cemetery, reserving the western corner as the private burial ground of the Ruffner family. The deed stipulated that if the town ceased to utilize the plot as a cemetery the title was to revert to the Ruffner heirs. Years later a family controversy arose, and lengthy court proceedings followed. During the litigation many bodies were removed by relatives and reinterred in Spring Hill Cemetery. The dispute finally settled, this tree-shaded plot is today a small public park, where the tombstones above the lone graves of Joseph Ruffner and his wife remain as the only evidence of its former use. In the center of the park there was erected in later years a memorial and roster of members of the Kanawha Riflemen, local pre-Civil War organization which, in that conflict, became a part of the Confederate Army.

Holly Grove Mansion

IN 1815, Daniel, fifth son of Joseph Ruffner, erected on the site of his parents' log homestead the splendid brick house long known as "Holly Grove Mansion," number 1710 Kanawha Boulevard, now the second house below the Executive Mansion. The land at that point then projected much farther into the river than at present, and although later the James River and Kanawha Turnpike passed the house, it still left a wide expanse of green lawn which sloped down gradually to a boat landing on the tree-shaded river bank. Thus, there was a far more appropriate setting for the generous proportions of the house than appears today when, shorn of its wide surrounding acres, it must rub elbows with its neighbors.

In those days such places were referred to as plantations and were truly all that the name suggests. There was the great log barn where the present Executive Mansion of West Virginia now stands, the granary, blacksmith shop, loom and weaving house, smokehouse, and all the other buildings necessary to this self-sustaining establishment, including a small separate office building near the front of the property. There were well laid off gardens of vegetables and flowers, and leading down a lane in the distance stretched orchards, fields of grain, and pasture for cattle and horses. North, near the hills and the entrance to what is known today as Ruffner Hollow and the road leading to the airport, were extensive vineyards in charge of a keeper whose little house stood where Piedmont Road now passes the

Hollow entrance. Nearby there was also a wooded area known as Ruffner Grove—a favorite spot for picnic parties, for speech-making and public gatherings.

The mansion, as its name implies, is partly hidden by ancient holly trees, which, together with a tall maple and towering boxwood bushes, add much charm to the dignified beauty of its setting. Constructed of large and heavy brick made in England, the walls of the house are eighteen inches in thickness, making possible generously deep window sills. Although a fire in 1832 destroyed virtually all of the interior woodwork, the walls remained undamaged, and repairs were made quickly.

Conforming to a style popular at the time in Virginia, Holly Grove was originally a square two-storied structure, with brick dining-room wing extending in the rear almost to the kitchen which was housed in a separate brick building. The large windows were trimmed with green shutters, and a small portico covered the front doorway which opened into a wide central hall whose rear door led to the brick-floored dining-room.

High-ceilinged square rooms open upon each side of the hallway, those on the right being connected with wide folding doors, above which an elaborate cornice, similar in design and workmanship to the front doorway, extends to the ceiling. These may possibly be all that remain of the original woodwork. The much plainer mantels, window and door casings appear to be of a later period and are almost certainly replacements following the fire of 1832.

The very attractive stairway at the end of the hall extends to the third floor, each shallow step having three small square spindles to support the graceful handrail of cherry wood. A full-sized window in the end of the hall, oddly enough, is divided by the stairlanding, the lower half of the window visible below, the upper half above the landing. One wonders if the stairway were originally placed differently.

When the house was built, the second floor hallway corresponded to that below, and opening on the roof of the portico was a wide doorway ornamented with fan-shaped window above and narrow glass panes on each side, furnishing not only light and ventilation for the second floor but giving a fine view of the river. A later owner apparently needed none of these things, and by erecting a partition across the front of the hall, shut them all away in a very small room. In the ceiling of each hallway there are circular medallions of plaster from whose centers lighting fixtures were suspended, that of the second floor being now concealed behind the partition.

Cellars of old houses, more or less immune to the whims of architecturally-minded owners, often tell a truer story than the rooms above, and the cellar of Holly Grove is no exception. Here may be seen the great stone blocks of the foundation wall into which is built a large open fireplace where an iron crane once swung. In the cellar the original wide floor boards, unseen from above where they are covered with modern hardwood flooring, are here visible overhead, supported by the heavy timbers on which they rest, all hewn no doubt from trees on David Ruffner's surrounding acres. The outside cellar door still wears the heavy box lock with its pencil-long key that was originally on the front door of the house.

As was customary at the time, persons with rooms not needed by their families frequently made them available to travelers. "Holly Grove," with its numerous bedrooms, its location on the stagecoach route, and its extensive acres furnishing ample food for man and beast, was ideal for such purpose. In a newspaper called *Western Virginian*, published in Charleston, under date of October 31, 1826, this announcement appeared:

> Western Virginian
> Chas., Wed. Oct. 31, 1826.
> To Travellers:
> The subscriber has opened a house of private entertainment at his commodious residence, situate one mile and a half from the town of Charleston on the road leading thence to Lewisburg. Every effort will be made to render the lodging of the traveller comfortable, and his diet palatable. His pastures are extensive and corn abundant. He will therefore be amply prepared to accomodate the cattle or hog merchant. For travellers on horseback, or in carriages, he will be able to furnish good stables well supplied with all kinds of provender for horses.
> Sept. 13.   Daniel Ruffner.

Many travelers gratefully accepted these unusually comfortable accommodations, and family tradition records that numerous persons of prominence were entertained. Daniel Boone, Henry Clay, Samuel Houston in his younger days, John J. Audubon, the famous naturalist, and in October, 1832, Andrew Jackson, President of the United States, visited Holly Grove.

Daniel Ruffner was a fitting owner for his great house. Tall and muscular, with a store of physical strength and endurance, he possessed a kind and charitable nature and an extraordinary fund of common sense and business acumen. No man was better known or respected throughout Kanawha County. Although he had no taste for public honors, he received an unsought appointment from the Governor, as justice of the peace, and held the office of High Sheriff.

In 1844, three years after the death of his wife, Elizabeth Painter, who was ten years his senior, Daniel Ruffner married Elizabeth Honeyman Singleton, a widow of Cincinnati. His seven children, all born in Charleston, were at that time grown and had homes of their own. Before his marriage and his removal to Ohio, where he later bought a farm in Fairfield County, he divided his Kanawha land equally among his children, who were:

Catherine—born September 24, 1799, married David C. Ruffner of Ohio;

(Colonel) Charles—born 1801, married (1) Anna Hedrick, (2) Elizabeth V. Wilson;

(Colonel) Joel—born 1802, married Diana S. Mayre;

Augustus—born 1805, married Mary Elizabeth Rogers;

James, Andrew—twins—born 1807. James married (1) Martha Morton, (2) Ellen McFarland; Andrew, unmarried;

Elizabeth—born 1810, married Nathaniel V. Wilson. To the second marriage were born five children:

Walter—born 1844;

Daniel, Jr.—born 1847;

Joseph—born 1848, married Mary A. Jackson;

Virginia—born 1851, married J. E. M. Sloughton;

William St. J. E.—born 1854, married Miss Montague.

When Walter, the eldest of these children, was accidentally drowned in a pond on his farm, this home became intolerable to Mr. Ruffner and he returned to Charleston, where he lived for a time in a house on Capitol Street. He then, in 1853, purchased a farm in Kentucky known as "Mt. Vernon," and there he died in his eighty-sixth year, just after the close of the Civil War.

In the distribution of property to the children of his first marriage, Daniel Ruffner had given "Holly Grove" to the twin son, James, who with his wife, Martha Morton, of Kentucky, lived there many years. They were the parents of three children: Andrew L., Meredith P., and Anastien W. Mrs. James Ruffner died in 1865, and a short time later her husband married Ellen McFarland, of Charleston. His death occurred the following year.

About 1859 or 1860 James Ruffner sold "Holly Grove" to his cousin, Silas R. Ruffner, son of Tobias Ruffner, who occupied the house for a longer period than any of the preceding owners. Silas Ruffner and his wife, Eliza Hadassah, had no children, and the house, after the death of the wife who was the survivor, became the property of a niece, Mary Ruffner. She later married Augustus McClung of Greenbrier County—bringing to an end the name of Ruffner in connection with this house.

Hard times then came upon this lovely spot. During subsequent ownerships it became a pawn in financial difficulties, and about forty-five years ago was sold for debts of its then current owner. It was purchased by Mr. James H. Nash, father of the present owner and occupant, Mrs. Nan Nash Grosscup.

Following his purchase in 1902, Mr. Nash made numerous alterations to the house, and to him goes the credit of its distinctive appearance today. In order to make it suitable for the use of two families, he worked out a clever partition involving no noticeable exterior changes or interior disfigurement. At this time the roof was raised and the former attic converted into a usable apartment. In making this change the curious discovery was made that the house was covered by three roofs, previous owners having merely laid one over the other, additional weight meaning nothing to the substantial construction of the early builders.

Other changes were the removal of the long dining-room wing and the substitution of an indoor kitchen for the separate kitchen building. The small front portico was removed, and replaced by a beautiful circular entrance porch with massive white columns extending above the second floor and with smaller columns supporting a white-railed balcony over the doorway. The red brick walls were painted gray, and with its green-shuttered windows, its tall white columns, the house, sheltered by fine trees, is today an attractive picture, while the old stone mounting-block at the entrance serves as a reminder that "Holly Grove" is also a treasured landmark of Charleston's early history.

Rosedale

WEST of "Holly Grove Mansion" are still standing the homes of two of the sons of Daniel Ruffner. The first, number 1538 Kanawha Boulevard, is called "Rosedale," and is still owned and occupied by Ruffner descendants—Mrs. William F. Mandt and Mrs. John O'Keefe.

On a street where the greater number of neighboring homes are imposing three-story modern structures, this small house, close to the ground and dwarfed still more by the enormous elm tree towering above it, is both unexpected and interesting. Weatherboarded and painted white for many years, few persons realize its charming exterior conceals the sturdy log walls of one of the early buildings erected on the original farm of the Ruffners. The time of its construction is problematical, as the more utilitarian farm buildings continued to be built of logs even after the use of brick for dwellings. It may have been erected as early as during the lifetime of Joseph Ruffner, Sr., who died in 1803, and whose log house stood on the site of "Holly Grove Mansion," or if not then, by his son Daniel, the succeeding owner.

In 1844, Daniel Ruffner, at the age of sixty-five, contracted a second marriage, and left the Valley to take up his residence in Ohio. Before his departure he divided his Kanawha lands among his children, his son Joel receiving the section upon which stood this log building.

Colonel Joel Ruffner, born in 1802, was a quiet man, prudent and careful, noted for good sense and integrity.

He did not seek public office, but was appointed justice of the peace for the county, a position which, though honorable, was not profitable, as no fees were charged. "O times, O customs!"

In 1827 he married Miss Diana Mayre, of Shenandoah, Virginia, and they became the parents of sixteen children, three of whom died in infancy. The children were all well educated. One daughter, following a European trip, conducted a private school; two of the sons lost their lives in the Civil War; a few of the children were unmarried, while others were married and lived elsewhere.

It was Joel Ruffner who converted the log building into a dwelling, which descendants believe to have been about the time of his marriage, and assume it to have been his home for many years before he became its owner. Originally, the two-room building, with a loft above, had been used in connection with a sawmill operated by the family. No basement was undertaken, but the building was raised enough to put a low foundation under it —no mean accomplishment, as one quickly realizes when examining a section of one of the logs removed from the rear wall during some recent alterations. It measures twenty inches wide by seven and a half inches thick and, now resting on two stones, serves as a bench in the flower garden.

The loft was divided into rooms and lighted by shuttered windows. Here the wide floor boards of black pine are undisturbed, and also remain in one of the lower rooms, although others have been overlaid with modern flooring. Changes have been the addition of a wing on the western end of the house, the enclosing of a rear porch that led to a summer dining-room, and the erection of a small square entrance portico surrounded by a balustrade. The handsome, beautifully paneled front door, with its old knocker intact, was reduced in size and utilized elsewhere a few years ago when the house was converted into a two-family dwelling.

The mantels are plain, the door casings grooved, with a circular design in the corner blocks; there is a low wainscot and a wide stairway with round handrail and ornamentation of small ivory inserts in diamond design.

The house still contains a number of pieces of "heirloom" furniture which have been there for many years—numerous small chairs, several tables, and an extremely heavy and handsome bow-front sideboard with wooden gallery, rope legs and columns, and sandwich glass knobs. Inside one of the drawers is written in ink: "Cost $180.00, July 15, 1823." This piece is thought to have come from Holly Grove Mansion.

During the Civil War, at a time when Federal forces occupied the town, it is said that General Lightburn, who was in command, rode up the turnpike one morning in 1862, and informed the Ruffners that the Confederates under General Loring were advancing from the east, and as the town would no doubt be under fire, advised retirement to the hills. This they did, along with the majority of the town residents. The Confederates arrived and took up their position on the south side of the Kanawha River, and the Federals being on the north side, the firing continued back and forth across the town all during the day. One of the Federal defense barricades was thrown up in front of "Rosedale," which fortunately escaped damage, except for one shell which lodged in the thick log wall underneath the dining-room window.

For many years a log barn, slave cabins, and other buildings stood in the rear of the house, and recently,

"The Stone House"

N.S.Hosterman

when a stone terrace was being laid, a twenty-five thousand gallon cistern was uncovered which had once supplied water for the Ruffner farms.

Shorn of its wide acres, today, dwellings and streets surround this small house, and on the upper side where once flourished an extensive rose garden that gave to the place its name, a tall iron fence encloses the grounds of an adjoining residence. Links with the past are the ragged old cedar standing near the street, and the large boxwood tree that leans slightly as though looking for support.

In the spring, "Rosedale" is at its best. Then the twisted branches of a wild plum tree become a cloud of beauty, while dogwood, holly, and flower borders add their share to the attractiveness of the well-kept grounds.

Augustus Ruffner House

CEDAR GROVE, the second Ruffner house in the exceptionally long fifteen hundred block of Kanawha Boulevard, was, like the others, bereft many years ago of its farm acres, and now situated on a town lot, is number 1506, the second house above the corner of Ruffner Avenue.

In 1844, when Daniel Ruffner, of Holly Grove Mansion, divided his Kanawha lands among his children prior to his removal to Ohio, the adjoining section below Rosedale was given to the fourth son, Augustus. As in the case of the elder son Joel, of Rosedale, there had evidently been an understanding as to the eventual ownership of these lands, since each son lived on his portion for many years before becoming its actual owner.

In 1834, the year following his marriage, Augustus Ruffner had built this substantial brick house which was called Cedar Grove, a name no longer used nor applicable, as the cedars, once so numerous along the river, have now virtually disappeared. Many of the fine old holly trees remain, however, but none more handsome than those in the lawn of Cedar Grove. Tradition says a tree was planted after the birth of each of the Ruffner children. At first thought, this bit of sentiment seems a very nice and uncomplicated plan, but on more careful reflection when one considers the definitely prolific tendency of the Valley's early families—a conspicuous example being near-by brother Joel with sixteen children —the implication of this Arbor Day routine becomes apparent. Results might eventually have assumed the appearance of a particularly successful project in reforestation! Fortunately in the case of Augustus Ruffner it all worked out very inconspicuously, as he had only three children.

The marriage in 1833 of Augustus Ruffner (1805-1856) and Mary Elizabeth Rogers (b. 1803), daughter of Dr. Henry and Leonora Lovell Rogers, linked together a chain of interesting family names and connections which are carried on still farther in the marriages of their children:

In 1860, the son, Colonel Henry Daniel Ruffner (1834-1925), married Sarah Alethea Patrick, at Forest Hill, the home of her parents, Dr. Spicer Patrick and Lavinia V. M. (Bream) Patrick;

A daughter, Leonora Caroline Ruffner, born 1836, married William A. Alexander, of Putnam County;

The second daughter, born 1838, married Dr. Lucius Comstock.

Several of these names—Rogers, Lovell, Patrick, and Bream—appear in connection with other houses in this book.

Augustus Ruffner was a man of alert and cultivated mind. He was engaged in farming and in the lumber business, owning a mill on Elk River. He must have absented himself from his duties shamefully, however, during the building of his home, else he could not have devised so many places to ornament with wood carvings —roof, gables, porch cornice, balustrades, and everywhere possible appear scrolls, circles, and all manner of cut-out patterns and fanciful swirls. The entrance is particularly ornate, with heavy French doors, whose lower section of wood and the upper of glass, have octagonally cut corners, made into panels surrounded by raised molding. Above the doorway extends a carved cornice supported by brackets. A porch, whose cornice is scalloped and otherwise adorned, is carried across the front of the house, and even the five steps leading to it are decorated with elaborate scrolled side panels.

The style of this house is a distinct departure from that of any other so far described in this book. It is not the customary oblong shape, but is narrow and fairly tall. Instead of the central hall opening from a small square portico, the doorway is at the upper end of a "porch" that frankly started out as such.

The interior arrangement begins with the small entrance hall whose steep and narrow stair against the outside wall crosses to the opposite side at the end of the hallway and has a window on the landing. A few additional steps lead to the only two rooms on the second floor. On the first floor there are two large rooms on the left, one at the end of the hall and two others in a rear wing. The land slopes perceptibly downward away from the river, so that an outside doorway from the dining-room requires a flight of steps to reach the lawn, and basement rooms at the rear of the house are almost entirely above ground. The wide floorboards remain in the house and also the high doorsills which keep one stumbling from room to room. The "parlor," of course, was the large square front room with its fancy black mantel. The long windows, floor length and shutter trimmed, contain nine panes of glass in each sash, and are still fastened with their early latches.

There is such a Victorian flavor about this much embellished and relatively unchanged century-old house that one has the urge to dress it up in flowered carpets and brocade draperies, and even go so far as to supply a pair of iron dogs to guard the entrance.

The house was later occupied by Colonel Henry D. Ruffner, son of Augustus Ruffner, and remained in the hands of the Ruffner family until recent years. Its present owner is Mrs. C. O. North, who has lately vacated the house, since when it is occupied by her tenants.

The Salines

ALTHOUGH, until 1946, the most traveled highway in West Virginia passed through the town now called Malden, six miles east of Charleston, few travelers were aware that this quiet village has been known by several names, and, as The Kanawha Salines, was once not only one of the most important communities industrially in western Virginia but was known far beyond the boundaries of the state. A few may have recalled it as the boyhood home of the Negro educator, Booker T. Washington; others may have noticed that many of the houses had an old and rather "quaint" look, but to the average motorist it was just another village along the road, and if remembered at all, it was for the very bad curve at the eastern end!

The first explorers and woodsmen who journeyed through the region found this site near the Kanawha River because of the Great Buffalo Licks, to whose brine-covered marsh wild game had worn a trail for more years than anyone knew. Strangely enough, possibly the first white persons to see The Licks were women—Mrs. William Ingles and her sister-in-law, Mrs. John Draper, who, with Mrs. Ingles' two young sons and an infant, reached the site in July, 1755. Captives of the most cruel and dreaded of Indian tribes, the Shawnees, they were being taken to the Indian village beyond the Ohio River, following the massacre of the first pioneer settlement on New River, Montgomery County, that of the Draper family. The savages hoped later to secure large sums for the ransom of the prisoners. Reaching The Licks, the Indians decided to stop for a few days of hunting, and while they were thus occupied, the captives were given the task of boiling brine to make salt, which, packed in grass baskets, was to be carried to Ohio.

The courage of these two white women among savages who had slain members of their families and destroyed their homes, was amazing. Horrified at the atrocities they had witnessed, and stunned by grief, they had additional suffering to endure. Mrs. Ingles, when but three days distant from the scene of the massacre, had given birth to a child. Her stamina and fortitude were such that she was able to resume her journey the following day, and because of these qualities, she gained a grudging consideration from the Indians, who recognized her as an exceptional woman. Mrs. Draper at the time of the attack upon her home had made a vain attempt to save the life of her own small child, only to see it ruthlessly killed before her eyes, while she received a broken right arm from an Indian bullet.

Their sole comfort, that of being together, was soon taken from the prisoners, for the sisters-in-law, as well as the children, were separated and sent elsewhere after their arrival in Ohio, Mrs. Ingles and her infant alone remaining together. Sensible and wise, Mrs. Ingles realized her good treatment depended largely on her attitude and her determination to make herself useful. Her ability to sew, to cook, to distill salt, to nurse and care for the sick, and her knowledge of making herb remedies enhanced her value immeasurably, and she was allowed more liberty and freedom than was accorded to other captives.

After several weeks, Mrs. Ingles and other prisoners, whom she did not know, were taken on a salt-making trip to Big Bone Lick, Kentucky, about a hundred and fifty miles from the Ohio camp. While there, with fewer Indians around her, she began considering the feasibility of an attempt to escape, knowing full well if she were caught she would be tortured and killed. It was a heartbreaking and perilous decision to make, as it meant leaving her infant child, facing a wilderness journey of several hundred miles on foot, without a gun, knife, or other means of securing food, and without clothing other than the garments she wore, as she dared not risk the slightest preparation that might arouse suspicion.

Finally, after confiding her thoughts to another prisoner, a Dutch woman older than she, they determined to risk it together. Awaiting a favorable moment, they escaped unnoticed and began a journey, the severity of whose hardships, though culminating in their eventual safe arrival at the cabin of a pioneer, is a tale which, if not historically verified, would be too fantastic to believe. For forty-two and a half days they fought their way mile by mile through the forests, climbing steep mountains, struggling through thickets and underbrush, walking countless additional miles along the river banks searching for a means of crossing, which was accomplished sometimes on logs, in an abandoned dug-out canoe, by wading, or by whatever means were presented.

The older woman, instead of being the comforting sharer of their common fears and trials, proved to be just the reverse. She became complaining and stubborn, and had constantly to be coaxed and cajoled. Aside from slowing their progress and being a great hindrance, she also became a menace. As the days passed and their hunger and hardships increased and their strength lessened, she blamed Mrs. Ingles more and more for their plight. Finally she became so deranged that she attempted to kill the younger woman, who was forced to flee from the madness of her companion, as well as from the constant danger of starvation and exhaustion.

Through the Kanawha Valley Mrs. Ingles retraced the route she had traveled as a prisoner. As she passed the Buffalo Salt Licks, one of the most clearly remembered landmarks of her former harrowing journey, she little dreamed that one day her great-grandson, John P. Hale, would operate "Snow Hill," the largest salt well in the whole region, within a few hundred feet of the spot where she had first boiled brine for the Indians, and that he would also recount in *Trans-Allegheny Pioneers* the whole graphic story of her flight, the sheer courage and remarkable accomplishment of which is unsurpassed in frontier history. Thomas, the eldest son of Mrs. Ingles,[*] after thirteen years with the Indians, was finally located and ransomed. In 1774, as a Lieutenant with the army of General Andrew Lewis, he again passed The Licks which his childish eyes had first seen years before when he watched his mother at her salt-making.

After the Battle of Point Pleasant and the passage through the Valley of many companies of men, The Licks were well known, and the following year they were included in the survey of five hundred and two acres along the Kanawha made for Colonel John Dickinson of Virginia. Although making no attempt to manufacture salt, he had evidently acquired the tract because of the potential commercial value of The Licks, as indicated in the terms of his sale of the property to Joseph Ruffner a few years later. It was stipulated the purchase price of that part containing the Licks should be

---
[*]The fine old floor clock owned by the Ingles family may be seen at the State Museum in Charleston.

contingent upon a successful development of salt production. Up to this time salt was extremely scarce and of such value as to form the basis of many an Indian treaty. Before the first settlement of the western country, salt was almost unobtainable at any price.

Mr. Ruffner expected at the time of his purchase personally to undertake the salt development, but upon the heels of this transaction came the purchase from George Clendenin of the thousand-acre tract of bottom land farther down the river, and once having embarked on the farming of its fertile acres, his love of the soil was too strong to forsake it for the uncertainties of a new venture. He compromised, however, by leasing the Licks to Elisha Brooks, who set about making a primitive apparatus by which he managed to have a salt well in actual operation in 1797.

This marked the end of an era. "The Licks," and all that the name implied, would soon be forgotten. Now one spoke of The Salt Wells, of Saltborough, of Terra Salis, or The Salines, and later and for a long period the thriving town that grew there was called "Kanawha Salines"—but all this came gradually.

The death of Mr. Joseph Ruffner, Sr., in 1803 brought about the termination of his lease with Elisha Brooks before Mr. Brooks had made much progress with salt manufacture, which was still in a very elementary stage. The Dickinson survey extended both below and above Campbell's Creek, and in Mr. Ruffner's will was given to three of his sons, David, Joseph, Jr., and Tobias. In accordance with their father's urgent admonition that they lose no time in carrying out his own unfulfilled intention to manufacture salt, the sons at once took over the operation of the Brooks well and began a serious study of the best ways and means of procedure.

David, the eldest son, had also been given the lower third of the large tract his father had purchased from Colonel Clendenin. His share began on the west at Elk River and included the forty-acre boundary of the "town" of Charleston and the Fort Lee property farther east. David was still living in the Fort Lee building which had been his home ever since he and his wife, Anne Brumbach Ruffner, with their three small children, had arrived in Kanawha on November 3, 1796, a year later than his father. Mr. Ruffner was then occupying his recently completed log house a mile farther east, leaving the newly vacated fort available for the newcomers. During the years of their occupancy of the fort, a fourth child, Lewis, was born to them.

After the death of his father, when David found himself embarking upon the career of a salt manufacturer, he realized he must be nearer the scene of activities, and in 1805 forsook Charleston. Building a home near the wells, he established his family at the new location, selling the fort property nine years later to Colonel James Wilson.

David and Joseph, Jr., appear to have been associated in that portion of the acreage lying above Campbell's Creek. Tobias built and occupied a home near the river upon the part below Campbell's Creek, and conducted his operations at that point.

The Ruffner brothers worked hard and steadily, but, with little actual knowledge and no experience, their progress was at times discouragingly slow, and while they and other salt-makers who followed them eventually became successful and wealthy, it was nothing of a get-rich-quick process. Instead, it was by the painful trial-and-error method—with the error percentage in the higher brackets. Nevertheless, with unflagging energy and persistence, unwilling to be content with the crude methods worked out by Elisha Brooks, the Ruffners were determined to find a better way.

Brooks had sunk three "gums" about eight to ten feet into the mire and quicksand, and from these, brine was dipped out by a bucket on a long "swope"—something of the "old oaken bucket" system. The brine was then distilled by boiling in a row of little iron kettles.

The Ruffners experimented with deeper drilling, making a tube from a twenty-foot oak log, bored with a long-shanked auger, three inches in diameter. The tube was sharpened, shod with iron, and driven to bedrock in pile driver fashion. At that time there was no method of getting through the rock. By welding a shank to a long chisel bit and operating it by a sweep, rigged as a spring pole bounced up and down by three men, they had driven to thirty-four feet by November 1, 1807. Encouraged when the flow of brine increased, they made the shank longer and drilled farther through the rock, until they reached fifty-nine feet. Getting a still stronger flow of brine, they ceased boring, and, to prevent surface water from diluting the brine, cased it in with a wood casing. From this, the first drilled well in the United States, rigged, tubed, and worked, the Ruffners, on February 8, 1808, made salt for the new low price of four cents a pound.

The next step was the use of coal for the kettle fires. At first the only fuel used for the furnaces was wood from the surrounding hillsides, but within the next few years production had increased so rapidly that these neighboring areas were stripped bare, and by 1817 expenses were mounting to an alarming extent, as longer distances must be traveled to procure sufficient wood, which, of course, burned rapidly, consuming huge amounts very quickly. David, casting about for a remedy, began experimenting in the use of "stone" coal, the outcropping veins of which were readily accessible. This was not so simple a solution as it sounds, for then nothing was known of combustion, and even the necessity of a draft had to be learned by repeated failure to make the fires burn without one. Then they found that by dampening the coal they got steam, and little by little its mysteries were solved. With this, the first industrial use of one of the State's most bountiful resources, under way, it was not long before the furnaces were converted to coal burning. By 1815 there were fifty-two furnaces extending four miles below, and three above that of the Ruffner operations, and the homes of the various salt-makers were rapidly clustering around the wells.

These salt producers, in order to protect themselves from outside importations, did a surprising and revolutionary thing. They banded themselves together into the first monopoly or "trust" in America, with the lawyer Joseph Lovell as originator. Formed on November 10, 1817, this organization was called the "Kanawha Salt Company." It was scheduled to go into operation January 1, 1818, and to expire December 31, 1822. Its officers and directors were in full charge, with authority to receive all salt manufactured by the members, fix prices, make terms, receive proceeds, pay expenses, purchase land, borrow money, and make a fair dividend of the net proceeds of sales according to the respective interests of the subscribers. The salt-makers who signed this agreement were John, Sam and John D. Shrewsbury, Leonard and Charles Ruffner, Isaac and Bradford Noyes, A. Donnally, Joseph, David, and Daniel Ruffner, Stephen Radcliff, A. Stockton, John Reynolds, Joseph Lovell, W. Steele & Company, and John J. Cabell.

The industry was now making great strides, and improvements and developments were constantly being made. Tin tubes for casing, made by a Charleston tinner, were found to corrode and were replaced by copper; the horsepower pump appeared, to be replaced in 1827 by a steam engine. About this time a temporary business slump occurred, but by 1831 new impetus was given the industry by an invention made by William Morris, grandson of the pioneer of Kelly's Creek. It was an uncomplicated device of the utmost simplicity that eliminated drill-sticking, and was of immense value in deep drilling. It was never patented, and Mr. Morris received nothing from it financially, but it was of the utmost importance then, and is still in use in all deep well drilling in this country. All wells below the town ran from eight hundred to twelve hundred feet deep, and those above from one thousand to fifteen hundred.

Some years before, Joseph Ruffner, Jr., had severed his business association with his brother, as well as his connection with the Kanawha Valley, and had removed with his family to Cincinnati, where he remained the rest of his life.

David Ruffner's two sons were now grown and highly educated men. The eldest, Dr. Henry Ruffner, had prepared himself for the ministry, and it was he who preached the first Presbyterian sermon and organized the first Presbyterian church in Kanawha County. He was likewise the founder of Mercer Academy, located in Charleston upon church property. In 1836 he was elected President of Washington College, now Washington and Lee University at Lexington, Virginia. He also became well known as a writer, particularly along anti-slavery lines, the *Ruffner Pamphlet,* published in 1847, creating a decided furor in the South.

(General) Lewis Ruffner, David's second son, after completing his education, plus a year of school teaching, became interested in the salt business, and went into it with great enthusiasm. After three years he had made several valuable improvements, chiefly that of a new furnace adapted to the use of coal. By this time his father was ready to relinquish active control of the business, and in 1823 Lewis Ruffner took over its management.

Tobias Ruffner, while of an inventive turn, and with several useful innovations to his credit, appeared to lack the business ability of his brother David, and became increasingly involved financially. This may have been partially brought about through an alarming situation which arose about 1825. American commercial shipping, for want of return cargoes, began loading with salt, either as ballast or as cargo, at a very negligible cost. It is readily seen what a depressing effect this practice would have upon local prices, and salt at the Kanawha wells dropped as low as fifteen to twenty cents a bushel —a price so ruinous that many wells were closed. The manufacturers were so aroused that in 1828 they sent a protest to Washington against a move to repeal the duty on imported salt.

In 1830 Tobias Ruffner determined to turn over his affairs to his sons, Isaac, Benjamin Franklin, and Silas. This proved a most fortunate change for all concerned. They operated the salt property so successfully as not only to relieve their father's monetary embarrassment, but to make each of them financially independent. Tobias then sold his share of the Dickinson survey to other salt manufacturers—the twelve acres below Campbell's Creek to John D. Cabell, and the other part above to Messrs. Lewis and Shrewsbury.

In 1833 George H. Patrick, of New York, introduced the multiple effect evaporator. Heretofore the salt had been an ugly red color, due to sediment and iron. By this new process the salt was pure white, and its making was facilitated to such an extent that the industry was revolutionized.

The peak of the industry was between 1845 and 1852. Annual Kanawha production increased from 600,000 bushels in 1814 to 1,419,205 bushels in 1840, and in 1850 to 3,142,100 bushels. It was strong salt, of a very fine quality, and most successful in meat curing. Of all the salt works in Ohio, Pennsylvania, Virginia, Kentucky, New York, and other states, the largest amount produced by any one was 300,000 bushels, while the Kanawha wells produced more than twice that amount. In 1851 salt from these furnaces was exhibited in London's first World's Fair, and later in the Paris Universal Exposition in 1868, winning awards and prizes in each.

The salt industry brought many other businesses in its train—the tin- and coppersmiths, the wagon- and barrel-makers (one hundred and thirty thousand barrels being used annually), blacksmiths (many wagons were in use for hauling wood, barrels and later coal), foundries (each salt furnace in its erection requiring about eight tons of cast iron), and the boat builders who made the large flatboats that carried the loaded barrels piled to alarming heights on long journeys to the Ohio and beyond.

The Kanawha Salines had become a busy town, with taverns, stores, churches, and an academy, and as a shopping center it far outdistanced the slow-growing neighboring town of Charleston. Progress, as such, is not without its disadvantages, however, and man had outdone himself in making this once beautiful landscape

"The Froms House".

an eyesore. The hillsides, formerly green and inviting, were now bare and covered with soot and cinders from the coal-burning salt furnaces. The river, once clear and lovely, had become oil-coated and ill-smelling—an unpleasant stream which the rough boatmen had given the equally unpleasant name of "Old Greasy." This condition was brought about because all salt drillers encountered petroleum in greater or lesser quantity. Being totally unaware that it had any value, they were concerned only in getting rid of it with the least effort, and the nearness of the river solved the disposal problem. The constant hauling of barrels of salt for loading on the flatboats made a sea of mud in winter and a cloud of dust in summer.

In 1826 The Salines received such widespread and unfavorable publicity through the publication of a book by Anne Royall, *Sketches of History, Life and Manners in the United States,* that a storm of protesting editorials broke forth in the local press. As a result of her journey from the East through the region, she devoted several pages to a description of Kanawha County and the salt works. Noted for her caustic pen, she not only excoriated the appearance of the locality, but apparently judged its inhabitants as a whole by the rough and undesirable part of the population that came and went at the call of easy money.

She wrote: "I never saw or heard of any people but these, who gloried in a total disregard of shame, honour and justice, and an open avowal of their superlative skill in petty fraud, and yet they are hospitable to a fault, and many of them are genteel." She had some good words to say of the women, both as to their virtues and their looks, but apparently felt they were in constant danger of coming to an unspeakably bad end, for she continued with the dire thought that "I would be sorry to see one of these amiable females become a widow in this iron country." Nevertheless she did hold out a little hope for them by remarking, "However, for the honour of human nature be it remembered, there are a few noble exceptions among the other sex, which may justly be compared to diamonds shining in the dark." This comparison was likely inspired by the gloomy and smoke-laden atmosphere of the Salines!

In spite of Mrs. Royall's unfavorable comments, and of the unfortunate and unattractive conditions with which the salt manufacturers were surrounded, there were indeed many "genteel" people who lived at The Salines—able, upright, and worthy citizens of whom the Valley is very proud, the names of many having later been given to a number of the streets in Charleston. A list of such pioneer street-names may be found in the appendix of this volume. The reader who scans these pages can readily see that much of the early history of the Valley is bound up in these names, names which have a meaning worthy of preservation—"city planning" to the contrary.

After 1852, with the development of additional salt wells along the Ohio River and their cheaper transportation advantage, the Kanawha salt market was greatly reduced, and the industry began to decline. The "trust" which, with frequent reorganizations had continued to function, in the end was largely responsible for this, chiefly through "dead renting" all the furnaces of its members to a group of New York men for a period of six months. This gave competitors a clear field to increase their market, and with the Kanawha furnaces idle and falling into disrepair, permanent inroads had soon been made into Kanawha production.

In 1861 the highest flood ever known to occur in the Valley destroyed many wells, and that, together with the disruption brought about by the Civil War, with the Valley first in the hands of one, and then the other, of the contending forces, meant the beginning of the end for many manufacturers. After the war, methods of operation and conditions of marketing had changed, and the lost momentum was never regained.

The hillsides are now green again, the river is beautiful and inviting once more, and the mud and dirt are gone long ago, with the discontinuance of the name of "Kanawha Salines." Today the highway hurries by on a newly constructed route completed in 1946 that bypasses the quiet little village incorporated in 1885 under the name of "Malden," and of the forty-two salt wells once crowding each other for miles above and below it, only one remains in operation today, that of J. Q. Dickinson and Company.

Located upon the river bank at the eastern end of town, Mr. Charles C. Dickinson, owner of the well and its surrounding acres, lives upon the property in a beautiful modern home whose architecture and setting of trees and boxwood bushes is reminiscent of Virginia homes of an earlier day. Mr. Dickinson is primarily engaged in banking and the coal industry but also continues an active interest and pride in the salt business begun by his great-grandfather, William Dickinson I. He has preserved a collection of the tools, drills, and crude devices used by each generation of salt-makers.

William Dickinson I, the Kanawha pioneer, came to the Valley with his brother-in-law, Joel Shrewsbury, after the War of 1812, possibly about 1814-18. In 1832, under the partnership name of Dickinson and Shrewsbury they erected a well on the site of the present operation, and at this and two other wells, engaged in the production of salt on a large and profitable scale for many years. During this time they also conducted a mercantile business at Kanawha Salines. As the years passed, they acquired other properties and extensive land holdings, and became men of large means. The partnership, together with the friendship, ended in a bitterly contested law suit, and was followed soon after by the death of Mr. Shrewsbury in 1859, and by that of Mr. Dickinson two years later.

This well, close to the river, was one of those to be destroyed in the devastating flood which swept the Valley in the spring of 1861, and with the war under way, there was no attempt made to restore operations.

William Dickinson II (1798-1881), with headquarters in Nashville, Tennessee, acted as selling agent for the company. After the death of his father, he came to the Kanawha to take charge of the latter's estate, and established his residence at the early Dickinson-Shrewsbury Homestead fifteen miles east of Charleston. Both of his sons served in the Confederate Army—John Quincy (1831-1925), enlisting in 1862, in Company A, 2nd Virginia Cavalry, under his older brother Captain Henry C. Dickinson (1830-1871). After participating in several serious battles, each was captured and held in war prisons until the termination of hostilities.

When released, John Q. Dickinson came to the Kanawha Valley and made a determined attempt to rehabilitate one of the long abandoned Dickinson salt wells. He persisted in spite of depletion of resources and other adverse and discouraging conditions which are the inevitable aftermath of war, and by the 1870's the well was rebuilt and production under way. It stands today as a conspicuous example of the tenacity of one man, as Mr. Dickinson alone of all the former manufacturers who made the attempt, succeeded in permanently re-establishing and again making profitable this early industry.

John L., the elder son of John Q. Dickinson, having finished his schooling, spent a few months as bookkeeper for the company, but soon left to commence his banking career. It was his younger brother, Charles C. Dickinson, who in 1898 undertook the management of J. Q. Dickinson and Company, and who, as owner and operator, continues production today. In these days of labor turnover and unrest, it is interesting to record that a member of each of five successive generations of one family has been employed at this operation.

About 1913 the first chemical plant in the Valley was built by a group of English businessmen, and today the Kanawha Valley, written up recently in *The Saturday Evening Post* as "The Magic Valley," is one of the largest, if not the largest, caustic and chlorine producing centers in the world. With salt an important constituent of alkalies and other chemicals, many wells are now privately operated on their own property under the most modern methods, for use of the various chemical companies. For all of the industry's golden past, the future salt production of the Valley, while less spectacular, will likely become far greater.

"Kanawha Court House" 1801

SINCE the census of 1800 showed Charleston as having a population of sixty-five persons, it was high time some progressive steps be taken, and in 1801 a post office, located at what is now the northeast corner of Kanawha Boulevard and Hale Street, was established, with Edward Graham as postmaster.

The settlement did not receive its official name of "Charlestown" until in 1794, and perhaps in 1801 the name was too new to be much in use. It may have seemed locally less significant, since the Clendenins, who had chosen it in honor of their deceased father, Charles, had recently sold their land to the Ruffners and departed from the locality; or with two other towns in Virginia having the same name, it may have been thought less confusing to give the post office a different designation. Whatever the reason, the post office was called "Kanawha Court House," and this name remained for a surprising number of years. It was changed in 1879, to conform to that of the town, the spelling of which had in the meantime become shortened by common usage to Charleston, and officially adopted as such in 1818.

A post office building was a useless waste of public funds. Any merchant with a vacant shelf in his small store and a box to hold the letters was well equipped to act as postmaster, and possessed all necessary requirements.

The use of postage stamps was many years in the future. Even envelopes were unusual, the letter merely being folded and sealed with wax, and the address written on the reverse side. The postmaster used a pen to write the postage rate in one corner, left blank for the purpose. The rate was determined by the distance the letter traveled, and it could be mailed without prepaid postage. Considering the amount might be as high as sixteen cents, the recipient was privileged to refuse the letter if, after examining the handwriting, he thought it likely that the contents would not be worth the charge. Such letters were then advertised in the weekly paper, and if the addressee still remained unresponsive toward a missive, it was destroyed by the postmaster — presumably unread!

It is fortunate this state of affairs did not continue into the radio and motion picture era. Had it done so, the reigning stars would have been torn between two unthinkable fates—pay for their fan mail and go happily bankrupt, or let the postmaster destroy it and, though financially solvent, be deprived of hearing the siren song of their public.

The duties of postmaster in the early eighteen hundreds could hardly be considered arduous, as the mail arrived only once in two weeks. It was carried over the mountains on horseback, but the rider was never so laden with letters that he failed to bring along the small but important purchases of medicine, tea, spices, and needles, requested by the housewives along his sparsely inhabited route.

The pound, shilling, and pence had been used in Kanawha until 1799, although tobacco was the principal legal tender. Money was scarce, and fractions of a cent were quite usual in pricing commodities, and also in fixing the rate of postage. Therein was where a good credit rating was a definite asset, although obtained in a somewhat more whimsical fashion than in the nineteen-forties. It was all a matter of being on the right side of the postmaster, who, it seems, was endowed with somewhat the same qualities as the family doctor. He knew everything about everybody, and acted accordingly.

If the postmaster felt a citizen met satisfactory standards of trustworthiness, he could give credit for the troublesome fraction of a cent that frequently occurred in the postage rate. Setting it down in his little book, he would add the total to the honest one's semi-yearly store bill. As it happened, Edward Graham, the first postmaster, may or may not have been a merchant, but he also was distinguished by being an attorney—the first in the town. He had received a license to practice on August 1, 1796, and was at once appointed State attorney at the munificent fee of $40.00 a year.

The name "Kanawha Court House" was not inspired by a visioning dream—the courthouse was unquestionably there, all forty feet of it, and it stood on the same site as the present courthouse. The judges' bench was a platform four feet high, extending across the end of the one-room building. Every magistrate was a judge, and at times the platform was somewhat congested. The clerk's office was a small building on the upper corner of the lot.

Near the courthouse stood the log jail, with two cells, one for debtors and one for criminals—a definite example of discrimination! At the front of the jail, near the south end of the courthouse, were the whipping post, pillory, and stocks. These unpleasant items of outdoor disciplinary equipment were in plain view of the populace, and perhaps more effective for that reason. The wheels of justice ground less slowly in 1800, and it was just a step from crime to punishment.

The little village straggled along the river, all but lost in the dense forest of poplar, beech, ash, and sugar maple trees that extended behind it to the hills, while along the river bank, towering above the thickets of paw-paw bushes, grew sycamores, cedars, and tall elms whose branches held clusters of mistletoe. About where Brooks and Hale streets now enter the Boulevard there were worn paths of deer and bear crossings.

Colonel Clendenin had operated a ferry across the Kanawha in 1794, and the franchise was extended to Joseph Ruffner when he purchased the Clendenin lands. The Valley was crisscrossed by small streams that wandered aimlessly toward the river. In later years they were bridged in various places—one at Capitol and Fife streets, one on Lee Street west of Court, and another between Clendenin Street and Elk River, where a deep ravine made it difficult to reach the Elk River ferry.

"The old State road," constructed to Kelly's Creek by 1790, had been opened to the Ohio by 1800, and four years later mail was being carried beyond Kanawha Court House to the Scioto, and by 1807 on to Chillicothe. Travelers now began to appear in the Valley. One of these was Lewis Summers, from Alexandria, Virginia, who in 1808 came to inspect lands and gain knowledge of the country for his father, who contemplated a removal to western Virginia. The mission was successful, and a desirable location was found in Putnam County. Settling there a few years later, the Summers family became one of the most outstanding in the Kanawha Valley. Like all early travelers, Mr. Summers kept a journal, from which one may gather interesting glimpses of conditions at that time.

Coming from White Sulphur Springs, he passed over Sewell Mountain, where he saw large bears and flocks of wild turkeys. He crossed New River at Bowyer's ferry, and found the country rough and uncultivated, with little means of subsistence for the inhabitants except game. Coming farther along to the Falls, the Valley widens, and he noted the better farms and homes. He visited the Jones and Morris families, and spoke of orchards and of good cotton being raised, at the same time mentioning the loss of sheep and hogs from bears and wolves. Visiting the salt works where sixty-four kettles were boiling the brine, he was hospitably received by the Ruffners. He dined with them, but evidently observed that his hosts had their problems, as he states they were financially embarrassed with the salt works.

Charleston, he describes, as composed entirely of log houses, with one exception, a house not yet completed. There was a tannery on Elk, and a small tub mill. He mentions the fact that there was no drinking water except from the river. Such, however, is hardly correct, as there were springs—one in particular on the south side of the river having been mentioned by Colonel Clendenin in a report to the Assembly as the site of an Indian attack.

While he says that fever and ague were prevalent in the fall (no doubt the dense undergrowth along the river harbored many mosquitoes, and malaria took its toll in the humid valley), Mr. Summers didn't seem to be suffering personally from any ailments. In fact, he appears to have been having a very good, one might almost say giddy, time. He describes a gay July 4th celebration, where there was much food, dancing, and many "handsome" ladies—some of the fair ones coming from as far away as Teays Valley; he spent a day with Mr. Hale and was his guest on a deer hunt thirty-five miles from Elk; he "swapped" horses with Mr. Reynolds, visited Colonel William Clendenin, and met a number of interesting men before journeying onward. And "though the circle is small," he spoke of it "as fine a society as I could find in Fairfax."

Shrewsburys and Dickinsons

THE STONE HOUSE

DAUGHTERS of two branches of the Dickinson family intermarried with three Shrewsbury brothers, and all came to the Kanawha, where they were important figures in the early development of the Valley. Even a few hours spent trying to unravel the intricacies of their marriages, particularly the many between cousins, and the complicated relationships of their large families, with constant use of the same names in different generations, is sufficient to convince one it could easily develop into a life work. It is impossible to mention one Shrewsbury brother without immediately becoming involved with all three, and it is likewise impossible to mention Dickinsons without including Shrewsburys. The whole relationship becomes a maze of repetitions. Even so, it is crystal clear compared with the complete opaqueness encountered in determining the location of their homes.

Before coming to the Kanawha, and for many years afterward, the Shrewsburys and Dickinsons were closely associated not only in personal relationships, but also in business affairs. They lived on the same lands, built their homes near each other, made countless purchases and sales of property, formed partnerships, and finally grew wealthy together in the salt industry. The story does not, however, end there, as they did not "live happily ever after." Instead, in later life the ties that bound the two families together were irrevocably severed and the partnerships were dissolved, with many years of bitterly contested litigation. Long after the death of the original participants, suits were still pending and partitions of their complicated land holdings were still being sought by various heirs.

Century-old wills and deeds are masterpieces of vagueness. In attempting to learn which of the Shrewsburys were the builders of the two existing family houses, innumerable deeds and other legal papers have been examined, only to find nothing more enlightening than mention of "the house where I now live." All possible identifying descriptions appear to deal entirely with long vanished landmarks, such as "the orchard," "a salt well," "a gum tree," or "a blacksmith shop." Fruitless hours have likewise been spent in looking for clues in county histories and biographical sketches. Equally unproductive have been interviews with descendants and persons suggested by them, as having knowledge.

Since the writer of this book could not, by even the most optimistic standards, be considered youthful, and since she entertained hopes of completing this volume in due course, she, of necessity, desisted from further efforts and contented herself with setting down such gleanings as she was able to gather, however incomplete. If the results seem a confused jumble to the reader, the simple fact is, they *are* confused, and there is no remedy.

Adam Dickinson came early to America, settling first in New Jersey, then in Pennsylvania, but removing in a few years to Augusta County, Virginia. His only son, Colonel John Dickinson, was born about 1731 and died in Bath County in 1799.

Although he never became a resident of the Kanawha region, the name of Colonel Dickinson is a familiar one in its early records. He was one of the first to patent lands, and owned large tracts in western Virginia and in Kentucky. In 1785 he entered the first survey that included the ancient Salt Licks at the mouth of Campbell's Creek, which he later sold to Joseph Ruffner. Many of his tracts were acquired for military services in the Indian wars, as he was a veteran of numerous encounters. One reads of his exploits in 1763 at the massacre on Kerr's Creek, Rockbridge County; later, of his commanding a company at Point Pleasant, and of being wounded in that engagement; and later still of his participation in 1781 in the Battle of Cowpens, South Carolina.

In May, 1767, Colonel Dickinson married Martha Usher in Philadelphia. Her background was a most romantic one: William Usher, an Englishman, while engaged as tutor in the family of Privy Counsellor Sir Edmund Perry, of Dublin, Ireland, fell in love with his daughter, Lady Mary Perry. They eloped and were privately married, after which she was disinherited, but was later forgiven. She came to America and joined her husband and brother who were living in Philadelphia, and there her only daughter, Martha Usher, was born.

The veracity of the story would seem to be borne out by the fact that the eldest daughter of Colonel and Mrs. Dickinson was given the name of Martha's mother, Mary Perry ("Polly"). The Dickinsons were the parents of five other children, and Mary Perry and two of her sisters became residents of the Kanawha Valley, where many of the descendants of their large families still reside. Mary Perry (1768-1853), was married in 1785 to Samuel Shrewsbury, and Martha Usher ("Patsy") in 1793 to his brother, John.

Jane, the third Dickinson sister, was married to

Lieutenant Charles Lewis (1774-1803), son of Colonel Charles Lewis, killed in the Battle of Point Pleasant. Their two sons, John D. Lewis and Charles Cameron Lewis, became well-known Kanawha residents. Lieutenant and Mrs. Lewis first settled in Mason County, four miles above Point Pleasant. After the death of Lieutenant Lewis, his widow, several years later, married Captain James Wilson, by whom she had a daughter, Ann Jane, who married Judge Joseph L. Fry.

In 1810 the Wilsons moved to Kanawha, where they lived six miles above Charleston, at The Salines. David Ruffner, who had previously resided in the old log Fort Lee building in Charleston, at the corner of Kanawha and Brooks streets, had also moved to The Salines. He and Captain Wilson made an exchange of properties in 1814, in which the Wilsons acquired the fort building and came to Charleston to take up their residence in it.

The next year Mr. Wilson decided to drill for salt, and put down a well on the river bank in front of his house. Drilling was not progressing satisfactorily, and Captain Wilson, irked at the lack of progress, announced he would have better brine or bore straight to hell. Shortly after this remark was made the auger struck a vent of natural gas, which became ignited and shot up in a blazing tower of fire. Captain Wilson, convinced he had tempted Providence far enough, and fearful of the outcome, abandoned all further efforts at salt drilling.

Colonel Dickinson, listed in 1791 as head of a family in the Cowpasture region in Virginia, was a man of means and prominence. He was selected as one of the first justices for the new county of Bath, formed in that year from Augusta, Botetourt, and Greenbrier, and was one of the first trustees of Hot Springs when it was laid off two years later. He served subsequently as sheriff of the county, and again as justice. His sons-in-law also took an active part in local affairs. Both Samuel and John served as justices, and in 1795 Samuel received from the Governor an appointment as sheriff, with his younger brother, Joel, as deputy.

On October 8, 1796, three years before his death, Colonel Dickinson conveyed a tract of seven hundred and four acres of land on the Kanawha to his two Shrewsbury sons-in-law. Including both bottom and hill land, it lay on the north side of the river a few miles east of Charleston, in the vicinity of the present towns of Malden and Belle. This tract is referred to in the early land books as "The Pioneer Property," "The Upper Steele Survey," then as "The Rogers-Shrewsbury Tract," and later in the Civil War period as the "Camp Piatt Property," and finally was partitioned into numbered lots.

The Shrewsbury name is an ancient one in England, and an early one in America, certain branches emigrating before 1700. The earliest directly traceable ancestor of the Kanawha branch appears to be Samuel, son of Reverend Nathan Shrewsbury. He came first to New Jersey, then acquired land and settled where Roanoke, Virginia, is now situated, but finding the climate there unsuitable, the swamps causing malaria to be prevalent, he abandoned the location and removed to Bedford County, Virginia. There, about 1760, he married Elizabeth ("Betsy") Dabney, who sprang from the old Hugenot family of D'Aubigne'—later corrupted to Dabney. They were the parents of ten children, three of their sons, Samuel, John, and Joel, becoming Kanawha pioneers. As these same names are applied repeatedly to their children, grandchildren, and all later

"The Brick House"

generations, for purposes of clarification these three will be hereafter referred to as the senior members of the family.

Samuel Shrewsbury, Sr., was born in 1763. When a lad of eighteen, fired by patriotism following the raid of the English cavalryman, General Tarleton, through the Valley of Virginia, in 1781, enlisted in the Revolutionary Army. Shortly afterward he was wounded at the Battle of Cowpens, South Carolina, where he is said to have first met Colonel John Dickinson, whose daughter he later married. Samuel and his brother, John, whose birth date is unavailable, must have been nearly of age, and were especially close in other ways. They not only married sisters, but were partners in all their activities and business undertakings, lived their lives as neighbors on the same lands, and finally died in the same year—1835.

Their brother Joel was also associated with them, but he was younger, born in 1778. His marriage in 1803 to Sally Dickinson, daughter of Joseph Dickinson, of Bedford County, and possibly a relative of the wives of his brothers, brought still closer the relationship of these three brothers. Samuel and John had moved from Bedford County to that part of Augusta which became Bath County, and lived there for a number of years, Joel joining them later. Two years after acquiring the Kanawha tract from their father-in-law, Samuel and John determined to settle upon this land. In May, 1798, they embarked for western Virginia, accompanied by their wives and children, mounted upon horses, their slaves, and their household goods and possessions loaded upon wagons.

After a long and tiring journey over what, though officially termed a road, was actually little more than a mountain trail along which the trees had been felled, they reached their journey's end, only to make the appalling discovery that they had failed to bring a timepiece—an omission which seems incredible today, but at that time actually could not have been so vital as it sounds. After all, there were no trains to "catch," no appointments to keep, and no radio programs to miss. One arose when it was daylight, worked until sundown, and went to bed when it was dark. Nevertheless, clocks were considered an essential, and a rider was promptly dispatched back over the way they had come to procure one. The nearest place he was able to purchase clock works was in Lynchburg. These he carried back to Kanawha, where a local cabinetmaker later fashioned a case of wild cherry—and thus was born a family heirloom.

Soon the newcomers had erected log houses for their families and were clearing land for farming on the seven-hundred-and-four-acre tract along the river. It was only a few years, however, until the new interest in salt drilling had replaced all others. Such farming as was necessary was done, but salt furnace and well rigging grew to be barnyard companions of cows and horses. The Shrewsbury land, lying in the midst of the production area, inspired the brothers to buy adjoining acreages, and a good deal of buying and selling went on, with the Shrewsburys becoming actively engaged in the growing salt business.

Less information is available concerning John Shrewsbury, Sr., than either of his brothers. He lived on the seven-hundred-and-four-acre tract, but the exact location of his house is undetermined. His family was smaller than theirs, but there were several interesting marriages. His son, Samuel, married Laura Angela Parks, whose mother was a relative of George Washington, and the daughter of another son, John, married Dr. Lawrence Augustine Washington, son of a full brother of George Washington.

County historians say that when the Shrewsburys first arrived on the Kanawha they camped in a walnut grove which afterward supplied interior woodwork and wainscoting for a "stone mansion," built later by Samuel, Sr. No location is given of grove or mansion, other than as being on the Colonel Dickinson survey. With the difficulties of handling and hauling heavy beams, timbers, and stone without mechanical equipment, it seems obvious that the sources of supply and the actual construction must not have been far apart. Not even one walnut tree can now be found to suggest the virgin hardwood timber then so plentiful, but soon to be consumed by the avaricious salt furnaces that were springing up like mushrooms along the river.

Although the grove is lost in the mist of the past, some indication of its existence remains, for in this locality there still stands an early stone house whose interior woodwork is of walnut. In spite of exhaustive efforts to identify it positively as the "Stone Mansion," built by Samuel Shrewsbury, the writer must reluctantly admit she can only say she believes it to be—and such data as has been found, tends to verify the belief.

The house is on the original seven-hundred-and-four-acre tract, and is located about thirteen miles east of Charleston, at the town of Belle, and about a quarter of a mile above Simmons Creek. An indication of its age is shown by the position of the building which has no relation to its present surroundings. Its back is turned to the present Route 60, and the entrance, which must have originally faced a long nonexistent road that once wound toward the river and continued along the bank to a ferry at The Salines, now stares into the side of a neighboring house. While the house—its building date unknown—is obviously very old, perhaps as early as 1810, its construction defies time. Though the eighteen-inch thick walls, made of sandstone quarried from a steep hillside across the highway, are weathered and brown, they are as sturdy and true as they were more than a century ago.

The term "mansion" seems a slight exaggeration, however, as the house, though two stories in height, is most primitive, and has only four large rooms and one very small one. Nevertheless, compared to the log dwellings which were its contemporaries at the time of construction, it must undoubtedly have appeared an impressive edifice. The building is oblong, the two sides alike, with an equal number of doors and windows.

Inside chimneys in the end walls furnish fireplaces for the four rooms, which are spaced two on each floor, with a small hall and steep stairway between, one end of which is partitioned on the second floor into a small extra room. There are three windows across the second floor, and two on the first, flanking the central door.

The interior woodwork is of the crudest sort, thick mantels and window sills, rough and unplaned, but the wooden ceilings appear to be whipsawed boards. The doors are heavy, and wooden pegs are in evidence. One of the lower rooms has wainscoting, although much of the woodwork was torn out and utilized as firewood by Civil War soldiers who may have occupied the house during the period of their encampment at Camp Piatt in the fields near Simmons Creek.

The most interesting feature of construction is the stone work. Random widths and lengths give a varied and attractive pattern to the walls, which are supported at the corners by huge blocks of cut stone.

It is unfortunate that so little is known of the history of this truly pioneer dwelling which has sheltered many generations of the Shrewsbury family, as well, no doubt, as many travelers and visitors passing through the Valley in early days when taverns were many miles apart. One such traveler who stopped here more than once was the popular Henry Clay, for whom many parents chose to name their children—the Dickinson and Shrewsbury families being no exception.

Samuel and John Shrewsbury lived harmoniously together on their seven-hundred-and-four-acre tract, with no formal division of their property until 1830, five years before their deaths. The occasion for a partition then apparently was their desire to divide the land among their respective children and grandchildren—which each proceeded promptly to do. John was particularly concerned in making provision for the widow and children of his deceased son, John, and Samuel was anxious to bolster the status of sons and sons-in-law who had become involved financially.

On December 14, 1833, Samuel, Sr., and his wife, Mary, gave several valuable tracts of land to their sons, William, Joel, Jr., Charles L., and to their daughter, Nancy, and her husband, John Rogers, Jr. Part of this land had been apportioned to John Shrewsbury, Sr., at the time of the division of the original tract, and he had conveyed it to Samuel shortly afterward. Part of it, lying on the waters of Campbell's Creek, had been purchased jointly by Samuel, Sr., John, Sr., and their brother, Joel, Sr., from William Tompkins, and part was Samuel's interest in land called "the dead property" which had been acquired in 1817 by the Kanawha Salt

Company. These various tracts included salt wells, furnaces, coal banks, and numerous houses, barns, and other buildings, in addition to the farm and house where Samuel, Sr., and his wife then lived—presumably the stone building, and in which they stipulated they were to continue to reside for their joint lives.

Other stipulations in the deeds were that John D. Shrewsbury be paid $3,500, James Craik $2,500, and all debts of Samuel and Mary Shrewsbury be paid. This attempt of the parents to help their children out of financial difficulties was only temporarily successful. Samuel, Sr., died the following year. Fourteen years later, through failure of the sons to meet certain obligations, the lands were sold at public auction, and on June 20, 1849, the Rogers-Shrewsbury tract was purchased by Joel Shrewsbury, Sr., and William Dickinson, I.

For many years Smithers, Crocketts, and other Shrewsbury descendants lived in the old house, but it finally passed out of the hands of the family. Its present owner is Mrs. Jessie Nelson, and it is today occupied by her tenants.

Once conspicuous because of its "modern" appearance, this ancient landmark now looks out of place and lost in its present surroundings of vast chemical plants whose towering structures represent the ultimate of modern industrial development, and one feels the days of the old stone house are numbered.

THE FRAME HOUSE

WHEN Samuel and John Shrewsbury came to the Kanawha in 1798 their brother Joel (1778-1859), was young and unmarried, and if he accompanied them, it was likely for the adventure of the trip, and to help them with the moving, rather than with any intention at that time of remaining. His chief interests were still in Bedford County, where in 1803 he married Sally Dickinson (1776-1842), daughter of a prominent and wealthy plantation owner, Joseph Dickinson (1742-1818) and his wife, Elizabeth Woolbridge (1744-1818). This family included two other daughters, Edna (Mrs. Archibald Stratton), and Nancy (Mrs. Jeffrey Robertson), and two sons, Pleasant, who lived in Franklin County, and William I, who was born in 1772 and who married Folby Candler.

According to the will of Joseph Dickinson, written the year of his death, he, his son, Pleasant, and son-in-law, Joel, were engaged in tobacco merchandising and milling in Bedford and Franklin counties, under the firm name of Joel Shrewsbury and Co. The death in September of Mr. Dickinson, followed two months later by that of his son, Pleasant, brought an end to the partnership. Then began an intimate association between the remaining son, William, and Joel Dickinson, which was to continue for many years.

The War of 1812 had been followed by a business recession and a slump in the tobacco market. With Joel's two brothers established in Kanawha, where salt production was growing beyond the experimental stage into a stable industry, the query of what to do after the death of his partners, was soon determined. With his sisters married, and now bereft of a brother and both parents in the same year, the family ties that held William Dickinson to Bedford County were broken. He was ready to join his brother-in-law, Joel, in a proposed move to western Virginia, and with their families to become permanent residents of the Kanawha colony.

Reaching the Valley, they settled in a spot fifteen miles east of Charleston, now known as Quincy. Many dates have been given as the year of their arrival, beginning with 1813, but actually the time is uncertain. Since the three deaths in the Dickinson family occurred in the early and late autumn of 1818, the following spring would seem the logical time for the pilgrimage to have taken place.

Still standing at Quincy is a white frame farmhouse whose early history is so closely identified with the two families that, after more than a hundred and twenty years, it is often spoken of as the "Dickinson-Shrewsbury Homestead," although the Shrewsbury connection was comparatively short, while the Dickinson association has continued to this day. The birthplace of the present owner, Mr. John L. Dickinson, great-grandson of his pioneer ancestor, William Dickinson I, this pleasant white frame house is enclosed by a picket fence and surrounded by beautiful meadows and the large barns and other farm buildings of the Quincy Dairy Company. Although Mr. Dickinson maintains a very charming home in Charleston, where he is actively engaged as president of The Kanawha Valley Bank, his valuable herd of Guernseys and the successful operation of his fine dairy farm are among major interests.

The homestead is a simple farmhouse type of dwelling. It is two stories in height, with outside chimneys of red brick, on each side of which pairs of twelve-inch-long windows under the eaves serve to light the attic. The windows, flanking the central doorway, are somewhat unusual. Especially large, each has a long upper sash containing twelve panes of glass, while the shorter sash below has but eight. The large rooms opening into a wide hall measure approximately eighteen by twenty-four feet. Two of them contain ornate plaster moldings which are obviously much later embellishments.

During the Civil War, with armies of both North and South passing through the Valley, many early homes were burned, and this one, directly on the turnpike, had a narrow escape, as the charred rafters in the attic testify. William Dickinson II was living on the farm at the time. When the northern troops came through and saw his son John's cattle branded "J.D.," the cattle were promptly destroyed, with the explanation that the initials stood for Jefferson Davis, which, had such been the case, would seem to have been carrying patriotic ardor a bit far!

Near the house is a small one-story cottage, said to have been built and occupied before the large house was constructed. Back of it is another small building whose fine old brick chimney, wide at the bottom, and narrowing toward the top, has a very definite similarity to the outbuildings that cluster around the restored dwellings of Williamsburg. It is called the wash house, but may have originally been used as a kitchen. An unexpected feature is its interesting windows, which are very long and contain three separate sash. Another building on the opposite side of the house, and in the rear of the shaded lawn, is the sturdy log meat house.

The family burial ground was located where the New York Central Railway now has its right of way, but before construction of the railroad, the bodies were all removed to the Spring Hill Cemetery in Charleston.

Soon after their arrival on the Kanawha, the brothers-in-law, William Dickinson I and Joel Shrewsbury, under the partnership name of Dickinson and Shrewsbury, had embarked on a long and lucrative business association. They acquired many tracts of land, built and operated several salt wells, and were the owners and proprietors of a store at The Salines.

The heart of the salt area being somewhat below Quincy, it became advisable for one of the partners to be in closer touch with operations. Apparently Joel later removed his family to that location, as a deed of December, 1833, states he was then living on the same tract as his brothers, Samuel and John, that is, on the original Shrewsbury seven hundred and four acres. Some years previously Joel and William had sunk a salt well at the upper end of the tract, but it was 1825 before they purchased the acre or so of land on which it stood—evidently a successful well, as the interval of time indicates a no-salt, no-purchase arrangement.

As time went on, Dickinson and Shrewsbury became men of much wealth and large estates, a condition bringing in its train complications and disagreements as to jointly owned property, which finally, in their later life, caused a disruption of their friendship and a severance of their business relations. The last years of their lives were spent in legal controversy with intensely bitter feeling which carried on into later generations, although descendants today can tell with a smile some of the things that were said and done in the vindictiveness of that far-off quarrel.

Joel Shrewsbury died first, in 1859, and Dickinson two years later. Half of Mr. Dickinson's estate went to a son, William II (1798-1881), who had continued his residence in Bedford County after the departure of his father for Kanawha, and had assumed responsibility of the family plantation on Goose Creek. Later, however, he became selling agent for the Salt Company, with his headquarters in Nashville, Tennessee. About the beginning of the Civil War, with uncertainty and confusion on all sides, he returned to Virginia. Coming to Kanawha, he established his residence at the old

Quincy homestead and took over the management of the salt wells and other family properties.

William Dickinson II had married Margaret C. Gray, who died in the spring of 1859, leaving four children: (1) Mary (Mrs. John A. E. Winkler); (2) Jane (Mrs. John A. Cobb); (3) Henry Clay (1830-1871), who married Sally Jane Lewis, daughter of John D. Lewis and Ann Dickinson Lewis. (Mr. Lewis, a grandson of Colonel Charles Lewis, who was killed at the Battle of Point Pleasant, was a man of high character and great energy. He lived to be eighty-three, and was four times married. On the river bank near Campbell's Creek still stands the vine-covered ruin of his once handsome brick house. Mr. Lewis was one of the wealthy salt kings of the Valley); (4) John Quincy (1831-1925), who married Mary Margaret D. Lewis, sister to the wife of his brother.

Henry Clay and his brother, John Quincy Dickinson, became men of prominence in West Virginia, where each, as well as their father, served as president of The Kanawha Valley Bank, of Charleston. Henry, one of the original stockholders, was elected its second president in 1870, three years after the bank was founded. His tenure of office was brief, however, as his death occurred within a year. He was succeeded by his brother-in-law, Charles C. Lewis, who in 1878 was followed by William Dickinson II, father of the deceased Henry Clay and of John Quincy. The latter, in 1882, after the death of his father (1881), became the fifth president. Colonel John Q. Dickinson lived to be ninety-four years of age and served the bank with distinction for the amazing period of forty-three years. After his death in 1925, his son, John L. Dickinson, succeeded him as president, and continues as such today. Thus has continued the unique precedent of family succession which was established with the second president in 1870. During these years this banking institution has become one of the largest and most important in the State, and is housed in one of the handsomest buildings in West Virginia.

The Brick House

WHERE the Joel Shrewsbury, Sr., house stood, the writer has been unable to ascertain. It was on the seven-hundred-and-four-acre tract near the homes of his brother, and a number of indications point to the possibility of it being the large brick house at Belle, that faces U. S. Route 60 just above the old stone house of Samuel Shrewsbury.

The writer embarked on a determined effort to trace its ownership, and for many weeks of investigation refused to believe that somewhere, sooner or later, the words "brick house" would not appear in early deeds relating to this property, particularly as it is an unusually good house, and when built, must have been as fine, or finer, than any other in the vicinity. But nothing more revealing than the vague words "houses" and "appurtenances" has come to light.

Numerous descendants of both Shrewsbury and Dickinson families—for it *could* be a Dickinson house—have been consulted without avail, so now the writer, unable to spend any more time on this apparently hopeless quest, frankly admitting she doesn't know, is going to take matters into her own hands and "attribute" this house to Joel Shrewsbury, Sr. She has not a doubt that so soon as this book is printed she will learn the house was built by someone named Jones or Smith, with the exact date thrown in for good measure, and both from a thoroughly reliable source!

These are the reasons for the "attribution": First, the house is on the Samuel and John Shrewsbury tract where their brother Joel is known to have been living in 1833. Second, it is a very large house, and Joel had a large family—his brother John had a small family, and the elder brother Samuel is identified with the stone house. Since the death of the two older men occurred in 1835, and they spent the last five years of their lives distributing their property among their descendants, with no mention of this house, it is unlikely either of them would have built a dwelling of such size and pretentiousness late in life, and if either had done so earlier, such would place the house in a period at variance with its architectural details.

Joel, on the other hand, as the younger of the three, and by far the wealthiest—being designated along with William Dickinson, John D. Lewis, and General Lewis Ruffner as one of "The Four Salt Kings" of the Valley —would, by 1833, have reached the time where the building of such a home was indicated. The owner of seventy-two different properties, thousands of acres of coal, and more than a hundred slaves, he must surely have lived in something more than an ordinary house. After all, what good is a King without a few superior accoutrements!

Although he lived upon it, Joel Shrewsbury did not become the actual owner of the property until some years after the death of his brothers, when the tract was sold at public auction in June, 1849, and was then purchased jointly by him and his partner brother-in-law, William Dickinson I. Joel was then seventy-one and his partner seventy-eight, so obviously construction of the house did not follow the purchase, as neither owner would likely have undertaken it at his age. The year when the house was constructed, one cannot say, but the type of architecture, and certain interior details, indicate the period as approximately within the eighteen-thirties.

The mantel in one of the lower rooms is somewhat similar to that in a lovely old Greenbrier County house called "Mountain Home," that was built in 1833. Massive and hand-carved, it too is supported by pairs of reeded columns and both are still painted the original ebony color—the height of style and elegance at the time, but a little overpowering for present-day taste. In the adjoining dining-room there is a mantel, now painted ivory, that is not quite so large, and has only one column at each end, with a different motif carved in the center. All the interior woodwork shows more careful attention to the niceties of detail than is true with respect of most of the early houses found in the Valley. The thick partition walls permit paneling on the inside of the grooved window and door casings. The doors themselves are very wide, and some still have their original large brass box locks of English make. The baseboards are unusually deep with panels under the windows.

One of the most attractive features is the stairway. One can stand at its foot in the wide central hallway and, gazing up the stairwell, see its graceful curve extending into the open third floor. The small round handrail and carving on the paneled staircasing are good details. The floors are composed of the original six-inch boards. Especially interesting is the deep-set central entrance doorway, with side lights and much elaborate carving, as will be noted in the illustration.

As for the exterior, this fourteen-room house, built of bricks burned on the premises, with walls three courses thick, is a substantial, well-proportioned structure of the customary oblong type, with steep roof pierced by pairs of tall brick chimneys at each end. A carved wood cornice extends across the front wall above the five shuttered and lintel-trimmed windows of the second floor. In the end walls there is a full window on the third floor, and pairs of closely spaced windows below it on each of the others.

Few structural changes are in evidence. The one-story brick kitchen, with its large end chimney and Dutch oven, originally separate from the house, has since been connected by a brick wall. Columns of the small entrance porch are plainly a replacement of earlier ones. An enclosed frame extension has been added, unfortunately, to one end of the porch, but these are the only changes.

The log slave cabins, barns, and farm buildings that were originally a part of the property, have long ago disappeared, and the open space that once intervened between this house and the old stone house of Samuel Shrewsbury is now occupied by two or three small residences. The ancient cedar tree that stands in the front lawn is taller than the house, and is the only tree on the premises.

After the death of Joel Shrewsbury in 1859 the Rogers-Shrewsbury tract was owned jointly by his heirs and by William Dickinson II, but who the occupants of the brick house may have been during this period, one does not know. The family of Robert F. Reynolds likely occupied it in 1862. Mr. Reynolds, born in Monroe County, Virginia, 1826, lived in Nicholas County until 1861, when he came to Kanawha, living first on the Thomas Newton farm in Malden district. After a year's time he rented a farm from Mr. Dickinson, subsequently purchasing portions of the Rogers-Shrewsbury tract, and also buying the interest of various Shrewsbury heirs. These purchases included the brick house in which he was evidently living in 1863, when he opened a store on the opposite side of the road.

Indications are that Mr. Reynolds was a Union man, as his property, during the Civil War, suffered no more serious damage than the loss of fences. And after the war, when General Grant became President, Mr. Reynolds was appointed the first postmaster of the community, and dispensed the mail from the end window of the huge dining-room of the brick house. When the railroad was built to this point, he was again appointed postmaster by President Harrison, and served as such until his death in 1911.

Robert Reynolds had married Bettie Burns in 1853, and they were the parents of five children. Mary, the eldest daughter, married Charles Gardner, and she and her husband established their home in her father's house. Now a woman nearly ninety years of age, Mrs. Gardner, with her daughters, is still living (1947) in this brick house which has been her home since her earliest childhood recollections.

Anne Royall, Early Charleston Resident

ANNE NEWPORT ROYALL was one of the most interesting and widely known women of her time, as well as one of the most feared. She had a caustic tongue, and, as writer of eleven books, and publisher of a Washington newspaper, was in position to give full and uninhibited expression to her opinions, of which she had plenty, and of a most definite character. She was a champion of causes, and unrelenting in her efforts to promote reforms in which she believed, regardless of personal or organized opposition.

Anne Royall was as modern as 1948, even though she was born in 1769, and had spent her childhood in frontier cabins and log forts. Her life is the more remarkable for its humble beginning. The fact that she visited every city and town of any size in the United States, talked with all men and women of consequence, and personally interviewed thousands of people, including each man who became President of the United States, from George Washington to Abraham Lincoln (although her death occurred before Mr. Lincoln was inaugurated), would be an amazing achievement even today, with the speed of present rail, motor, and air transportation. Mrs. Royall's travels were accomplished by stagecoach, steamboat, on horseback, and on foot.

During the years of her editorship of the Washington newspaper *Paul Pry,* and its much later successor, *The*

Huntress, which covered the period from 1831 to her death on October 1, 1854, Mrs. Royall lived in Washington, and was a recognized force, and one might say, in the opinion of many, somewhat of a menace.

In her writings she attacked with equal vigor, men and causes of which she disapproved, and though courageous and completely honest, her remarks were not always couched in the best of taste, were excessively personal and lacking in diplomacy. On the other hand, Anne Royall was not a vulgarian, and did not write a gossip news sheet, as the misleading name *Paul Pry* might indicate. Though critical, she was sincere.

Her "Pen Portraits" of members of Congress and other important persons were unprecedented and naturally created a sensation, as at that time the personalities of men in public life were sacred from candid appraisal by the press. These sketches were at times most complimentary, but at others, just the reverse. For that reason, they were anticipated with trepidation by official Washington and read with avidity by the public generally. Today they furnish a source of reference concerning the outstanding men of that period which is both personal and unusual.

Although her education had its deficiencies, of which she was quite aware, Anne Royall was well versed in history, and had due respect for verified facts. She also was familiar with certain of the classics, among them Shakespeare, Voltaire, Goldsmith, and Addison.

While the books written by Mrs. Royall may not be classed in the strictest sense as literature, they are good reading. Never dull, they possess clarity, humor, and spirit. Primarily descriptive of her travels throughout the United States, they give an interesting picture of the country and its inhabitants, and of customs, conditions and events prior to 1832, and are now sought as rare and expensive items in the field of Americana.

Anne Royall lived for several years in Charleston, West Virginia, and for this reason her story is included in this volume. The elder of two sisters, she was born in Maryland, the daughter of William Newport, of whom little is known, and few references to him are made in Anne's writings. Evidently he was a man of some education, as he taught her the rudiments of reading, and he, and later his wife, Mary, somehow supplied the child with a few books—an achievement worthy of note in a primitive frontier cabin.

Although Mr. Newport was affectionate enough with his family, he was unapproachable so far as other people were concerned, and appears to have been a rather unhappy man. In Sarah Harvey Porter's book, *The Life and Times of Anne Royall*, she says there was reason to believe he was of royal blood through the bar sinister. Be that as it may, he was thought to have been a Tory, and was engaged in some secret business that involved long journeys and mysterious comings and goings. Mrs. Newport was a small and pretty woman, with much strength of character. Her daughter Anne inherited her attractive appearance and had fair hair, blue eyes, and the white teeth and glowing skin of perfect health.

About 1772 the Newports moved to Virginia where Mrs. Newport had relatives named Anderson, living on Middle River. After three years, in company with other pioneers, the family left Virginia and settled in Pennsylvania. Indians were prevalent there, and for safety's sake the two little daughters were placed with families who lived some distance apart in fortified houses. During this time, Anne attended a log cabin field school—without, as she said later, learning anything except how to play a game called "Under the juniper tree." The only information as to the younger sister is that she became the wife of a man named Cowan and apparently remained in Pennsylvania. She had a daughter whom she named Ann Malvina Cowan.

Mr. Newport died while his children were young, and his widow afterward married a Mr. Butler, by whom she had a son, James. This son became a Colonel in the War of 1812.

The Butlers moved to Hannestown (Greensburg), Pennsylvania, county seat of Westmoreland County, then a settlement of thirty log houses, a courthouse, jail, and fort. In 1782 this place was attacked, burned, and pillaged by Indians, with much slaughter and many prisoners taken. Few persons escaped except those who were in the fort, as the majority of the women and children were helplessly trapped in one of the cabins where they were attending a social gathering.

Mr. Butler was one of those killed in the massacre or died shortly afterward. With the cabins destroyed and the meager possessions of the settlers burned or carried away as loot, Mrs. Butler was faced with the necessity of escaping from so dismal a spot. By 1785 she had somehow made her way back to Virginia, where she may have left her young son James with her relatives, as no further mention is made of him.

Mrs. Butler was ill, and according to the account of a woman who saw her, suffering from "blood poisoning" when she left the vicinity of Staunton. Accompanied by her daughter Anne, she journeyed on across the mountains over what was then little more than a rough pack-horse trail to the Sweet Springs, in Botetourt County (now in Monroe County, West Virginia), where she hoped to be relieved by the curative waters.

Destitute, sick, and weary, Mrs. Butler presented herself at the home of Major William Royall on the slopes of Sweet Springs mountain, where she was given employment in a menial capacity. This placed the poor woman in an unfavorable light in the eyes of the slaveholding neighbors, and at once stamped her as a person of very low degree, giving rise to the gossip and unkind remarks which soon surrounded her pretty daughter, who was now sixteen years old.

Major Royall, a distinguished Revolutionary officer and friend of Washington and Lafayette, was a cultivated older man, who had come from a prominent family on the Tidewater to live the comfortable life of a gentleman of means near the Mineral Springs, whose medicinal properties were just beginning to be known. Observing Anne's alert mind and her desire to learn, the Major encouraged and directed her studies. With access to his large library and under his tutelage, she eagerly absorbed books and learning, and developed into the intelligent and self-reliant woman that made possible her future career.

Although Major Royall was many years her senior, they were surprisingly congenial, and on November 18, 1797, were married. Anne's devotion and admiration for her husband were genuine and lasting, and are revealed in the frequent references to him in her later writings. The Royalls entertained a great deal, and as hostess to many noted persons who came as visitors to the Virginia springs or to attend the courts, Anne, now a mature woman of twenty-eight, gained poise and assurance as the wife of a man of wealth and position. Although her husband accorded her every courtesy and respect, and saw to it that others did likewise, and although she conducted herself decorously and dutifully,

Anne Royall was not accepted socially by the local gentry, nor by her husband's relatives. Even so, their marriage was a happy and companionable one.

The Major died in December, 1812, after a lingering illness. He had made a will in 1808, by which he left his estate to his wife for her lifetime, and then to William Archer,* son of the Major's half brother. He and Mrs. Royall were named as executors of the will. The only other bequest was to Anne's niece and namesake, Ann Malvina Cowan, "when she becomes of the age Eighteen, one bed and furniture, one cow and calf, and one tract of Land lying and being at the Mouth of Elk river as per patent bearing date, etc., found in the county of *Kennahway* or Four Hundred in lieu thereof if she *chuses,* to her and her heirs forever."

This niece had made her home with the Royalls for a number of years, and while there, it is said she had been sent to a "Young Ladies Academy," and given advantages she would otherwise have lacked. In return she evidently made herself useful in the household, as there is a deed recorded in 1811 in which Major Royall gives her one hundred and ninety-three acres of his Elk River land "in consideration of her service and attention." The deed refers to her as "of Kanawha," so she had apparently left Sweet Springs by that time. The land is described as "being known by the name of Old *Magazin*," and as adjoining land of John Reynolds. The name "Magazine" is still applied to the locality, which is not far from Charleston proper.

Major Royall had not been long dead, when his widow became the target of slanderous accusations which were

---

*In later life William Archer served as a Representative in Congress.

to recur again and again, and to follow her to a greater or less extent the rest of her life. The Roanes, relatives of Major Royall, at once brought suit to have the will set aside, asserting, among other unpleasant things, forgery, fraud, and that there had been no marriage. For some unexplained reason the marriage record, which could at least have refuted the latter charge against Anne, could not be found, and remained mysteriously invisible until some years after the suit was decided against her.

Some time after the suit was brought, Anne left Sweet Springs and came to Charleston, where by deed dated August 9, 1813, she made a joint purchase with John Reynolds, a well-known Charleston resident, of a one-acre lot on Front Street. The lot was number eleven, next to Fifth Street on the town plat, now the east corner of Summers Street and the Boulevard. It was purchased from Patrick Keenan, who was then living on the property, in what must have been a fairly large house, as eight years later it was in use as a tavern. Here Mrs. Royall established herself for about four years, and continued to live in a somewhat pretentious manner, spending much of her time traveling and making notes of all that she saw and learned. Her retinue consisted of two men servants, a maid, and a courier. But Mrs. Royall was not a good financial manager, and having lived with a wealthy and generous husband for fifteen years, she had no experience in handling money. Being spontaneous and sympathetic, she continued to disperse largesse in whatever direction her impulses indicated, without provision for what a less favorable day might bring forth.

In August, 1813, Mrs. Royall and Ann Cowan made an agreement with William Hensley to experiment for three years in drilling for salt on the Elk River lands. It appears to have been an unsuccessful venture, and revenue from that source a futile hope. On February 8, 1815, Mrs. Royall signed an agreement and a seven-year lease with Keenan for lot number eleven—which would indicate the purchase money had not been forthcoming and he was taking this method of obtaining it in yearly rental payments of four hundred dollars.

The litigation over the will dragged on year after year, and Mrs. Royall soon began to pile up debts and to find herself in difficult straits. By 1816 Ann Cowan had married Newton Gardner, and was probably either residing on her Elk River land, or living with her aunt. Mrs. Royall, in need of funds to help defray her legal expenses, turned to her niece's husband for assistance. While Gardner made her a loan of something less than one hundred dollars, he had no idea of being philanthropic, and did not hesitate to secure her signature to a bond with a double indemnity clause should she fail to repay the loan at the specified time.

By the next year matters were no better, and on January 3, 1817, Mrs. Royall conveyed her half interest in the Front Street lot to her co-owner, Mr. Reynolds. With funds from the sale of other property given her during his lifetime by her husband, Mrs. Royall soon left the mountains of western Virginia and embarked on an extensive tour through the deep South, accumulating data as she traveled and adding constantly to her voluminous notes. She was in Alabama in 1823 when, after ten interminable years filled with unhappy experiences, she at last received word that the jury, first deciding in her favor in the action against the will, had been reversed by a higher court. While in the main upholding the claim of the Royall relatives, the court acknowledged Anne's marriage by awarding her dower in the estate. This, however, was an insignificant amount compared to the expense of years of litigation and accumulated debts.

Now that an adverse decision was finally reached, Mrs. Royall's creditors began pressing their demands, among them Gardner, the husband of her niece, who brought suit to recover his debt. This must have been a keen bit of cruelty to Anne Royall, when recalling the many years his wife had spent as a member of the Royall household, and particularly the final generosity of Major Royall in bequeathing her a legacy.

But Mrs. Royall was to grow used to cruelty, and the day was coming when she would learn to fight back with the telling weapon of her pen. Deprived of her status as the legatee of a husband whose large estate would have assured her a home and security, maligned by gossip, her character besmirched, and with the din of creditors' demands forever in her ears, it is small wonder that she grew bitter and abusive.

Mrs. Royall loved the far South—Louisiana, Georgia, and particularly Alabama. The gracious, easy hospitality and kindness soothed somewhat the harsh treatment she had received at the hands of Virginia, but she could not remain there.

Fifty-four years old, physically ill from the effects of the treatment she had received, alone, penniless, and debt ridden, her circumstances were indeed distressing. Anne Royall was a woman who enjoyed luxury and ease, but if need be, she could, and did, live undaunted in poverty and hardship. She wasted no time in self-pity. Her courage and tenacity were dominant qualities, and she soon determined what she must do. Saying good-bye to the comfort and pleasure she had enjoyed, she secured a horse and set out for Washington, in an attempt to obtain a pension as the widow of a Revolutionary officer. Forced to abandon her horse en route, she finished her journey by stagecoach, frequently indebted to strangers for her stage fare. Indigent, she was forced to ask for scraps from tavern kitchens along the way, and to sleep wherever opportunity afforded. Such experiences might have overcome a more fastidious woman, but not Anne Royall. She was a child of the frontier, and what she could not help, she accepted. She was resilient.

Eventually, after six months of travel, Anne, weary and shabby, arrived in Alexandria, Virginia, in the middle of December, and there she found a true benefactor in the person of the proprietor of a hotel, to whom she appealed for help as the widow of a member of the Masonic Order. This man provided her with comfortable rooms and a servant to wait upon her, although she says he paid a high rent for his house and had a family of ten children. Here she began sorting her masses of travel notes and compiling them into manuscript form for publication. In the summer of 1824 she went to Washington, and fortunately once more encountered a family with instincts of kindliness. They kept her for six months without remuneration, as she was unable to pay them until considerably later.

In her attempt to obtain proof of her husband's military service, she made futile trips to Richmond (possibly also visiting Sweet Springs and Charleston), only to find the records destroyed by fire. This necessitated securing letters from persons who knew Major Royall personally and could vouch for his service—one such letter was from General Lafayette, for whom the Major had great admiration.

Again came up the ever troublesome matter of Anne's missing marriage record. There seemed no end to the hindrances encountered, but at last the claim was filed. She visited the Secretary of State, John Quincy Adams, who invited her to call upon Mrs. Adams, which she did, and with his promise to support her pension claim, she had done all there was to do for the present. Regularly thereafter, year after year, she kept the claim alive with letters of renewal, although the claim seemed doomed to oblivion.

Assisted by her ever staunch friends of the Masonic Order, she next started on a trip through Pennsylvania, New York, and the New England states, to collect further material, and to solicit subscriptions for her forthcoming book. Printed anonymously, her first book, published in New Haven under the title of *Sketches of History, Life, and Manners in the United States*, made its appearance in 1826. It had a decided success and was widely read.

Residents of western Virginia, familiar with the history of Anne Royall, were agog to see what mention would be made of their locality. A Boston paper gave the history a favorable review which was copied in Charleston papers, but it was late in the summer before a copy of the book appeared locally. When it did, the citizens were outraged to find that instead of glowing compliments heaped upon their heads, the lady had some very unpleasant things to say about them.

In her description of the salt works, Mrs. Royall says very few of the proprietors had received any advantage from "this great bounty of nature . . . . . owing perhaps to want of capital in commencement, want of skill, or want of commercial integrity, or perhaps all three," and goes on to describe the rough looking men, the ill-used oxen beaten by their drivers, and the dismal smoke-blackened landscape. As for the inhabitants of The Salines, she rather leaves the impression they were not much better than a band of cutthroats. It is true the boatmen and waggoners were a rough lot, and the place had undoubtedly become an eyesore, but at the same time the greater part of the masculine population of Charleston was deep in the salt well business, and such comments were not to be endured in silence.

Mrs. Royall refers to Kanawha as being inferior, but as producing one genius in the person of Henry Ruffner, professor at Washington College (Washington & Lee). She berates the neighboring Greenbrier countians unmercifully, and says they "lack every requisite for commercial purpose, without capital, system or enterprise, nor do they seem ambitious of either. If their sons can get a fine horse* and saddle and a fine broadcloth coat, and their daughters a fine dress and bonnet to show out at preaching on Sunday (which is probably attended with no better consequence), it is the height of their ambition"—this Mrs. Royall seems to attribute to an aping of the wealthy planters and visitors who flocked by the thousands to the mineral springs of White Sulphur, Blue Sulphur and other resorts—"such eternally is the effect of ignorance, which always chooses the worst and rejects the best; the ignorant always choose the tinsel, it is the bait that takes the vacant mind."

The press was greatly agitated, and the editorial wrath of the Charleston newspaper, *The Western Virginian*, was at white heat. Mrs. Royall's past life was dragged forth and flayed anew. Compared to the newspaper's angry and libelous outbursts, the opinions ex-

---
*Greenbrier bluegrass produced General Lee's "Traveler," and is still the home of fine horses!

pressed in her book were mild and tepid. Such present-day legal props as use of the word "alleged" were totally lacking.

All statements were made as though factual, and ugly words in all their starkness were used with appalling freedom. In speaking of Major Royall, for instance, the issue of September 20, 1826, says: "with him she had lived several years as his paramour, and in the last stages of imbecility and dotage had contrived to inveigle him into a marriage . . . . . Such was the infamy of her character and so notorious the prostitution of her person, that during her residence in Charleston she was never admitted to the fashionable society of the place." Among numerous other accusations hurled upon her is that of having been confined in Greenbrier county jail for debt—a statement for which no verification in clerks' office records or otherwise has ever been found, a circumstance leading one to assume it was a bit of wishful thinking on the part of the irate editor.

All of this bothered Mrs. Royall not at all. She was through with western Virginia. Even so, all of her comments were not unfriendly. In referring to the people as a whole she says they are unsuspicious, kind, and hospitable to strangers, and is particularly complimentary to the women, whom she commends for their beauty and their many good qualities. The little town of Charleston is mentioned as having four stores, two taverns, a courthouse, jail, and Academy—the last three of brick—a post office, printing press, and "some very handsome buildings."

Mrs. Royall traveled the length of the Kanawha River, and her description of the lower, more fertile bottom lands, the crops grown, and conditions encountered, is very informing. She inspected the site of the Battle of Point Pleasant, and saw the bleaching bones of Indian skeletons where the river bank had slipped away and exposed their burial place. She talked with the frontier heroine of early days, Anne Bailey, then growing old and living in that vicinity, and mentions receiving a rather broad hint for a "dram," which was duly given.

Continuing her indefatigable travels, Mrs. Royall wrote tirelessly for the next five years, during which time ten other volumes followed in rapid succession. A novel called *The Tennesseean,* not comparable to her other works, was published in 1827, *The Black Book,* in three volumes, was a continuation of travels in the United States, and followed in 1828-29; *Pennsylvania,* in two volumes, in 1829; *Letters from Alabama* in 1830, and the three volumes, *Southern Tour,* in 1830-31.

With the establishment of her newspaper in 1831, Mrs. Royall wrote no more books, but devoted her time to journalistic efforts. She was constantly engaged in advocating some reform or espousing some current controversial question. In repayment for much assistance given her at the hands of the order, she fought long and valiantly for the cause of Freemasonry during a period when it was in disrepute, due to a local happening in New York state which plunged the east into an anti-Masonic uproar. She fought against union of the church and state at a time when it was actually proposed and secretly worked for. These and many other engrossing subjects kept her alert and active as long as she lived.

Financially, she was more down than up, in spite of the wide sale of her books and periods of seeming prosperity. She was generous and impulsive, and was never able to keep her affairs on any sort of even keel. The pension for which she applied was not granted until after a change in the pension law allowing the eligibility of widows married before 1794. Coming, as it did, after many years of constant and fruitless efforts on her part, and when she was in her eightieth year, it was of little benefit to her. She died not long after, on October 1, 1854, and is buried in the Congressional Cemetery in Washington.

Viewed against the background of her time, Anne Royall, as the first woman journalist, stands out as a unique, colorful, and amazingly courgeous person.

"Cedar Grove" and Virginia's Chapel

WILLIAM TOMPKINS, JR. (1793-1857), one of a family of seven children, was born near Richmond, but after the death of his father, his mother remarried, and removed to Kentucky. Following service in the War of 1812, William, a young man in his early twenties, doubtless lured by stories of the fast developing salt industry on the Kanawha, arrived in the Valley in 1815. His brother-in-law, Aaron Stockton, left Kentucky also, and in 1816 had purchased several parcels of land between the Burning Springs and Kanawha Falls, and later sold a part to Tompkins. The section at the Burning Springs was in the salt area, and here, a few miles above Charleston, Tompkins was soon engaged in operating his own furnace. Energetic and ingenious, as time went on, he invented several appurtenances of drilling, and inaugurated a number of improvements in salt furnaces. His most outstanding achievement came many years later, when in 1844 he began what is said to be the first commercial use of natural gas for fuel.

Mr. Tompkins was twice married, the five children of his first marriage dying in infancy. His second marriage in 1831 was to Rachel Maria Grant (1804-1882), daughter of Captain Noah Grant, a Revolutionary officer, who had been one of the party to throw the tea overboard

Virginia's Chapel

in Boston Harbor. She had arrived at The Salines four years previously to visit her brother, Peter Grant, a member of the salt manufacturing firm of Armstrong, Grant & Co. Another of her brothers was Jesse R. Grant, father of Ulysses S. Grant.

The Tompkins family lived at the Burning Springs for several years while the numerous salt furnaces continued to blacken the hillsides with coal smoke, and to line with money the pockets of the more astute producers. Mr. Tompkins, after twenty-five successful years, had accumulated a substantial estate, and, ready to build a larger home for his growing family, selected a location some miles farther east beyond the fumes and soot of The Salines, on one of the acreages acquired from Aaron Stockton.

It was an historically significant region, as these were once the lands of the Morris family, whose fort and primitive log houses, clustering around the mouth of Kelly's Creek, constituted the Valley's first permanent settlement. The place later came to be known as the Boat Yards, and there dugout canoes were made for travelers going down the river, and afterward flatboats and barges were constructed for the salt-makers to carry their barreled product to distant markets. Boat-making continued until the Civil War period, and was in full swing at the time Mr. Tompkins began construction of his new house. He chose a site on the western side of Kelly's Creek, facing the Kanawha River across a wide intervening strip of bottom land. While the turnpike curved past his door, the house was placed well back from the road in a wide lawn in which grew walnut, holly, and other trees. The hillside above the house was banked with cedar trees and suggested "Cedar Grove" as an appropriate name for the estate. Although a great snowstorm in 1891 virtually denuded the hillside, two or three old cedar trees still stand in the lawn.

In more recent years the small community that grew around the mouth of the creek adopted the name of the house and was incorporated as Cedar Grove in 1902. The house was completed in 1844, and construction certainly began the year before. It is built of brick burned on the premises, and rests on a foundation of large cut-stone blocks. Another huge stone serves as doorsill for the wide entrance, which is approached by a broad flagstone walk.

"Cedar Grove" conformed to the prevailing standards as to size, with sixteen rooms and full attic. The long entrance hall has stairs against the right wall, crossing to the left at the rear. The graceful walnut handrail is supported on each step by two flat spindles—there doubtless being no facilities for making a round spindle. The bill for the woodwork is still preserved. Work took a full year to complete, and was done at a cost of $970, the carpenter taking up his abode on the place while he executed the slow task of carving by hand, mantels, the wide paneled doors, with casings for them and for the windows, stairways, and all other necessary woodwork, including the ever-present shutters which trim the large windows.

The kitchen was a separate one-story building, reached by a flagstone passageway in which the well had conveniently been placed. Across the rear of the house, in true southern style, were two long upper and lower verandas. These are now partially removed. Other alterations have been made from time to time, and, as so frequently happens, the original good lines of a well-proportioned early house became obliterated. "Cedar Grove" suffered this fate when a long and disfiguring first-floor porch replaced the original square double portico that covered the entrance. The upper section with carved balustrade was left intact when the lower was removed to make way for its present rambling successor, which not only crosses the front of the building, but wanders around the end. It will be noticed in the illustration of "Cedar Grove" that the artist did some remodeling also, and mentally restored the portico to its former place.

Interior changes are less noticeable. As usual the large mantels came to be considered "old-fashioned," were promptly whisked away to upper rooms or barns, and replaced by smaller ones with fancy iron grates. The six-inch hand-grooved floor boards remain, but in certain rooms have been overlaid with new flooring. The house yet contains pieces of handsome furniture which have been there ever since its completion. Among them are a mahogany sideboard in Duncan Phyfe style, chairs that came from Philadelphia, and a pair of carved pedestal tables refinished in 1842 by the makers of the sideboard to harmonize with the other pieces. Correspondence concerning the refinishing is still preserved by the family, along with many letters and papers belonging to the early occupants of "Cedar Grove."

Especially cherished and now owned by various descendants, some of whom still live in the Kanawha Valley, are the numerous pieces of a magnificent silver service designed by Mrs. William Tompkins, Jr. They were made by different firms in Cincinnati, Philadelphia, and Baltimore, and for that reason show small variations in design, but all are equally beautiful. The first profits made from his salt well were given by Mr. Tompkins to his wife in silver coin, and it was this coin that she had melted and made into the table service, which consisted of one dozen goblets, one dozen tumblers, a large tray, water pitcher, tea and coffee pots, bowl, cake basket, and various other pieces. It seems fairly obvious that the salt well didn't do too badly!

The original acreage of the "Cedar Grove" property was much greater than at present. At one time there was a formal flower garden on the west side of the house beyond a small brick building used as an office by Mr. Tompkins. In the rear of the house were slave quarters, workshops, barn, corn crib, and the various structures necessary to the maintenance of a plantation, while beyond were fruit orchards and fields of wheat, corn, and other farm crops. Although Mr. Tompkins owned thirty or more slaves, a number of them worked at the salt well, and he frequently employed additional men for the farm work. The daily wage at that time for mowing and binding was seventy-five cents, with the day beginning at sunup and ending at sundown.

President Ulysses S. Grant and his wife came to the Kanawha in July, 1874, to visit his relatives. Arriving in Charleston by packet, the President was greeted at the levee by a cannon salute and a large crowd of citizens, and was conducted to the home of his cousin Mary, Mrs. Thomas B. Swann, who lived on what is now Kanawha Boulevard, below Bradford Street. The next day the President and Mrs. Grant were to be driven twenty miles up the river to "Cedar Grove" to visit his aunt, Mrs. Tompkins, mother of Mrs. Swann. Mrs. Tompkins, with preparations in full swing for the arrival of her guests, had gone to Charleston to pay her respects and to accompany them to her home. Mrs. Grant, however, became indisposed and the decision was made to abandon the proposed journey. It was necessary that word be sent to "Cedar Grove," and also notice be given to all the expectant neighbors who were even then waiting along the roadside to see the President and his wife as they passed.

Rachel Brown (Mrs. C. B. Couch, of Charleston), the eleven-year-old granddaughter of Mrs. Tompkins, was a very capable and dependable child for her years, and upon numerous occasions had been entrusted with the responsibility of making the trip from "Cedar Grove" by boat to Charleston to deposit in the bank sums of money amounting to as much as $500. It is therefore not surprising that she was the one chosen to be driven alone in the family carriage to "Cedar Grove" with the message that the President was not coming. Feeling grownup and important, to be sent on this mission, it made a decided impression upon her, and she naturally remembers it very clearly, as well as other details of President Grant's visit to Charleston.

"Cedar Grove" owes its war-time preservation to the fact of the Grant relationship, as otherwise a house so conveniently accessible on the turnpike, traveled by Federal troops, must surely have suffered the same destruction inflicted upon many others throughout the Valley. But as the home of the widowed aunt of General Grant, "Cedar Grove" was untouched. Armed with a letter from the General himself, written for her to display to any questioning trooper, Mrs. Tompkins was safe —although she did not trust even the Confederates when it came to cows and horses, and had the animals driven up the creek and hidden when soldiers were in the Valley!

Mr. and Mrs. Tompkins were the parents of ten children, eight of whom reached maturity. Virginia, born 1835, was an especial favorite of her father. When she finished her schooling he wished to make her a present, and asking her to suggest the thing she most desired, received what seems an extraordinary reply for a young girl to make—that she would like for her father to build a church. Her unique request was granted, and before long the work was underway.

Using bricks left from the construction of "Cedar Grove," Mr. Tompkins and his daughter chose a spot near their home, but a little farther east beyond a curve in the road. There, on the lower side, and close by the turnpike, he built a small church which he called "Virginia's Chapel." It bears the date "1853" above its white doors. It is simple and unpretentious, trimmed only with a brick cornice under the eaves of the sloping roof. It is lighted by three narrow Gothic windows on each side and a fanlight over the doors. The interior is furnished with plain walnut-trimmed pine benches. Later the building was lengthened slightly and another window added on each side, and at the same time a small cupola made of wood was placed over the arched doors of the entrance. The contrast of the box-like wooden structure atop the brick walls seems a little odd at first, but one becomes used to it. Built for all denominations, the chapel was used indiscriminately for a time, and then exclusively by the Methodists, who, after a reorganization of their congregation, sponsored the alterations. Its early name of Virginia's Chapel was dropped, and it became best known by the designation of "the little brick church." Larger churches have been built at towns above and below it, and now the fate of this small chapel, which served as a Confederate hospital during the Civil War, seems to hang in the balance. Upon the outer walls are placed two bronze plaques to two Kanawha Valley pioneers and their wives. One, to William Morris, Sr., the other to his son, Major William Morris, veteran of the Battle of Point Pleasant, who is buried in the church yard, where many graves and their leaning tombstones are lost in a tangle of honeysuckle and crepe myrtle. It seems a great pity that steps are not taken to preserve this small chapel and plot of ground where lie many of the early inhabitants of this locality.

Virginia Tompkins married the Reverend John C. Brown, a descendant of Mary Brown, whose family were massacred by Indians and whose tragic story is recounted in *The Captives of Abbs' Valley*. Mr. Brown was a member of the faculty of Lewisburg Seminary, now Greenbrier College, and, like his father before him, ministered to congregations at Kanawha Salines, Coalsmouth, Buffalo, Campbell's Creek and elsewhere. He and Mrs. Brown were the parents of eight daughters —a blessing, which, educationally speaking, from today's viewpoint, would be somewhat staggering, since present crowded conditions of all institutions of learning make the education of only one or two daughters a major accomplishment. Eight would be beyond imagining! The problem could not have been a simple one, even in Mr. Brown's time, and perhaps he solved it through his professorship in a girl's school!

One of the brothers of Mrs. Brown was Captain William H. Tompkins, an officer in the Confederate Army, and a participant in the Battle of Gettysburg. After the war he was engaged between 1869-1876 in operating his deceased father's salt well. He then became interested in river transportation, first as captain of a boat on the Ohio and Kanawha, and afterward as captain-owner of the "Virgie-Lee," named for his two daughters. It was the largest packet on the Ohio.

The wife of Captain Tompkins was Ellen Carr, daughter of Major James L. and Sallie Cook Carr, prominent residents of Charleston. After his retirement from steamboating, Captain Tompkins and his family made their home in Charleston. The other five children of Mr. and Mrs. Tompkins, of "Cedar Grove," were: Beverly, Charles C., Ellen R., who married Colonel Oliver A. Patton, Henry Preston, and John Grant. They all married and had children. Many of the Tompkins descendants are still residents of the Kanawha Valley, and "Cedar Grove" has remained in the family ownership and occupancy.

"The White House" Tavern

IN 1789-90 William Morris, Sr., the Kanawha pioneer of Kelly's Creek, built a large frame house about a half mile east of the creek at a small place twenty miles above Charleston, now called Glasgow. The architect and builder, Charles Venable, while engaged in the construction, fell in love with Mr. Morris' attractive daughter Catherine (Kitty), whom he later married. Frame houses were still very new in this region, and such a structure was no doubt considered the last word architecturally, and being three stories in height, was nothing short of a skyscraper, particularly as it stood on a high bank overlooking the Valley. Erected for use as a tavern, court records of November 9, 1791, show Mr. Morris was "permitted to keep public entertainment at his house."

A painted house was almost startling in a locality accustomed to log cabins, so it isn't surprising that this white painted tavern became known as "The White House."

Mr. Morris died in 1792, and his will* was disaffirmed by his widow, January 7, 1793, who elected to take her legal dower in lieu of the provision made for her in the will.

Some years later, 1816, "The White House" and an extensive acreage along the Kanawha River were purchased by Aaron Stockton from John Morris, who was

---

*As an interesting example of an early will, and the first one to be recorded in Kanawha County, the will of William Morris, Sr., will be found in the appendix.

moving to Missouri. This Morris was probably the sixth son of William Morris, Sr. The name of John's wife is given in the deed as "Mary," and in Laidley's *History* as "Polly"—there seems no affinity between them, but even so, in early court records these two names are often used interchangeably in referring to the same person, in connection with other families. The Stockton purchase embraced several parcels of land from Campbell's Creek eastward, including two hundred and fifty acres on Kelly's Creek, and beyond the "White House" to the Kanawha Falls, where stood a sawmill. Built by the Morrises, this mill no doubt furnished the lumber used in construction of the tavern. John Morris also sold several slaves to Stockton, and on April 19, 1817, issued a power-of-attorney to him, apparently departing for the West.

Aaron Stockton was born in 1776 in New Jersey. He came to Kentucky, where he married Elizabeth Tompkins, sister of William Tompkins, and after serving in the War of 1812, removed to the Kanawha Valley. Although a much younger man than Stockton, Tompkins also was a veteran of the war, and he either came with Stockton or at approximately the same time, as he is said to have arrived at the Burning Springs in 1815. They both became active in the salt business, part of the time as associates. In 1827 Stockton sold Tompkins the Burning Springs tract on which Tompkins then lived, and also other of the lands acquired from John Morris, in the vicinity of Kelly's Creek. Stockton became identified with the Kanawha Falls locality, as he operated the sawmill, ran a ferry, and was proprietor of a well-known tavern, where as "Colonel Stockton," he was a popular host to the stagecoach passengers.

Tompkins, now owner of "The White House," opened its doors once more to the public, with his brother Colonel

Henry Tompkins in charge. The first stagecoach line between Lewisburg and Charleston was established in 1827, with one trip a week, and a fare of seven dollars for the one hundred and ten miles. The trips gradually increased to two and three a week, and for a time were on a daily schedule. The register of the tavern has been preserved, and is in possession of Tompkins' descendants, and those who leaf through it find rewarding enjoyment. Many interesting names are found on its pages, particularly in the 1840's. There were rich planters from New Orleans who came by steamboat as far as Guyandotte on the Ohio, and there took the stage for the trip over the mountains to the fashionable Virginia Springs, accounting for a number of French names, among them "J. Destronde and lady and servant," and Monsieur D'Aberdiel, of New Orleans. One party was so plutocratic as to travel from the Blue Sulphur Springs to Louisiana by special stage. Families came from South Carolina, Maryland, and elsewhere to display the charms of attractive daughters, and as a regular tour was made of the various spas, many famous belles alighted at the taverns along the way; then there were politicians en route to Richmond or Washington; persons on their way to attend the courts; some were sightseers, and often there were local residents going short distances for visits, or on business.

Colonel Tompkins enjoyed talking with his guests, and while doing so, made mental character sketches of them. He especially inquired as to their political leanings in the Presidential campaign of 1844, and conducted his own "Gallup poll" by carefully noting under their registered names "for Polk" or "for Clay." He had various little ways of gathering information, and rather insisted that the patrons not only write their names in his book, but likewise their destination, and adroitly maneuvered them into stating the purpose of their journey. If for any reason they failed to do so, he simply wrote down his own conclusions. For instance, under the name of the Reverend Bishop Osburn who was on his way from Point Pleasant to Greenbrier, the Colonel wrote "Look out girls!" Under the names of L. D. Shields and G. F. J. Traytree from Natchez, Mississippi, he noted, "Shields is a hot Democrat and Traytree is a Whig and a Kentucky broker." One assumes this little whimsy was indulged in during the intervals between stagecoaches, and that a fresh page was presented to each incoming group of arrivals. But many of the guests were innocently willing to add a few details after their names, and were spared their landlord's comments. There was "Henry Clay and servant en route from Kentucky to the Virginia Springs," and "Monsieur Felix Peelere, Paris, France, destination 'Tour DuMonde.'" Two others, frankly sightseeing, were William H. Thompson, U.S.A., "Going to Falls of Kanawha, searching out the picturesque," and the Reverend Edward Winthrop, "Going to look at Hawk's Nest."

Additional names were John Johnson, of Piqua, Ohio, who was returning home from the Whig National Convention in Baltimore; Charles Lee Adams, of Maine, and T. O. Shawnessy, of Dublin, Old Ireland. On May 31, 1842, the name of Lord Harbeth, of England, appeared. Other distinguished patrons were Baron von DerStraten, of the Belgian Legation, residence Belgium, destination Washington; Rufus King, twice candidate for Vice President of the United States, and later Minister to France; Andrew Jackson, Thomas H. Benton, Benjamin H. Wade, and John C. Breckenridge.

Colonel Henry Tompkins died in January, 1845, after

which "The White House" closed its doors to the public. About 1874 the building was demolished and a brick residence, given the name of "Melrose," was erected on the site by Mr. John Tompkins. The only part remaining of the original tavern is a portion of the kitchen, but still substantial and useful is the huge cellar with walls of large cut stone blocks extending into the hillside immediately behind the house. The covered well in a corner of the front lawn is still there, and no doubt was once a welcome sight to those passing on the dusty turnpike. In later years the faded bricks of "Melrose" were concealed with cement, and there is nothing in its present appearance to indicate that it marks the location of one of the Valley's early taverns.

Levi Welch House

THE name of Welch is one of the earliest encountered in the annals of the upper Kanawha Valley. It was Alexander Welch, County Surveyor of Greenbrier, who came over the mountains from Lewisburg to lay off the little town at the mouth of Elk for Colonel Clendenin. On the plat which he made in 1794, or earlier, his name appears as owner of lots eleven and twelve. Facing the river at the corner of Third Street, now Court, they were in the center of "Charlestown." He did not become a resident, however, as the first of the Welch family to settle in Charleston was the merchant, George Welch, who arrived about 1811. His two sons, Levi (1784-5—1849), and John (1789-1856), possessed many similar characteristics. They were men of extreme accuracy, and excelled as reliable bookkeepers and accountants, John serving as deputy clerk for several years. Both were salt producers and merchants—occupations so frequently combined that one wonders, with such competition, how storekeeping could have remained profitable.

About 1825 John Welch married Julia, sister of the Charleston merchant, James C. MacFarland, and of their four children to reach maturity, two were daughters, Cornelia H. and Eliza. James, the eldest son, was killed in the Battle of Scary Creek on July 17, 1861. His brother, George Lewis, born 1833, also served in the Civil War, and was twice wounded. From 1862 to 1865 he was on the staff of General Seth Barton.

In 1872 George Lewis married Caroline Donnally Kenna, daughter of Edward Kenna and Marjorie Lewis Kenna, and a sister of the Honorable John S. Kenna, member of the United States Senate.

Levi, brother of John Welch, was born in Washington County, Pennsylvania. He is described in George W. Atkinson's *History of Kanawha County* as possessing "a mind of extraordinary strength, quickness and vigor, whose accuracy in all transactions, fidelity, and promptitude were proverbial." Mr. Welch was for many years proprietor of a store in Charleston, where the early homestead of the Welch family stood on Summers Street in a deep and shaded lot adjoining the alley beside the present Capitol Theatre building. In the heyday of the salt boom, Levi left the slower growing town on the Elk, and moved to the crowded and busy Salines, where money flowed out of pockets and into stores with far less persuasion on the part of the storekeeper. He became owner of a salt well, and an associate with other operators. He also acted as manager for different companies, and was invaluable as their accountant and bookkeeper.

One of his partnerships was with Colonel Andrew Donnally in two salt wells. Another was with Dickinson, Armstrong and Company. This firm had purchased a large area of river front land at The Salines which, according to the "Saltsborough" plat, dated March 4, 1830, comprised eleven lots, Numbers 1, 3, 4, 5, 6, 7, 8, 13, 15 and 16, secured from David Ruffner and his wife, Ann, in 1831, and Lot 14 obtained from another source the year following. The only two buildings then on this land were a tailor shop and a tavern which Mr. Ruffner* was to remove within three years. There was

---

*Reference was made to a church Ruffner expected to build in the vicinity, and which subsequently materialized in 1840, as "The Kanawha Salines Church."

a partnership agreement that provided in the event of the death of any of its members, those surviving became owners of the jointly-held property. Thus Levi Welch, the last survivor, came into possession of the various lots as sole owner on September 1, 1844. Lots 7 and 8 were at the upper end of the tract, and faced the river, with Lots 15 and 16 adjoining them in the rear. This block of four lots had streets in the front and rear, and an "alley" on the lower side. Upon the upper corner—Lot Number 8—Mr. Welch erected a brick residence, and beside it, on Lot Number 7, a large store building. Construction, no doubt, was begun soon after Mr. Welch became owner of the lots, and was possibly completed in 1845.

The store building is long since gone, but the house remains. Large and comfortable, it is well built and pleasantly situated on a tree-filled lawn surrounded by a hedge. It faces the river—once the salt-makers' highway—but the road that passed its door and led to the old ferry has been partially undermined by the wash of floods, and since abandoned, the present highway now being located some distance away, at the base of the hill. The brick walls of this house are eighteen inches thick, giving winter warmth and summer coolness to its occupants. It is two stories in height, with an ell extending toward the rear, the doors of which originally opened on a long double veranda running its length. Another porch shelters the front entrance, the doorway surrounded by glass panels overhead and on the sides. The heavy door, unlike those usually seen, with panels arranged horizontally, has a single very wide vertical panel down its entire length.

The exterior of the house is in excellent condition, with few changes, and its original interior is still intact.

Watch House

It is a dwelling of many doors, all wide and put together with wooden pegs, those between the high-ceilinged double parlors being long folding doors. Carefully executed workmanship is apparent in the paneled inside casings of the deep-set windows, and in other details. The parlors open into the wide entrance hallway, whose proportions are those of a long room. The graceful stair against the outer wall, crosses at the end of the hall to the opposite wall, and terminates in a circular well. The seven-and-a-half-inch boards of the fine ash flooring at once attract attention, and are one of the pleasing features of the interior. A door at the end of the hallway opens into a small cross-hall from which a second stair leads to the floor above.

The kitchen was originally a separate building, near which was a large cistern that furnished water for the household. On the grounds still stands a two-story brick building containing four rooms, built as quarters for the house servants.

Levi Welch was married about 1821 to Catherine G., daughter of Goodrich and Hannah Slaughter, and they were the parents of one son, John S. Welch, and several daughters: Julia, who married James H. Fry; Miriam, who in 1859 became the second wife of Lewis Fry Donnally; C. Amelia, who married John B. Smith, of Louisville; Lolla V. Welch, Camillia Welch, and, strangely enough, there seems to have been another daughter named Camillia. The author does not attempt to explain it, but on a legal paper signed by the Welch sisters, their brother, and their husbands, the name "Camillia Welch" appears alone, indicating she was unmarried, while opposite the name of Charles Hedrick, who presumably was a son-in-law, appears the name of "Camellia Hedrick," and, moreover, opposite that of

John B. Smith is "C. Amelia Smith." Perhaps the simplest explanation is that some clerk was not quite up to par the day he recorded this document.

In the summer of 1849 the Kanawha Valley was visited by its second epidemic of cholera. A frightening terror! Some of the victims, seized when at work in the fields, succumbed before they could reach their homes. Levi Welch was one of those stricken by this dread disease, from which he died on August 23, at sixty-five years of age. Leaving no will, his estate was handled through the courts, and in the distribution of property, the brick homestead was assigned to the widow. The appraisal of the estate indicates the Welch home was well furnished. The list of personal property enumerates a number of interesting items, among them 96 yards of Brussels carpet, 90 yards of "ingrain" carpet, stair carpet, three pairs of embroidered curtains, a gilt mirror, sofa, secretary, 50 yards turkey red chintz, 10 windsor chairs, and six beds—one of which was described as "a truckle bed, bedding, and bedstead." He had two horses, a carriage, wagon, dray, and three cows. There were twelve slaves listed, several of whom were infants and children. A memorandum stated Mr. Welch had given his piano to Mrs. Charles Hedrick during his lifetime, and after his death her husband returned it to the four Welch daughters, then unmarried.

The Welch house was later occupied for a number of years by the William D. Shrewsbury family, Mrs. Welch having apparently joined her daughter, Mrs. John B. Smith, in Louisville, Kentucky. On August 13, 1878, Mrs. Welch and Mr. and Mrs. Smith, who had previously become joint owners of the property, sold The Salines "Homestead" to Anastasia M. Hubbard, of Malden, for one thousand dollars—for four lots, a large brick dwelling, store building, two-story brick slave quarters, and other outbuildings, the amount seems so low as to appear ludicrous and unbelievable in comparison with present day prices of real estate.

Mrs. Hubbard held the property only three years. In May, 1881, with a comfortable profit to her credit, she sold it for nineteen hundred dollars to Lucy P. Oakes, wife of Ebenezer Oakes II, whose father, Ebenezer I, was a son of the Revolutionary soldier, Thomas Oakes, veteran of the Battle of Bunker Hill, who served throughout the war. Born in Vermont, Ebenezer I arrived in the Kanawha Valley when a half grown lad. He soon became a farmer and lumberman, and was the champion woodchopper of his generation. None could equal his record of five cords of wood in one day. His wife, originally from Marietta, Ohio, was Drusilla Drown (1805-1893), whose grandfather, John P. Duvall, was one of the early land surveyors in this region.

Mr. and Mrs. Oakes were the parents of several children: James W., Eliza (married F. Calvert), Allen, John C. (lived in Texas), Drusilla (married C. Calvert), Ebenezer II, Ira, and Leonidas. Mr. Oakes, Sr., died in 1873, when past seventy years of age, at the old Oakes farm three miles below Charleston, where their early log house is still partially intact. Ebenezer II was only a boy when he began work for a coal company, continuing in its employ for five years. He then became bookkeeper for Joel Shrewsbury. After 1860 and the death of Mr. Shrewsbury, he was employed as general manager for the Snow Hill salt furnace for sixteen years, and then for one year with the Daniel Boone furnace.

During the boom days of the salt industry there was

no bank at The Salines, and a place of safety for money and papers became a vital necessity. In the front hall of the Oakes house today is the answer to this problem. It is a large square box, approximately forty inches in height, and the same in depth, made of heavy oak wood and bound with strong iron straps. There are three locks, one being for a secret compartment—a veritable pirate's chest. This interesting old relic has been handed down from father to son—Ebenezer Oakes, II, to N. B. Oakes.

After decline of the salt industry, Ebenezer Oakes II was engaged in a transfer and grocery business in Charleston, until 1881, when he moved to Malden (The Salines) following purchase of the Welch property. There, under the wife's name of L. P. Oakes, a merchandising business was begun in the former Welch storeroom. The property was acquired in the name of his wife, whose maiden name was Lucy Parks Coleman, a daughter of Captain N. B. and Almira Anderson Coleman, of Virginia. Mr. and Mrs. Oakes were married in 1879, and their children were Almira, Lulu, who married F. G. Harris, Frances, Ebenezer III, who died in childhood, Nelson B. and Willard L. Oakes.

Kanawha Salines Church

Kanawha Salines Church

COLONEL DAVID RUFFNER, son of the pioneer Joseph Ruffner, and one-time resident of the log Fort Lee building in Charleston, was a man of strong religious feeling and one whose actions supported his beliefs. He was apparently the leading spirit in establishment of the Presbyterian Church in the Kanawha Valley, contributing not only his land, but his means, for the erection of more than one church building.

Colonel Ruffner was not only deeply concerned in the religious development of the community, but was also interested in its educational progress, and in 1818 conveyed a large plot of ground in Charleston upon which was constructed a preparatory school for young men. The brick building erected immediately upon this site was located on Virginia Street near Hale, and the school, called Mercer Academy, functioned successfully until the beginning of the Civil War, when all such schools were bereft of students. Later, when the town was shelled by Federal batteries, it was destroyed.

The building was completed in the spring of 1819. In it, on March 14, a small group of people met, and, under the leadership of Dr. Henry Ruffner, organized the "Kanawha Presbyterian Church," Dr. Ruffner (1790-1861), serving as temporary pastor. A son of Colonel David Ruffner, he was a brilliant and well-educated young man, having first attended Dr. McElhenney's Academy in Lewisburg, and afterward graduating in 1813 from Washington College (Washington and Lee University) at Lexington, Virginia. He then studied theology, and following a year or so of travel, was licensed as a minister. His pastorate of the newly organized church was brief, as Dr. Ruffner left Charleston in 1819 to begin a long period of professorship in Washington College. For twelve years, beginning in 1836, he served as President of the College. Dr. Ruffner did not abandon the ministry but continued preaching regularly at the Timber Ridge Church in Rockbridge County.

During these years Dr. Ruffner also engaged in writing, and contributed many articles to the *Southern Literary Messenger* and other publications. One of these, written in 1847, was his "Address to the People of West Virginia . . . showing that slavery is Injurious to the Public Welfare and that it may be gradually abolished, without Detriment to the Rights and Interests of Slaveholders, by a slaveholder of West Virginia." It was an amazingly forthright, penetrating, and farseeing document, as well as a courageous one. This indictment, known as *The Ruffner Pamphlet,* received widespread publicity and brought forth violent repercussions throughout the South, where it became a target of constant political attack, particularly in 1859. It is significant that the author's personal popularity remained undimmed in the midst of the controversial tumult.

In 1848, with the reluctant consent of the trustees, Dr. Ruffner resigned his thirty-year association with the college and returned to Kanawha. He could not long content himself without his usual occupation of teaching, however, and soon built a private school for young men which he called Mt. Ovis Academy. It was located in the hills at The Salines and no doubt his log house stood near-by, as he referred to it as "My forest home on the Kanawha Mountains" when delivering the centennial sermon of the Timber Ridge Church in 1856. The school, hidden away and inaccessible, was none the less well patronized and continued to function until 1861. It numbered among its students Nicholas Fitzhugh, prominent lawyer, W. S. Laidley, author of the *History of Kanawha County*, and members of the Donnally, Noyes, and other well-known families.

Dr. Ruffner's father, Colonel David Ruffner, one of the earliest of the salt producers, had lived at The Salines for many years, and was the owner of various properties. He resided on his farm on the western outskirts of the town near Georges Creek, and though no buildings remain, the site is marked by the tall pine and holly trees of the small fence-enclosed burial ground that shelters the graves of Colonel and Mrs. Ruffner.

It was on this farm near the mouth of the creek that David Ruffner erected a log structure which was called the Ruffner Meeting House. Built as a Presbyterian Church, it was nevertheless used by all denominations. Presbyterian services were held alternately with those in Charleston, the two congregations functioning as one with the same minister serving both. The meeting house was in use until 1839 when Colonel Ruffner determined to supply more permanent church quarters. As usual he proceeded alone, and according to his own ideas. Contributing a lot on the river bank, some distance east of his farm on Georges Creek, he laid out the plans and specifications for a new brick church building which he proposed to erect with his own means. Assuming that matters would proceed satisfactorily, he departed for Richmond to attend a session of the Legislature, but when he returned, finding the construction was not to his liking, he forthwith had one entire wall torn down and rebuilt. In spite of this delay the work went forward, and the little church was completed and dedicated on December 13, 1840, by Colonel Ruffner's son, Dr. Henry Ruffner, and the Reverend James M. Brown.

It was a very simple oblong structure with three shuttered windows on each side, and shorter ones in front above the two doors. A small belfry of wood sat astride the steep shingled roof and a lantern hung on a hook beside the door. The interior was equally plain, with the pulpit merely a slightly elevated platform at one end, and an overhanging slave gallery at the other.

Old records of the church give the names of a number of Negroes who were baptized and taken into the membership. It has been said that Booker T. Washington, educational leader of his race, was one of those to attend services here. Possibly such is true, but he was not born in Malden nor a "slave boy in the Ruffner family," as has been so frequently stated. It was after the Civil War when he was brought to The Salines by his mother, and though he was employed for a time in the home of General Lewis Ruffner, it was his stepfather who pocketed the money from his labors there and at the salt wells, and not a white owner.

In 1833 Colonel Ruffner had contributed a large lot in Charleston adjoining the property of the Mercer Academy to the "Kanawha Presbyterian Congregation," and upon it had been erected a substantial high-ceilinged brick church with wooden spire, tall circular topped windows and doors, and slave galleries along the sides. The land conveyed extended to the Kanawha River and as far as McFarland Street. The manse, described in this book as the Dr. Spicer Patrick house, still stands on this lot.

With completion of the new church at The Salines

and the congregation housed in permanent quarters, a severance from the Charleston group seemed advisable, and, on September 1, 1841, the separation was effected and the Kanawha Salines Presbyterian Church was organized with two elders and forty-eight members. Two years later, in 1843, the Rev. Stuart Robinson was installed as its first regular pastor. This church has continued in active use ever since, and a few years ago proudly commemorated its centennial with a three-day celebration.

The years have brought few structural changes. The shutters are gone from the windows and the old lantern from the doorway. The picket fence is replaced by a hedge and an iron gate swings between brick pillars salvaged from a dismantled century-old house that stood near-by. Roof replacements have been necessary from time to time and heating and lighting facilities have been modernized. A Sunday school addition has been added in the rear of the church with a connecting door, and here are still used twelve or thirteen of the original oak church benches—crude, narrow, with plank seats and straight backs — uncomfortable and uncompromising. Carefully preserved are the early communion goblets and tankard, the collection plates, and baptismal bowl. Also preserved is the old hand-pumped organ, the first in the Valley—though surely not installed until after the death of Colonel Ruffner as he did not permit the use of a wicked musical instrument in the House of the Lord, and would allow no voice but his own to "raise the tune" in the singing. But, after all, as the donor of the church, his opinions were entitled to priority. Anyway, the members probably sang much better without the distracting squeaks and wheezes of the organ.

Facing the early road that ran along the river bank,

the location of The Salines church seems today somewhat precarious. In spite of the fact that the building stands with its back turned indifferently to the Kanawha and still appears to be on solid ground, not too distant sections of the river bank and road have fallen away in swirling flood waters. An enormous and beautiful sycamore tree stands guard by the doorway as though it would hold back the river from the small house of worship that its long branches have sheltered for so many years.

Colonel Wood House

NOT all of the Kanawha salt-makers lived at The Salines. Some of them lived on the opposite side of the river where a number of the deeper wells were located. Among these was Colonel Henry Hewett Wood (1810-1883), who, with his wife Ann Ruffner Reynolds (1814-1879), resided at what is now designated as South Malden, in a large brick house which he built in 1829-31. Located on the river with its back towards the street, its present address is 6560 Roosevelt Avenue, S. E. Its owners and occupants are Mr. and Mrs. Charles Cunningham who have recently restored and redecorated the interior.

Mrs. Cunningham, one-time resident of the famous Colonel Andrew Donnally, Jr., home in Charleston, salvaged several of its mantels and doors when it was being razed to make way for the United Carbon building, and one of these fine old mantels has been installed in the parlor of the Wood house. This parlor is an interesting room, distinctly formal in character. Its high ceiling is decorated with a raised plaster molding of acanthus leaf design that is also carried around a wide recessed square, centered with a plaster medallion from which the lighting fixture is suspended. The long windows reach the floor, and add further to the note of formality.

The parlor is on the left and opens into the central hallway, the entrance to which is from a long low veranda across the front of the house. The two original rooms on the right side of the hall are large and square, one, the dining-room, paneled in walnut. Beyond these is a one-room wing with long bay window, obviously a later addition, its outside door indicating its possible use as an office. Extending toward the rear, a two-story ell, with bedroom above and pine paneled room below, opened onto a double veranda running the length of the ell. Both of these porches are now gone. A portion of the ell, now lowered in height, eliminates the upper room, and the brick-floored kitchen is converted into a garage.

Interior details of the house are especially good, with paneled and grooved window and stair casings, wide doors, and fourteen-inch-thick partition walls affording space for paneling inside the door casings. The entrance door is unusually wide and is completely surrounded by square glass side lights of alternating colors in dark blue, red, green, and amber—a combination which could hardly be called unobtrusive.

It is rather surprising that a house so well constructed as this appears to be, should be built virtually without a foundation, and yet such is the case, the entrance porch being barely a step above ground. The facade is wide, with a steep roof, under which a deep wood cornice, supported by brackets, extends around the entire structure. There are pairs of short windows across the front of the second floor, and between them a still smaller window where once a door opened on the porch roof, which then was surrounded by a wooden balustrade.

Old trees remain in the wide stretch of lawn between house and river—one in particular, an unusually large holly, presenting a very venerable appearance. The well house is in the side yard. The house faces the river and, when built, its occupants had no neighbors nearer than the Donnally family, whose large farm adjoined on the west. Today this tall brick dwelling with its back to

Colonel Wood House

M Stoakerman

the street looks oddly out of place surrounded by a little community of modern homes crowding each other on their narrow lots.

Colonel and Mrs. Wood had four children, all born here: Lavinia Cabell, mother of C. A. and Hewitt Cabell; Bettie, wife of J. H. Huling, member of Congress, and former mayor of Charleston; Margaret, who married William Donnally, son of Colonel Andrew Donnally, Jr.; and Elizabeth (1833-1880), who married William R. Cox, Jr. (1825-1870), whose father, a farmer and salt-maker, had come to Charleston from Campbell County, Virginia, about 1823. One of his farms lay in the center of Charleston's present business district, and the route taken to drive his cattle to the river for water came to be called Cox's Lane, and is now Capitol Street.

Colonel Wood came from New York to Kanawha. Strangely enough, he became an ardent Southern sympathizer, and, along with many others, lost a sizable fortune in the Civil War. He later sold his brick house to Mrs. Sallie Lewis Dickinson, after which it was purchased by Lawrence Christy, and was finally acquired within the last few years by its present owners, Charles and Emily Hogue Cunningham.

Dr. Spicer Patrick, distinguished early physician of Charleston, and his third wife, Virginia Harvie, who was a granddaughter of Chief Justice Marshall, are grandparents of Mrs. Cunningham, who has inherited a beautiful silver service originally owned by the Marshall family in Richmond. This treasured possession, with other interesting family heirlooms, is displayed in her century-old house at South Malden. Among them are pieces of furniture once owned by the Patton family of "Elm Grove," and purchased with the house by Andrew B. Hogue, relative of Mrs. Cunningham.

Dr. Richard Ellis Putney House

A NAME long associated with The Salines was that of Putney, borne by three pioneer brothers who came to America and settled in different states. One of the three, Ellis Putney, married Miss Ellis, of Cumberland County, Virginia. The first son, Dr. Richard Ellis Putney, was born in Buckingham County on March 13, 1794, and came as a resident to Kanawha Valley between 1812 and 1814. He was well educated and became one of the best-known physicians of the region, where he lived and practiced at The Salines for fifty years, until his death in 1862.

In 1815 he married Ann Ruffner (1792-1852), daughter of David Ruffner, prominent salt-maker and landowner, who had moved from Charleston to The Salines, and, at his own expense had erected, in 1840, the Kanawha Salines Presbyterian Church. Ann Ruffner Putney made all the bread used in the communion services at this church. The custom was followed by her daughter-in-law, Alethia Todd Putney, who continued the practice for many years, and whose own daughter, Mrs. I. J. Stanley, carried it on after the death of her mother, each using the original family recipe.

Dr. Richard E. Putney and his wife were the parents of seven children. A son, Dr. James (1816-1876), who married Mary E. Reed, followed his father in the medical profession, and he likewise practiced in Malden for a correspondingly long period, where he resided in a brick house now used by the Salina Lodge—earliest Masonic lodge founded in the Valley.

The second son, Richard Ellis, Jr. (1818-1895), was the local postmaster during the Taylor-Fillmore administration, and in addition was a lawyer and a selling agent for salt manufacturers. His wife was Alethia Todd, and their son, Alexander Moseley Putney, married Birdie Rebecca Littlepage, daughter of Adam B. and Rebecca Wood Littlepage, of "Littlepage Mansion," on Two Mile Creek. Mr. A. M. Putney was donor of a lot at Reed, a short distance below Malden, upon which was erected the Putney Memorial Church.

Of the two other sons of Dr. Richard E. Putney, David H. died at twenty-one, and Lewis, born 1826, married Julia Bedell, of Georgia. There were three daughters: Ann Electa, born 1822, who married Samuel Doyle; Frances N. (1824-1862), who married Moses Norton; Susan Eve (1829-1913), who was the wife of James Thayer.

The Thayer family owned a foundry and machine works operated at The Salines during the years of salt well drilling, and from 1870 to the present time, at Charleston, where the business is located on the south side of the Kanawha, at the site of "Willow Bank," early home of the Quarrier family.

The home of Dr. and Mrs. Richard E. Putney still stands. According to a memorandum made by their granddaughter, the house was erected in the summer of 1836.

In view of the deep personal interest of this Presbyterian family in all that concerned the Kanawha Salines Church erected by Mrs. Putney's father, where her husband, an original member, had long served as an Elder, it seems particularly fitting that their early home be under its present ownership—that of the church itself, with the house used as the manse for its pastor.

The dwelling is situated on the north side of former Route 60, about midway in the town, and is distinguished by its attractive doorway with fanlight above. The one-story porch, trimmed with three arches, is also pleasing. The house, constructed of brick, is of medium size, two stories in height, with a lower wing in the rear. The five front windows of the second floor are original, with six small panes of glass in the upper sash and nine in the lower, and are trimmed with shutters. The center window is arranged in a somewhat unusual fashion, with very narrow side windows placed close to it and forming a group. The roof is fairly steep, with inside chimneys at each end. The house is painted yellow and the shutters a soft blue, a welcome change from the early red and green then used so invariably as to make any other color combination appear nothing short of eccentric.

Putney House

Colonel Donnally House

DURING the Indian wars the name of Donnally was a significant one in the mountains of western Virginia and was known to the most remote inhabitants. The Donnally fort was long their refuge, as it then marked the limit of the western frontier. A hundred miles east of the present Charleston, it stood a mile or so north of U. S. Route 60, ten miles from Lewisburg.*

Andrew Donnally, Sr., had come to America from the north of Ireland about 1750 with the Scotch-Irish immigration of that period. He first settled in Augusta County, where in 1766 he married Jane McCreery, daughter of John McCreery who had arrived a few years previously.

Mr. Donnally was a man of unusual physical strength and courage, had much natural ability, and was known for his remarkable sagacity and judgment of men. With such qualities, it is not surprising that he was selected as County Lieutenant and high sheriff when the new county of Botetourt was formed from Augusta in 1769. Carrying with it the title of Colonel, the office was one of importance. The appointment, made by the Governor, went only to citizens of outstanding qualities, and was held during good behavior. The County Lieutenant was the intermediary through which county matters were brought to the Governor, and it was he who commanded the militia and presided at the county courts. These

---

*Doors to this old building may be seen in the State Museum at Charleston, and in the Museum at Lewisburg will be found one of the locks.

duties entailed much traveling, in the process of which Colonel Donnally began acquiring land, and as the years passed, he added extensively to his holdings, becoming a man of large means.

In 1777 the new county of Greenbrier was formed from Botetourt and Montgomery, and embraced a vast area west of the Alleghenies. Colonel Donnally, who had been living in this territory for several years, automatically became a nonresident of Botetourt and a resident of Greenbrier, and as such, found himself once more appointed County Lieutenant for a new county. He continued to serve in this capacity under the State of Virginia's first two Governors, Patrick Henry and Thomas Jefferson.

It is thought to have been in 1771 that Colonel Donnally built the double log house and stockade fort upon his Greenbrier lands. Located in a narrow mountain valley, it was a lonely spot, since, while a few settlers had ventured a little farther west, for several years the fort was the last white outpost. After the Battle of Point Pleasant in 1774, Fort Randolph was built at the mouth of the Kanawha, but even so, it was a hundred and fifty miles from Donnally's Fort.

In the fall of 1777 the Shawnee Chief Cornstalk had come to Fort Randolph reputedly to warn the garrison that, treaties to the contrary, all the Indian tribes, as allies of the British, had determined on warfare, and while he had opposed the decision, he and his tribe would abide by it. If this news were true, the situation was serious, and Cornstalk and one or two others who had accompanied him were held at the fort by Captain McKee as hostages. Cornstalk was noted as a brave and fearless warrior, but at the same time he had led raids into western Virginia that had meant death, torture, and captivity for many settlers. Only three years previously it was Cornstalk who had commanded at the Battle of Point Pleasant, and his was the voice that hurled taunts and derision at the Virginians while the battle was in progress. To them Cornstalk was no hero. During the interval while he was held as hostage a white man was killed by Indians not far from the Fort. Among the rangers were relatives of the slain man, and they became so overwrought that they rushed to the garrison, and before it could be prevented, killed Cornstalk and his companions.

It was a most unfortunate happening, and one which was to cost the settlers much in loss of life and property, as it promptly brought retaliation from the Shawnees who, the following spring, embarked on a revenge raid against the Greenbrier settlements, launching a preliminary attack on Fort Randolph, which they besieged unsuccessfully for several days. After killing the cattle and loading themselves with as much meat as they could carry, the Indians then departed up the Kanawha Valley toward the more distant mountain settlement. Confident of their objective, Captain McKee realized the outcome might easily prove disastrous for the scattered inhabitants, as the Indian party numbered about two hundred. He at once dispatched two men to warn the settlers. But these men meditated too much on the large number of Indians, and succeeded in frightening themselves into returning to Fort Randolph in two days.

Their action created a situation that was desperate. Two other scouts, Hammond and Pryor, then volunteered and, disguised as Indians, set out on the now doubly hard and doubtful mission of attempting to overtake and pass the Indians who already had better than two days' start.

Traveling night and day with the least possible rest, these men finally overtook the savages as they were slaughtering hogs at the deserted cabin of a family that lived not more than ten miles from Donnally's. Succeeding by this narrow margin, the scouts hastened on, and there was time for a number of families to reach the Fort, and for messages of warning to be sent to Colonel John Stuart and others who lived farther east. Before dawn the Indians had arrived and were concealed behind trees and boulders around the stockade.

Colonel Stuart, his guest, Colonel Samuel Lewis, and Captain Matthew Arbuckle, the Commander of Fort Randolph, who was then visiting his family near Lewisburg, spent the night attempting to muster a company of volunteers to go to the aid of Donnally Fort. This was not an easy task, as men were scattered, and were trying to get their families to the Fort and to protect their animals and stock. However, by the next day a company of sixty men had been assembled and reached Donnally's by two o'clock in the afternoon. By approaching the Fort from the rear they missed an ambuscade laid for them and get safely in the stockade without injury.

The Indians had begun their attack at daybreak, and those in the Fort, though far outnumbered, had made a valiant stand, with twenty or more Indians killed as against only four white men. With the arrival of the volunteers, the savages began dragging away their wounded, and soon abandoned the attack. One of those conspicuous in defense of the Fort was a Negro slave, Dick Pointer, who belonged to Colonel Donnally. He was given his freedom as a reward for his part in the encounter.

In the deposition of Leonard Morris, taken years later in relation to other matters, it is stated that Colonel

Donnally purchased Kanawha River lands of John Pryor in 1776. It may be the Colonel was even then contemplating a move farther west, particularly as four years later he resigned his commission as Greenbrier County Lieutenant. The resignation, however, was not accepted, and he still carried on his duties, one of which, according to a message sent to Governor Jefferson in 1781, was the sending of Greenbrier troops to serve in the Illinois campaign of General Rogers Clark. Other duties also began to press upon him. In 1782 he was made a trustee of the newly established town of Lewisburg. In 1783 he served alone as Greenbrier delegate to the General Assembly, and again in the two following sessions represented Greenbrier jointly with George Clendenin.

By 1789-90 Colonel Donnally had definitely made his decision to move to the Kanawha Valley, and, selling his fort property, left the mountains and removed to Point Pleasant. His stay there was brief, however, as the evacuation of the Fort Randolph garrison in 1779 had rendered the location a dangerous one. He then came to the mouth of Elk, where he settled in the vicinity of Fort Lee. During the short time of his residence at the Point the Indians had been much in evidence and various depredations had occurred—a son of the Colonel's former slave, Dick Pointer, had been captured and taken away prisoner, eventually becoming one of their tribal chiefs.

In spite of all that he had suffered at the hands of the savages, Colonel Donnally felt the murder of Cornstalk was unjustifiable, and when he heard a man boast of having fired the fatal shot, the Colonel relieved his feelings by knocking the braggart down. After reaching Elk River, the Donnally family lived near the mouth of Elk for a short time, but soon Colonel Donnally settled permanently about a mile above the Fort on the south side of the Kanawha. His well-built and sturdy log house stood near Venable Branch, now best known as the Union Mission Hollow. When Colonel Donnally moved to Kanawha he was for the third time a resident of a newly formed county, and when Charleston, the county seat, was established by act of the Legislature on December 19, 1794, he was appointed one of the trustees.

Colonel and Mrs. Donnally were the parents of six daughters and two sons. The daughters were: Mary (Polly), who in 1791 married Reuben Slaughter, son of Goodrich Slaughter, first surveyor of Kanawha County; Sally, who married Samuel Henderson in 1801; Katherine, who married Captain John Wilson in 1803, and Elizabeth and Nancy.

One of the sons died young, but the other, Andrew Donnally, Jr., not only inherited his father's name, but many of his qualities, and duplicated his public career, serving repeatedly as a legislative representative from Kanawha, as clerk of the county, justice of the peace, and as Colonel of the militia and high sheriff. With similar names, similar careers, and similar titles of Colonel, writers of Kanawha history must keep a watchful eye on dates to avoid confusion of generations.

Colonel Donnally, Sr., died about 1825, and he and his wife were buried at an unidentified location near their home. The old Donnally cemetery, situated above the bridge in Kanawha City, at 57th Street and Kanawha Avenue, was restored in recent years by members of the family and the local chapter of the Society of Colonial Dames, but many tombstones had been carried away years before by unknown persons, and there is no way of knowing the number of graves in the plot.

Andrew Donnally, Jr., was born in the Greenbrier fort October 17, 1778, a few months after the Indian attack, and died in Kanawha in 1849. In 1801 he married Margery (1781-1850), daughter of Captain John Van Bibber. Her sister, Chloe, had married Jesse Boone, son of Daniel Boone, and during the years of their residence in Charleston the Boones lived on the Donnally lands near the upper end of Kanawha Avenue, just above the present Libbey-Owens glass plant. Daniel Boone left the Kanawha in 1795, and Jesse and his family departed in 1797. Two other of the Van Bibber sisters married well-known Charleston residents—Colonel John Reynolds and Goodrich Slaughter.

Andrew Donnally, Jr., and his wife were parents of thirteen children, four of whom died in infancy. This large family numbers among its descendants those bearing the names of Goshorn, Kenna, Ashby, Morris, Cotton, Washington, Littlepage, Starke, Welch, Ruby, Venable, Fitzhugh, Truslow, and many others equally familiar to present Charleston residents.

The Andrew Donnally, Jr., house on Kanawha Boulevard at the corner of Broad Street, was demolished in 1942 to make way for the United Carbon Building, but many persons who read these words have nostalgic memories of a fine old brick building shaded by tall trees on the river bank in the days when there was no boulevard, but just pleasant Kanawha Street.

There has been much speculation as to when the house was built. Some say it was the first brick building in Charleston, and others debate whether it was earlier or later than Holly Grove Mansion, whose date is thought to be 1815, but in any case it was one of the earliest and best of the brick houses in the city.

Broad Street was only a short lane when the near-by

Miller house was built, and there may not even have been a lane when the Donnally house was erected, in which case it may then have appeared to much better advantage than in later years after the street was cut through, leaving the jutting wing of the one-story kitchen flush with the curb. Originally there was a large surrounding acreage on the lower side extending nearly to McFarland Street, and in the rear it reached Virginia Street, with room for slave quarters, a barn, vegetable garden, and pasture field.

The bricks for the building were burned on the nearby river bank, and the walls were strongly held with handmade angle irons visible here and there. All the wood sills and joists were hand-sawed, and the nails made by the local blacksmith. Double inside chimneys stood high above the steep roof, and every room had its fireplace. There were no windows in the end walls except one in each end of the attic, but across the front they were very wide, and were trimmed with green shutters.

The square porch, supported by six small carved posts, and ornamented with much fancy scrollwork, bespeaks a later period, and may have replaced an earlier one of plainer type.

Two large rooms opened from each side of the wide central hallway, those on the left being connected by enormous folding doors the full width of the rooms. The ceilings were exceptionally high, and though the foundation was low, the height of the inside walls and a full attic above made the house appear very tall. Behind the house stood one of the most magnificent of Charleston's once numerous elm trees. Its great branches extended far beyond the width of Broad Street, and covered a large section of the grounds. A second elm stood in front of the building, and trees of other types were in the side yard.

Colonel Donnally, Jr., apparently did not reside long in this house, but enlarged his father's old homestead on the south side of the river, and lived the greater part of his life there. One reason for this preference was probably the nearness to The Salines, since he was in the salt business singly, and as co-owner of several wells. He had a ferry franchise, and the upper location was convenient. He later became interested in steamboating and, with the boat "The Fairy Queen," inaugurated a packet service between Charleston and Cincinnati. Having added greatly to property inherited from his father, Andrew Donnally possessed a large estate, owning at least one hundred thousand acres of land, and a hundred and fifty slaves.

The more modern brick dwelling in the town proper was occupied by later generations, and was especially identified with the families of Fry, Goshorn, and Rand. George Goshorn, a Welchman, came to Charleston about 1822, and first lived on the Kanawha River bank at the end of Goshorn Street, which was named for him. He operated a ferry at that point and also a hotel, and became financially successful. He later purchased the Donnally house, and no doubt made various alterations in it at that time. The wide folding doors between the two large rooms on the left of the front hall are similar to doors in Holly Grove Mansion, which were installed in 1832, when interior woodwork was replaced following a fire. Those in the Donnally house were obviously of the same period and workmanship, likely that of the Whitteker brothers who were the leading architects, builders, brickmakers, carpenters, and painters of the time. When the house was demolished, one of Mr. Goshorn's innovations was still intact—a panel of glass above the wide front door with his name etched upon it in fairly large letters. An elaborate iron fence was later placed across the front and down the side of the lot, and, as in the case of the fence around the neighboring Miller house, was possibly made when the Thayer foundry was established almost directly opposite on the south side of the river.

The Goshorn family were residents of the house at the time of the Civil War, and an amusing story is told concerning their successful efforts to outwit soldiers who were foraging for anything that was edible. When rumor spread that gardens, cellars, barns, and outbuildings were being stripped of food and animals, the Goshorns determined to save their cow for their own uses, and plans were made accordingly. With the assistance of the entire family, the cow was cordially invited into the house, and being unused to such hospitality, was a bit shy, and came somewhat reluctantly. However, by means of much persuasion and cajolery, and with many compliments showered upon her, she was led, pushed, and otherwise propelled step by step up two flights of stairs to the attic. Here, surrounded by deep layers of hay and all manner of attentions, she took up her abode until danger of raiding parties had subsided. The family meanwhile continued to be supplied with milk.

This splendid old house was long a landmark, and in the final years of its life, under the name of "The Tallyho," was an attractive and popular rendezvous for luncheon and dinner parties. At the time of its demolition the good-looking mantels and doors were rescued by Mrs. Charles Cunningham, who was one of the more recent residents of the building, and she has since installed one of the mantels in her present home, the Henry Wood house, described elsewhere.

Charleston
1820-1840

THE majority of the brick houses described in this book were built between 1820 and 1840. Pioneering was of yesterday. The James River and Kanawha Turnpike had been completed, and now the stagecoach, rocking and creaking, tore through the Valley at perilous speed—not that the passengers were in such a hurry, but the driver liked it that way, as his skill in handling the four- or six-horse team showed off to much better advantage, and made the whole thing more sensational. Besides, he now carried the mail, and that old practice of making purchases of coffee and pins for the housewives along the route was definitely of the past. The post office authorities said it took too much time, and, except for medicines, it was prohibited. Relay stations were spaced at regular intervals, and gave the exhausted passengers an opportunity to rub liniment on their bruises and otherwise fortify themselves for the next flight. A few of these stage stands are still in existence, and are mentioned elsewhere.

The first Charleston newspaper, *The Spectator*, appeared in 1818 or 1819, only to suffer a quick demise and be succeeded immediately by the *Kanawha Patriot*, the *Western Courier*, and the *Western Register*, all before 1830. Charleston was incorporated on January 19, 1818. The Mercer Academy had been founded the same year, and five years later was sustaining a "Law Department." There was a library by 1823, and Presbyterian, Methodist, and Episcopalian church buildings by 1834. A branch of the Bank of Virginia had been established in 1832, and was housed in a dignified building on Front Street, with colonial columns at its entrance.

There were three sawmills on Two Mile Creek by 1815, two of them with corn cracker attachments, and the Ruffners were operating a steam flour mill and sawmills by 1832. A milk crock and whiskey jug factory was in operation. The town had a drug store in 1825, several tailors, merchants, a hatter, cobbler, a clock and watchmaker, two or three physicians, lawyers, a cabinetmaker, and a number of carpenters and brick masons. Several taverns were in operation, and a brick courthouse, built in 1817, replaced the early log building, although it lacked a bell until 1826, when Benjamin H. Smith, Matthew Dunbar, and Joseph Lovell were appointed to draft a plan for a cupola in which to hang one.

The names of the "gentlemen justices" of the county who were present at the court of March 8, 1830, furnishes a list of some of the prominent citizens of the time: David Ruffner, Daniel Ruffner, John Starkes, Joel Shrewsbury, James C. MacFarland, Claudis Buster, John Wilson, Thomas Matthews, James Staton, Van B. Reynolds, Levi Welch, Andrew Parks, Andrew Donnally, David Melburn, John Slack, John Harriman, Lewis Ruffner, William Morris, Jesse Hudson, Charles Brown, and John P. Turner.

There was a wheelwright and carriage factory on the south side of the river operated by Colonel Alexander Quarrier, who also maintained the ferry at the present Goshorn Street.

The Virginia Assembly had built dams and dredged the channel of the Kanawha, and in 1823 stream navigation had come with arrival of the steamboat "Eliza" in Charleston.

Other improvements were on the way. The telegraph was just around the corner, and a few years later a line was constructed from The Salines via Charleston to Point Pleasant and Gallipolis.

By Act of February 19, 1833, James C. MacFarland, Samuel Chilton, John P. Turner, Aaron Whitteker, Spicer Patrick, George Goshorn, James Y. Quarrier, and Henry Rogers were appointed commissioners to raise, by lottery, money not to exceed $10,000 to be applied to paving the streets of Charleston.

With such modern advantages, and a population of twelve hundred people in 1840, "the Town at the Mouth of Elk" was becoming cosmopolitan.

The Elms

AFTER the little settlement of Charlestown was designated as the Kanawha County seat, an area on lower Front Street was selected for the public buildings, and the first log courthouse was erected in 1796 on the site of the present court building. The clerk, John Reynolds, who lived a short distance farther east, conveyed a forty-foot square plot of his property to the county, and upon it a small clerk's office building was constructed of stone.

Another lot owner with whom the county had some dealings was John Alderson, one of the first justices of the county and also one of the first trustees of the town. Alderson Street, which is named for him, is situated between Court and Summers streets, and extends northward from Kanawha Boulevard, crosses Virginia Street, and comes to an abrupt stop at the entrance to "The Elms," one of the fine old homes of early Charleston.

Enclosed by a high stone wall, its shaded grounds are filled with many trees and shrubs, a cool and restful oasis on a warm summer day. Except for a fleeting glimpse from Virginia Street, "The Elms" is almost hidden by the business buildings that have grown up around it as the years have passed, and which have completely concealed its once pleasant view of river and hills beyond.

The house, large and substantial, is made of cut stone blocks, and is approached by a long straight path, while the brick-paved driveway that led to the carriage house, curves to the left.

Across the front of the house, a wide double veranda, supported by six columns on each floor, terminates in a pointed roof, and suggests the architecture of the southern plantation house. The tall chimneys, the circular-topped doorway, the balustrade around the second floor veranda and the fan window above it are interesting details. The rooms are on each side of a wide central hallway. Alterations and additions have been made from time to time, and rooms added as families grew, but the small slave house and the covered well are reminders that this house is one of the oldest in Charleston.

"The Elms" was erected in 1822 by John Francis Faure, who was born in the town of Le Prey, France, in 1784, and had served as an officer under Napoleon. He came to America in 1816, where, after the prescribed number of years residence, he made application and in 1828 became a citizen of the United States. Mr. Faure was an architect and designed the house for his bride, the widow of Samuel Dryden,* who, before her first marriage was Miss Eliza W. Quarrier, daughter of Colonel Alexander Quarrier, outstanding Kanawha pioneer. Mrs. Faure's death occurred in 1837, and not long afterward the property was purchased by Judge James H. Brown, one of West Virginia's most eminent jurists. Since then "The Elms" has been identified solely with the Brown family, its present occupants being grandchildren and great-grandchildren of Judge Brown—the Misses Jean and Ceres Brown and their brother, Benjamin B. Brown, and his family.

In 1848 James H. Brown came from Cabell County to Charleston, where he became a distinguished lawyer and

---
*John Dryden, a son of Mrs. Faure's first marriage, was for many years clerk of the County Court of Kanawha County.

citizen, serving as Judge of the Circuit Court of Kanawha, as a representative in the Legislature, as a member of the First Constitutional Convention, and for years as Judge of the State Supreme Court, and also as its President.

Judge Brown was twice married, first to Miss Louise M. Beuhring, and they were the parents of four daughters and two sons. Following the death of his wife, Judge Brown late in life married a widow with two children, Mrs. Fayette A. Lovell, who was a daughter of William D. Shrewsbury.

James F. Brown followed his father in the legal profession and became the senior member of the oldest and one of the most outstanding law firms in the State, that of Brown, Jackson & Knight, of Charleston, and his own son, Benjamin B. Brown, is the third in line not only to carry on the family legal tradition, but to maintain his residence at "The Elms."

Oxford Brewery, at Hook.

Dr. Patrick House

THE phrase, "few and far between," more than applies to the early physicians of Kanawha Valley. Although few in number, they were surprisingly well-qualified, educated men who, traveling on horseback or by whatever means were presented, managed to cover an amazing amount of territory. Not only were they indefatigable professionally, but several of them took an active and prominent part in public and political affairs. Of Dr. Spicer Patrick is such particularly true.

Dr. Patrick (1791-1884), son of Jacob Patrick, of Scotch descent, and Sarah Spicer Patrick, of English ancestry, was born in New York and came to Charleston as a medical practitioner in 1816. His skill as a physician was of the highest order, and during an epidemic of cholera which visited the Valley in 1832, he performed outstanding service.

A vigorous man of intelligence and ability, Dr. Patrick served as a legislative delegate several times between 1846 and 1854, inclusive, and was also a member of the Virginia Secession Convention of 1861, voting against the Ordinance of Secession. In addition to these public duties, he sat as a member of the Kanawha County Court from 1839 to 1851, and, after formation of the State of West Virginia, was elected Speaker of the House of Delegates at the first legislative session of June 20, 1863. He was also active in church affairs, being a vestryman of the Episcopal Church for a great many years.

Dr. Patrick was three times married—first, in 1822 to Lavinia V. M. Bream (1805-1843), a stepsister of Mrs. Henry Rogers, and daughter of Major and Mrs. James Bream, prominent early residents of Charleston, a sketch of whom is given elsewhere. There were six children born to Dr. and Mrs. Patrick, three sons and three daughters: Dr. Alfred S., James B., and John; Mary, who married R. C. M. Lovell, son of Joseph Lovell; Sally, who married Colonel H. D. Ruffner, and Lavinia, who married Major William Gramm, U.S.A.

The second wife of Dr. Patrick, whom he married in 1844, was the widow of Colonel Robert M. Steele. The third marriage, to Miss Virginia Harvie (1821-1915), occurred in Richmond in 1852. As he was a delegate to the Assembly that year, as well as for several years previously, he doubtless had made many social acquaintanceships in his frequent visits to Richmond. Miss Harvie was a granddaughter of Chief Justice Marshall, and in Charleston today, a granddaughter of Dr. Patrick is the possessor of china and silver from the Marshall home. Four children were born of Dr. Patrick's third marriage: Susie, Harvie, William, and George.

There is a deed on record from Thomas Fife to Dr. Patrick in 1830 for property now designated as number 1008 Kanawha Boulevard. Mr. Fife was a builder and had already started construction of a dwelling on the premises, which was completed by Dr. Patrick, who resided there for more than twenty years. It is a large building, with deeply recessed entrance doorway only a few feet from the public sidewalk. Constructed of brick, with steep roof and tall chimneys, the original architectural outline is difficult to trace, as alterations and additions in later years have greatly changed its appearance. Across the front wall groups of oddly bowed and shutterless windows stare into the afternoon sun, while on the lower side of the house, marks of shutters that once hung at the windows are still visible. Much of the original interior woodwork, and a number of the wide paneled doors remain, but for the most part, except for the large size of the rooms, there is little to suggest a house of 1830.

Dr. Patrick sold the property to the Presbyterian Church in 1855 for use as a manse, and having constructed a new frame dwelling below Charleston just east of Two Mile Creek, he removed there the following year. This estate was called "Forest Hill" and was one of only six houses existing on the west side of Elk River as late as the Civil War period. Dr. Patrick's nearest neighbors were the Littlepage family who lived in a large stone house at the foot of the bluff near the creek. "Forest Hill" stood on the side of the hill in the vicinity of present Beech Avenue, above the north end of Patrick Street Bridge, an impressive steel structure which bears his name, and which spans the Kanawha at this point as a link in U. S. Route 60. Here Dr. Patrick lived the rest of his life, busily engaged with his many activities. "Forest Hill" was later sold and became known as "Beechwood," a favorite picnic park and gun club.

The brick house in Charleston has continued as a Presbyterian manse since sold by Dr. Patrick almost a century ago. In the division at the time of the Civil War, it fell to the so-called Northern branch of the denomination, and now on what was once the rear of the lot, facing Virginia Street, is the beautiful stone Kanawha Presbyterian Church building, connected with the manse by a pleasant enclosed private garden.

Miller House

ONE of the first of Charleston's early frame houses is still standing, although now it is indeed a sorry looking spectacle, with its windows broken, and its door swinging open in the wind. If it were in a more isolated spot it could easily become a haunted house. Even in the eleven hundred block of Kanawha Boulevard on a sunny morning, one steps across the threshold in a sort of gingerly fashion, and doesn't have much enthusiasm about seeing what is on the second floor. There was a time when this residence, best known as the "Miller House," was a very charming home, surrounded by flowers and comfortably shaded by magnificent elm trees —which, like all the other elms that beautified Kanawha Street, were recently killed by an incurable disease, leaving the street distressingly bare and the homes much less inviting.

This house was built about 1830 by Aaron Whitteker, the skillful builder of many of Charleston's early dwellings. His practice was to purchase a lot, erect a good-looking house, and promptly sell. The deed for this lot referred to it as being "adjacent to Charleston." Broad Street, then called Summers Lane, extended only a short distance back from the river, and, leading to the Summers and Ryan houses, marked the eastern boundary of the town. The Miller house, facing Kanawha Boulevard and the river, is now the second one above the eastern corner of Broad, but originally it stood alone, as no other houses were built in the block until afterward,

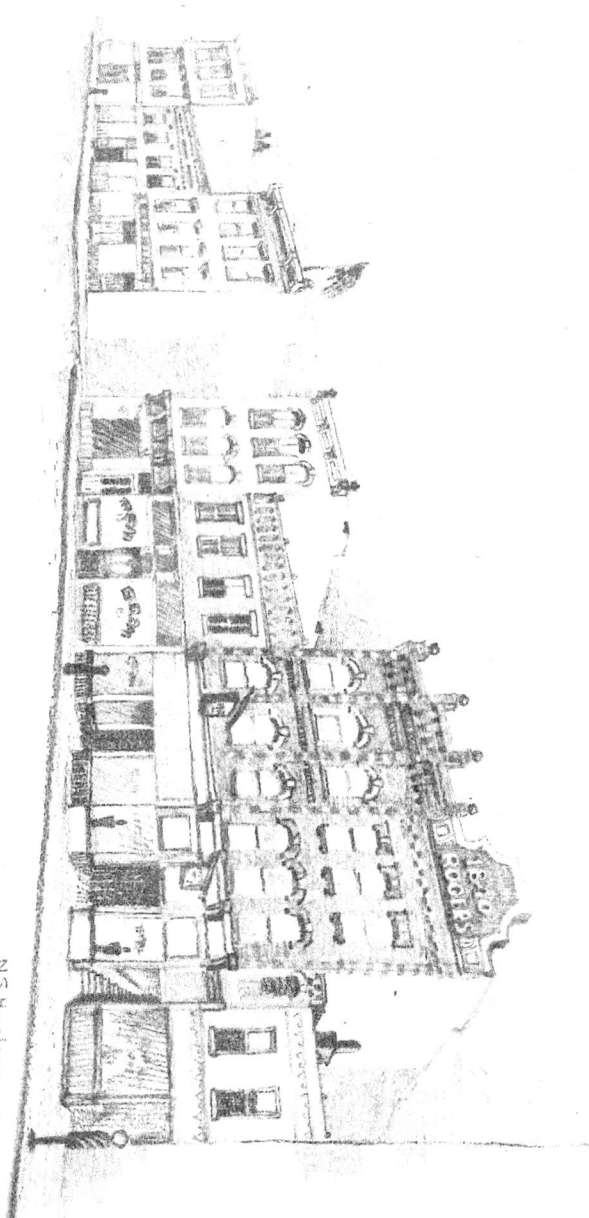

Rogers Pharmacy and Neighbors
On Early Front Street

N.S. Hosterman

when the brick dwellings of the Noyes brothers were erected.

The Whitteker property was first purchased by one of the salt-makers, Thomas Friend, in 1838, and though he owned it until 1855, it is never referred to otherwise than as "the Miller House." Samuel A. Miller (1819-1890), to whom Friend sold it in that year, was a young lawyer who had come to the Kanawha Valley in 1840, and five years later had married Helen M. Quarrier, daughter of Alexander W. Quarrier and Caroline W. Shrewsbury Quarrier. Mr. Miller first read law with Judge Summers, and later became his partner.

Enlisting at the beginning of the Civil War, Mr. Miller rose rapidly to the rank of Major in the Confederate Army, and in 1862 was elected from the Kanawha District to the Confederate Congress. With the coming of the Federal forces into the Valley, Major Miller's wife and children fled for safety farther south. After the termination of the war they returned to Charleston, but Major Miller, precluded from practicing his profession, went to Canada for several months. With the abolition of the test oath in 1872, he formed a partnership with his brother-in-law, William A. Quarrier, and resumed his legal practice. Later he was associated with Ex-Governor E. W. Wilson, and then with D. C. Gallaher, being recognized as one of the eminent lawyers of the town.

The Miller house was of excellent material and construction, much of it put together with wooden pegs. During plastering repairs in 1896, the wide and irregularly-shaped lathes were found to be riven and split by hand, some ten or more feet in length. Rather tall, with a steep roof above a full attic, there is a lower two-story wing extending from the rear of the house.

A porch across the front has interesting octagon-cut columns, and a dentil molding around the top. The porch was formerly on the upper side of the house, but was moved later to the front. Green shutters hang at the windows, which were the usual style of small-paned sash.

A white picket fence once enclosed the yard, but was replaced by a well-designed and, incidentally, very lovely one of iron—said to have been the first piece of ornamental ironwork made by the Thayer foundry, a well-known business concern first in operation at The Salines, and which removed to Charleston in 1871. This fence, too, is long since gone, although a portion of it was rescued by Mr. and Mrs. Walton Shepherd who utilize it on the terrace of their attractive home near the Edgewood Country Club.

The entrance doorway is on the upper side of the house and large square rooms with fireplaces are on the left. The doors are fine and paneled, and the unusually wide floor boards are still intact. For all of its having been open to weather and vandalism for several years, much of the woodwork is still surprisingly well preserved.

There was ample opportunity to demonstrate the durability of its construction, however, years ago, for the house has had what surely must be a unique distinction, that of having been twice moved from its original location. First it was moved backward to the rear of the large, deep lot, and turned around to face Broad Street. The land upon which it stood was later sold to the First Presbyterian Church for the erection of the church school building. So again the Miller house was hauled backward, and shifted about to its former location, except for being placed farther away from Kanawha Street. It continued to be occupied as late as the early days of World War II, when it was used as headquarters for the "Bundles for Britain" organization, but the "Old Miller House" is now destined in the near future to be demolished to make way for a large office building.*

*The Miller house was razed in the late summer of 1947.

Rogers Pharmacy

IN this volume will be found a composite drawing of a group of the century-old two- and three-story business buildings on Charleston's early Front Street, now Kanawha Boulevard. Located in the first and second blocks west of Capitol Street, the buildings, as shown in the drawing, are not all in their exact sequence. In order to present a more varied architectural pattern, two or three structures of similar style were omitted from the drawing, and the other buildings pushed up to fill the gap.

The outstanding characteristic of design seems to be the over-window decoration. Some windows have an extended cornice supported by brackets; on others a cement trim resembling an Egyptian headdress extends halfway around the windows. Simplicity was not popular. One rather low two-story building is much trimmed with rows of pointed lace-like cornice across the front. Two are decorated with fancy brick work and the corners of the roof adorned with balls and urns.

The most interesting historically, as well as one of the most ornamented, is a substantial three-story brick building, topped with a rounded pompadour on which appears in raised letters the name "Rogers," and underneath, the date 1840. This building now houses the Stalnaker Drug Company, successor to the Rogers Pharmacy, the two completing a cycle of more than a hundred and twenty-five years of unbroken service to this community.

Dr. Henry Rogers, a practitioner of experience in eastern cities and in Richmond, married Leonora C. Lovell, who was born in London of distinguished English parentage. Her mother, whose maiden name was Lady Mary Shapton, had married Joseph Lovell, but was soon left a widow with four small children. She then married Major James Bream, and in 1804 they came to America where they lived for many years in Richmond.

Mrs. Bream's son, Colonel Joseph Lovell, Jr., was educated in America and became an outstanding man in every respect. He came to Charleston in 1814, and having studied law, was soon engaged not only in the practice of law, but in salt manufacturing, merchandising, and legislative politics.

It was not long before he persuaded his mother and stepfather to bring the rest of the family and join him in Kanawha. His brother-in-law, Dr. Rogers, may have come at the same time, as he shortly afterward founded the first pharmacy in Charleston. It was located on the river bank where the ferry crossed the Kanawha, near the present boatlanding. Here he dispensed his pills and potions. He also evolved and sold a family medicine chest, complete with forty remedies, apothecary scales, and other essentials, which found its way into many remote households where a doctor was as intangible as Santa Claus—nice, but not there.

In order to decorate his windows and to display the customary sign of the apothecary shop of early days, Dr. Rogers procured, in Williamsburg it is said, several very handsome blown glass showcase bottles. They are enormous in size, graceful in shape, with pointed glass stoppers, and are beautifully etched. These choice specimens, although high on a dimly lit shelf, may still be seen in the Stalnaker Drug Company. It is said the Williamsburg Foundation has offered to purchase them at a really fabulous figure, but the offer has been declined. After the death of Dr. Rogers in 1837, his son, J. H. Rogers, an able businessman, salt-maker, inventor, and collector of documents and relics which are still displayed in the store, followed as owner of the pharmacy. He first moved it to 248 Front Street, against the advice of friends and associates, and then, no doubt with all manner of dire predictions from the same sources, three years later embarked on the epochal venture of erecting the three-story Rogers skyscraper. In due course the construction was completed, and the drug store duly ensconced in its new and permanent quarters, almost opposite the location of the first little pharmacy established years before. Here it has remained, and continued in operation even throughout the Civil War period, despite the shelling from the opposite side of the river that destroyed many neighboring buildings.

Still in existence is a large well-preserved and interesting oil painting done at this period and from this approximate location. It shows the sweep of the river, the rock cliff on the south side, and clustered at the base of the hill along the bank, the tents of the Union camp, while approaching the north shore is a boat filled with soldiers, the American flag flying in the prow. This painting, dated 1863, is owned by Mrs. James Foster, and hangs in the home of her daughter, Mrs. John F. Kay, who lives in the hills not far from the scene it depicts. The artist, an aunt of Mrs. Foster, was Miss Margaretta Doddridge, whose home then stood where the Kanawha Hotel is now located. Mrs. James (Emma Doddridge) Foster is a descendant of the Honorable Philip Doddridge, prominent West Virginia lawyer and member of Congress, for whom Doddridge County was named, and brother of Joseph Doddridge, author of the valued book of West Virginiana, *Doddridge's Notes.*

James A. Rogers, son of J. H. Rogers, succeeded his father in ownership of the pharmacy in the eighteen eighties, and in 1909 the Rogers family ownership ended with the purchase of the business by its present owner, Mr. T. B. Stalnaker.

Mr. Stalnaker has taken great pride in preserving and adding to the large collection of historical articles begun by his predecessors, and for those who are museum-minded there is much of interest to be gleaned from browsing through it. Naturally, first on the list of items preserved are the early medical and pharmaceutical books, ledger and account books, scales, mortars, drug mills, and recipe books pertaining to the Rogers Pharmacy. There are legal documents and papers that relate to the early settlement of the locality, among them a deed dated 1795 from Colonel George Clendenin, builder of Fort Lee, for one of the first lots sold after he laid off the forty-acre town of Charleston. There is a tax receipt dated 1804 for one of the enormous Kanawha Valley tracts held by George Washington. There are many Indian relics, quantities of Civil War mementoes—canteens, guns, bullets, swords, cannon balls, and Confederate money.

On the walls hang enlarged photographs of scenes in early Charleston. One is of Front Street, unpaved and muddy, with citizens standing on the sidewalk looking the way citizens in group photographs always look—half scared and not too intelligent. Some of them are draped in fraternal regalia, indicating that a special celebration of some sort was the occasion for the photography.

Many objects of associational interest are found in the

collection—the bronze ink well of West Virginia's first Governor, keys to the vault of the Branch Bank of Virginia, Charleston's first bank which was burned in the Civil War shelling of the water front buildings. Perhaps the Rogers Pharmacy was purposely spared, as it supplied many drugs and remedies to the medical officers in the army camp on the opposite side of the river. Whatever the reason, it exists today as one of Charleston's most noteworthy landmarks, and as the oldest drug store in West Virginia.

Elm Grove

The Quarrier Family

AS the object of this book has been to deal primarily with early houses that still exist, the names of many pioneer families whose homes are long since gone have of necessity been omitted. A few, however, of those who were particularly outstanding have been included.

One such is the Quarrier family. Its members are still residents of Charleston, where the name "Quarrier" is given to a street—one of the most important in the city, which extends from Capitol Street on the west, to the second block beyond the State Capitol building on the east, its lower section being filled with many of the better shops and business and professional office buildings, hotels, churches, and schools, and its upper section a desirable residential area.

The Quarrier family, of Scotch-English and perhaps French origin, records the marriage of a son, born in 1711, to Margaret Alexander. Since then the name "Alexander" has been almost synonymous with "Quarrier" through all generations and branches of the family to the present time. This Margaret's mother was related to Admiral Keith and Lord Grey of England, and the name Keith has also been carried on, beginning with the elder brother of Alexander Quarrier I, the American pioneer, who, born in 1746, was the only one of four brothers to leave his homeland.

Two years of Alexander's boyhood were spent in England with his relative, Lord Grey, following which, after his return to his home, he was apprenticed, at the age of fifteen, to a coach-maker in the City of Edinburgh. After the usual seven years' training, he emerged well qualified and ready to embark on the coach-making business for himself. Immediately, at the age of twenty-two, he sailed for America, where he established himself in the highly skilled work that was to occupy him for the rest of his life. He first settled in Philadelphia, but in a few years the Revolution began, and his personal affairs were laid aside for military duties. He organized a volunteer company and went into service as its commander. By the end of the war he had risen in rank to that of colonel, a rank which brought him into contact with the important higher officers, including General Washington, whom he greatly esteemed, and for whom he subsequently named two of his children.

In 1783 Colonel Quarrier married Elizabeth Dannenberry, and they were the parents of eight children,* one of whom married James Grant Laidley, thus uniting two Scotch pioneer families through this marriage of the daughter of the first Quarrier in America and the son of the first Laidley. A son of this marriage, James Madison Laidley, was the builder of "Glenwood," a fine old Charleston house pictured in this book.

A disastrous fire wiped out the coach-making establishment of Colonel Quarrier shortly after his marriage, and in 1785 he left Philadelphia and removed his family to Richmond, where he began business anew, remaining for twenty-six years.

Colonel Quarrier had accumulated a large library. An inveterate reader, he was a well-informed and interesting man. Although he was one of temperate habits, he lived well and unstintedly, and was considered something of an epicure, who entertained many of the states-

---

*See Appendix for list of children.

men of the new republic. Possessing a keen concern in the political questions of the day, he numbered among his wide acquaintance such public men as Jefferson, Madison, Chancellor Wythe, and John Marshall. He named one of his sons for James Monroe, a personal friend, and governor of Virginia at the time.

The death of Mrs. Quarrier occurred in 1797. In Prince William County, the following year, Colonel Quarrier married Sally Burns, a relative of the Scotch poet, Robert Burns. This marriage also produced eight children.

In 1811, at the insistence of Colonel Andrew Donnally and Major John Reynolds, then representing Kanawha in the General Assembly, Colonel Quarrier moved his family to the Kanawha Valley, where they lived for a few years on Major Reynolds' farm just east of Charleston at Burning Springs branch. Leaving this location in 1816, he journeyed down the river to Charleston, where he erected "Willow Bank," a simple frame house on the southwest side of the Kanawha, a little below the present Chesapeake and Ohio station and opposite Goshorn Street.

Colonel Quarrier continued in active business all his life. As late as June 18, 1822, when he was seventy-six years old, he was advertising in a Charleston paper, *The Western Courier:*

"Wheelright

"The subscriber living on the Western bank of the Kanawha river opposite Charleston informs the public that he carries on the Wheelright Business in all its branches. All kinds of carriages made or repaired on moderate terms at short notice.

"Alexander Quarrier"

He also operated a ferry from his place to the opposite side of the river. In his idle moments the Colonel worked on mechanical devices. He had a decided inventive trend, and experimented with putting a steam engine in a one-passenger coach. This forerunner of the automobile was something of a success—at least it operated sufficiently well for him to ride around his premises and demonstrate its wonders. He intended to patent his invention, but died without having done so. George Stephenson had, a few years before, invented the steam locomotive in England, and the engineer operating it for him was Ralph Swinburn, who later lived in Kanawha. Mr. Quarrier may have received from this source firsthand news of Stephenson's invention which inspired his own experiments with steam.

Continuing his interest in politics after coming to Kanawha, Colonel Quarrier not only served as Justice of the Peace, but as Clerk of the Court—setting a precedent of family succession in that office. His son and three of his grandsons held clerkships in Virginia and West Virginia courts for an aggregate of one hundred years. At the time of Colonel Quarrier's death in 1827 when he was eighty-one years of age, he was serving as President of the County Court.

Mrs. Sally Burns Quarrier, who survived her husband twenty-five years, was instrumental in organizing the first Episcopal Church in Charleston. In *Old Churches, Ministers and Families of Virginia,* published in 1857 by the influential religious leader, Bishop William Meade, she is mentioned as being the mother of the church, and with "Mrs. Colonel Lovell" as being the only two communicants in the town when he made his early visit through this region.

"Willow Bank" at the time of the Civil War was

The Elms

utilized as army headquarters by the Federal forces, and President McKinley and Rutherford B. Hayes, then minor officers, were stationed there. The old house stood until 1870 when it was demolished by Mr. Otis Thayer, purchaser of the property, to make way for his high-ceilinged brick residence, and the business buildings of the Thayer Foundry. The Thayer family have continued in ownership until within the past two years, when that part of the property embracing the residence was sold.

Elm Grove—The Craik House

ELM GROVE is a pleasant name, and has a feel of spaciousness. It is the last name in the world one would imagine as ever having belonged to the small, one-story house close to the sidewalk and crowded against its neighbors, that is now numbered "1316 Lee Street." Few of Charleston's present generation have even noticed it, and fewer still have recognized that in spite of its present unflattering position, it has individuality and a certain charm.

To a modest degree reminiscent in type of "Arlington" —the Custis home overlooking Washington where General Lee was married, and where his family resided much of the time until 1861—this little house originally had a more imposing setting and in a different location. Until 1906 it stood in an acre and a half lot that faced a hundred and fifty-four feet on Virginia Street—called Second Street when it was built—and extended to a depth of approximately four hundred feet to Quarrier Street, its site now occupied by the Kanawha Valley Hospital, business buildings, and by Dunbar Street.

Midway in the picket-fenced lot, and surrounded by a violet strewn lawn and the handsome elms that gave to the place its appropriate name of Elm Grove, the white frame house was flanked on the upper side by a flower garden and on the lower side by a little square office building used by its early lawyer and doctor owners. In the rear were the vegetable garden and fruit trees, the servants' quarters, the poultry houses, and the log barn and carriage house, which stood on the ground now occupied by the United Fuel Gas Company building, at Quarrier and Dunbar streets.

The architectural style of the residence was unusual. Of frame construction, only one story in height, it was long and low, although it then stood much higher above ground than at present, and had basement rooms used for kitchen and storage. An important square portico, whose large columns supported a high pointed roof rising considerably above that of the house itself, gave the building distinction. A front hallway ran across the width of the house, and opening from it were an unusually large living room and four other rooms which had access to the gallery extending across the rear of the dwelling. Above the front windows which were small, with nine panes of glass in the upper part of the sash and six in the lower, there was barely room under the low eaves of the flat roof for a narrow and rather crudely carved cornice that extended across the front of the house.

So nearly as can be ascertained, the house was erected by the Rev. James Craik, possibly in 1834. According to a deed of March 14 in that year, he purchased the lot for $476 from Ezra Walker, a scholarly man who had taught school at The Salines a year or so before, and who later became superintendent of the James River and Kanawha Turnpike, extending from Covington, Virginia, to the Ohio. The deed referred to a "parcel or lot of ground" with no mention of buildings.

The next deed is dated June 10, 1846, from Craik to Isaac Reed, and the consideration is given as twenty-two hundred dollars. The "tenements" are mentioned, and also the fact that Craik had resided on the lot until his removal from Charleston. Accordingly, it seems almost conclusive that he purchased a vacant lot and built the house. In 1829 James Craik married Juliet, youngest of the ten children of Samuel Shrewsbury, Sr.

The Craik family had, through many years of association, become closely identified with George Washington. Marianne, daughter of Sarah Ball Ewell, half sister of the President's mother, Mary Ball Washington, was the wife of Dr. James Craik (1730-1804), Washington's personal friend and physician, who accompanied him on various journeys. One of these trips, undertaken in 1770, was to inspect lands and locate surveys in the Ohio and lower Kanawha River region.

Dr. and Mrs. Craik had a family of six sons and three daughters. The second son, George Washington Craik, was secretary to President Washington during the second term. His wife, whom he married in 1805, was Maria Dorcas Tucker, daughter of Captain John Tucker, of Alexandria, Virginia. A son of this marriage, named for his grandfather, was James Craik, who had prepared to be a lawyer and had received his license to practice, but abandoned the law in favor of the ministry, in which he continued the rest of his life. He served as rector of St. John's Episcopal Church in Charleston from 1839 to 1844, when he removed with his wife and large family to a new pastorate in Louisville, Kentucky. Because of his comparatively short ownership, "Elm Grove" is much more closely associated with later owners.

One of the owners of the house was Captain George S. Patton I, grandfather of the great field general of World War II, who bore the same name, and who possessed many of the same characteristics. Captain Patton, of Richmond, was a young man of ability, good looks, and social attainments, as well as a man of honor and high courage. A graduate of Virginia Military Institute, he was well trained for future duties then unanticipated—his desires centering on a legal career. With this in mind, he moved to Charleston, the county seat of Kanawha, about 1856, where he engaged in the practice of law, part of the time an associate of Mr. Thomas Broun.

On October 1, 1858, Isaac Reed sold the Craik house to the Pattons—the deed being in the wife's name, Susan Glasell Patton—and here, soon after, was born their son, George Smith Patton, Jr. (II), father of General George S. Patton III.

Richmond had a well-known military and social organization called "The Light Infantry Blues," to which all the young aristocrats of the town aspired, its bright uniforms, parades, and balls being an important part of their lives. When Mr. Patton came to Charleston from Richmond he was induced to organize a similar company, and soon the Kanawha Riflemen came into being. Perhaps the newer group lacked the social opportunities supplied by the larger city, but it did not lack in dash and zeal, and the two companies engaged in a good deal of rivalry—the Blues even coming to Charleston to show off their proficiency. But the Kanawha Riflemen held their own. With Patton as captain, and Andrew Moore, Nicholas Fitzhugh, and Henry D. Ruffner as lieutenants, they made a good showing.

The boom in the salt industry was still a reality, fine homes were built in the Valley, and leisure had come to many. The Riflemen had money in their pockets to purchase the snappy gold-braided green uniforms designed by their captain, and as the group was composed of the most prominent young bloods of Charleston, it isn't surprising that the less eligible referred to it as "The Kid Glove Company." The organization was primarily a drilling club, and Patton, with his military training, was a disciplinarian, even somewhat of a martinet, and kid gloves to the contrary, he saw to it that the company learned to drill, and do it well. Any absence from the weekly drill meant a fine.

The Riflemen turned out on all possible occasions, and made a very impressive appearance as they drilled and paraded on holidays, and at public functions, fairs, and political meetings. They were also in demand at places other than Charleston and traveled about with great swank.

The company was reorganized in 1858, and again in 1861, when, with the commencement of the Civil War, its services were offered to the state of Virginia. Accepted, kid gloves and green uniforms were laid aside, and the men in sober Confederate gray, left Charleston as Company H, 22nd Virginia Infantry.

On July 17, 1861, the company, in conjunction with Hale's battery, under Captain Patton as commanding officer, had its initial encounter with the enemy in the Battle of Scary Creek, twenty miles northwest of Charleston. In comparison with the great and terrible battles later in the war, this engagement was of small consequence, but at the moment, it was important, and with staunch resistance of the Riflemen, the Federal advance into the Valley was temporarily halted. This advantage, had it been followed up by the political general in command, Henry A. Wise, might have had more far-reaching results. Instead, he immediately ordered the withdrawal eastward of the entire Confederate force, a decision for which he was severely criticized. Captain Patton had received a wound in the shoulder and his company suffered casualties, but fewer than those of the Federals, who lost a number of men and suffered the capture of three colonels and several privates.

Captain Patton, now promoted to Colonel, was given another command, and when the Kanawha Riflemen,* with Richard Q. Laidley as their captain, evacuated the Valley, it was to return but once during the war, in the fall of 1862.

Colonel Patton was killed in action at Winchester, Virginia, in 1864, after having been commissioned a Brigadier General on the field shortly before his death. Mrs. Patton had probably left Charleston and with her children, refugeed farther south during the war, as she is noted as being a resident of "Gouchla" County, Virginia, in September, 1865. At that time she sold her Charleston house to Andrew B. Hogue, and it has since been referred to, even so late as today, as the Hogue house. It was owned and occupied by various members of this well-known family until 1921.

In 1906 when a street was cut through "The Elms" property from Virginia to Quarrier, the house was removed and taken farther east to its present location on Lee Street. The name given the new street was Dunbar —for Judge Dunbar who owned the adjoining lot.

---

*A memorial to the Kanawha Riflemen is placed in a small park on Kanawha Boulevard. For a roster of the members see the appendix.

Rand House

THE Rand house and the Ruby house, two of Charleston's most attractive early homes, were always spoken of as though they were twins, and in a sense they actually were. Possessing similar architectural characteristics, they were designed and erected by the same man, at about the same time, and stood on adjoining lots for more than a century. The lots themselves were originally under the same ownership.

As time went on, lot owners, builders, and house occupants all came to be related by blood, friendship, marriage, and by business association: a state of affairs which, for the writer attempting to describe these houses and tell something of their background, creates a complex and confused picture, and one not greatly clarified by such data as is available—even court records only serve to add to the general murkiness of the scene.

Apparently the only way to begin the story of the many inter-related persons who are in various ways associated with these houses, is to start with the lot owners, and to begin with the childhood formula: "Once upon a time there were two brothers, and their name was Noyes"— actually there were four, but only two, Isaac (1785-1871) and Bradford (1788-1850), are concerned with these houses.

The Reverend James Noyes was the ancestor who had come from England to settle in Massachusetts at an early date, and it was from the branch of his descendants who located in Columbia County, New York, that the Kanawha family originated. Isaac, the eldest of the four brothers, was first to come to the Valley in 1804, where, like most of the young men of his age, he hunted and trapped, engaging in the profitable business of fur trading. While in the East disposing of his pelts, he made the acquaintance of another young fur trader named William Whitteker (1775-1853), whose family also had moved from Massachusetts to New York, and the two naturally discussed the advantages of the states they had known.

Isaac's enthustiastic description of the Kanawha region was very convincing, and Whitteker decided to return with him and see it for himself. The result of this long journey, made partially by boat, but from Baltimore on, by foot, was that William was favorably impressed, and returned to his home determined to come back to stay permanently. His interest did not waver, and after his marriage in the autumn of 1806 to Mrs. Philena Cobb, of Boston, they said good-by to the East, and a few days after Christmas reached Charleston. The following year Bradford Noyes repeated the same procedure as his brother Isaac, and he also returned from an eastern trading trip with Aaron, another Whitteker brother, in tow (who later married Betsy D. Quarrier, daughter of Col. Alexander Quarrier).

These pairs of brothers naturally drifted into joint enterprises of one sort or another—they purchased lands, went into the salt business, became merchants, builders, and engaged in other occupations. They were joined gradually by various members of their families. Charles and Franklin Noyes (1793-1856) came; Levi, a third Whitteker brother, arrived, and also Thomas, who had a sawmill at the mouth of Elk River, where his nephew, Norris S., son of William Whitteker, was head sawyer and superintendent of boat building for eleven years. All these young men were industrious, and their various ventures more or less successful.

The Whittekers bored the first salt well on the south side of the Kanawha. It was opposite the site of Malden, and inaugurated development of what proved to be one of the best of the salt well areas. Their well had been drilled to a depth of only seventy-five feet when a good stream of brine was struck, so that the initial expense was low. The well continued profitable for six years, its salt selling for $1.00 a bushel during the War of 1812. When this well ran low, a second one was drilled on the farm of Isaac Noyes, a short distance away. This proved a more difficult undertaking, and after drilling to a depth of seven hundred feet, with no salt found, the Whittekers abandoned it. A few years afterward, Isaac Noyes sank it fifteen feet deeper, and encountered a large stream of excellent brine.

Bradford Noyes was also a salt-maker, and in 1816 Aaron Whitteker made a bargain to supply him with wood for his furnace in return for one-half of the salt. Coal for the salt furnaces was then not in use, and the amount of wood needed to keep them going was immense. In order to carry out his agreement, Whitteker engaged the best wood-choppers he could find, at the then satisfying wage of fifty cents a cord. Putting Mr. William Wood in charge as manager, Aaron, with two flatboats which he and his brother Thomas operated, delivered a boat load of wood to the furnace every day for three years—flood, drought, snow, or ice to the contrary.

The appearance of the Valley after the Whitteker devastation was wrought—plus similar activities by other operators—is horrible to contemplate. He not only cleared all the timber from the old Charles Brown farm

("Brownstown"—Marmet) on the south side of the river, comprising several hundred acres, but he swept the hillsides bare, beginning at Magazine branch on Elk River, for four miles up the Kanawha. This took walnut, cherry, oak, and maple trees three feet and more in diameter. "Oh woodman . . ."—but it's too late!

The undertaking successfully accomplished, Aaron Whitteker then turned to house building and storekeeping. In 1819 he built a brick storeroom thirty-two by twenty feet, which, except for the one belonging to James C. MacFarland, was the only store in Charleston. This edifice stood on the river bank until it was destroyed by fire in 1870, and there for twenty-five years Aaron held forth, surrounded by, shall we say, a pleasing variety of stock, consisting of shoes, hardware, dry goods, groceries, and innumerable other salable items. During this period he also erected a two-story brick building that housed the Miller Drug Company and a dry goods concern. In addition, he also erected a number of dwellings in the town.

The Whittekers were builders—whatever else they did, they all, sooner or later, got around to building. William Whitteker's son, Norris S., born in Charleston in 1807, built many of its best residences, two of which were the Rand and the MacFarland (Ruby) houses. He had first spent a few years as a keel and flat boatman, but he soon followed the family precedent and learned carpentry, brick-making, painting, and every other trade then current that related to building. He was a man of tremendous physical strength and endurance, and into everything he undertook was thrown his vast store of energy and vigor. Such was true in the cause of temperance, in which he was keenly interested, and, in its behalf, is said to have made hundreds of speeches.

Norris S. Whitteker was a strong Union man, and at

the beginning of the Civil War received an appointment from Lincoln as postmaster of Charleston, and continued as such until the autumn of 1866. This was a difficult position, as Charleston was an important military point during the War, and the post office handled an enormous volume of mail, his registry book showing a record of several thousand letters passing through this office daily. In 1832 Mr. Whitteker married Leticia Morris, daughter of Carrol, a son of Major William Morris, Jr.

The old Whitteker homes stood on Capitol Street, where many early residences were located — those of James A. Lewis, Joel and Alexander Quarrier, and others. The lovely old brick house where Aaron Whitteker spent his last years was afterward the home of the Jefferies family. There in 1862 Mr. Jefferies found the lost flag of the Kanawha Riflemen, made the year before by Charleston women, which he presented to the Confederates when they again occupied the town.

While the Noyes brothers were not builders, they were engaged in other of the same pursuits as the Whittekers—they manufactured salt, were merchants, and dealt in lands, all of which proved lucrative, and they became men of wealth and much property.

Isaac and his brother, Bradford, jointly purchased a large tract of land along the Kanawha extending back to the hills, between the present Bradford Street and the line of Morris Street, then non-existent, but when cut through later was designated as Eastern Avenue, denoting the extreme eastern limit of the town. There was excluded from the tract only the two houses then in the area—the Summers and Miller houses near Broad Street.

Soon afterward, on the upper part of this property, Isaac Noyes erected a small, low, brick house placed far back in a beautifully shaded location, where he and his invalid wife resided. It was later the Thomas B. Swann home where President and Mrs. Grant were guests in 1874. Beyond it, on the extreme eastern boundary of the tract at the corner of Bradford Street, was erected in 1835 the residence of the other brother, Bradford Noyes, which later became the home of his son, James. The house, subsequently demolished, was supplanted by the ornate residence of Colonel John Q. Dickinson, but behind it still stands the simple two-story brick house built as servants' quarters by Mr. Noyes. It, too, will soon be gone, and also the Dickinson house, as the site is to be occupied by a large apartment building.

The brothers conveyed an acre or so of their tract to William J. Rand, husband of Ella Noyes, daughter of Isaac, and upon it Norris Whitteker was engaged to erect a large brick residence.

On January 1, 1834, William Whitteker acquired the adjoining lot where his son Norris constructed another equally large and well-built dwelling. This, William sold in 1836 to Mr. Henry Devol MacFarland.

In county histories will be found the statement that both houses were built in 1831, and a third house near-by, no longer existing, was built in 1832. Such may be correct as to the Rand house, but according to the deed to Whitteker, and the one from Whitteker to MacFarland which speaks of the "brick tenement recently erected" by Whitteker, it seems more likely that the date for the second house was somewhat later, possibly 1835.

It is only since this volume has been in preparation that the Rand house, long vacant, and having become untenable and ghost-like, was razed, but not, fortunately, before a drawing was made of it. It was Number 1306 Kanawha Boulevard, and the Ruby house, described later as the MacFarland house, was 1310.

The Rand dwelling, like its neighbor, was placed far back in a deep level lot, and was approached by a central walkway, on each side of which were several tall holly trees, planted when the house was young, and now they alone survive. Large, and definitely colonial in style, this square building was suggestive of the southern plantation house. Its deep double verandas extending across the front were supported by tall columns extending from the ground level of the lower porch to the pointed roof. The roof of the house proper was rather steep and had an odd little row of arched wire trim across the ridge. Outstanding features were the pairs of tall square chimneys piercing the roof on either side. They were trimmed with collars of graduated brick, and topped with pairs of tile chimney pots.

In 1807 Isaac Noyes married Cynthia, daughter of Major William Morris, Jr. The number of their children is uncertain, but there were at least two daughters: Roxalana, who married Colonel B. H. Smith, prominent Kanawha lawyer and legislator, member of the Constitutional Convention of 1850-51, and nominee in 1866 against Arthur Boreman, successful candidate for first Governor of West Virginia. A Whig, and fervid Union man, Colonel Smith's influence was instrumental in preventing damage to the Rand house, then the home of his wife's sister, Ella, whose husband was William J. Rand.

The Rand family had come to America from Great Britain and settled in Massachusetts, where William Rand I was born in 1776. He and his wife, Lucy Jackson, moved to Vermont. Of their seven children, six reached maturity. Jacob, born 1799, became a well-known educator in the Kanawha Valley, and Christopher, born 1800, who married Nancy McArthur Pines, of Kentucky, and had a large family of ten children, came to the Valley in 1819, where he was a merchant and salt manufacturer at The Salines. A younger brother, William J. II, born in 1809, also came to Kanawha, where he married Ella, daughter of Isaac Noyes, Sr.

While William J. Rand II followed the popular trend and engaged in salt-making, he abandoned it later for merchandising and banking. His family consisted of two daughters and one son, Isaac Noyes Rand, who, as a Civil War veteran, saw much service. Mustered in as a member of the Kanawha Riflemen on May 8, 1861, he was later on the staff of General Echols, and with the rank of Major, was in command of a brigade to which the 22nd Virginia Regiment belonged. After the War, Major Rand became interested in mining operations in Texas, and with his wife, Anne Norvell, and their five children removed to that state in 1882. Major Rand's sister Elizabeth married Noyes S. Burlew, and they were later residents of the Rand house on Kanawha Boulevard.

The Burlew family was of French origin. The parents of Noyes S. and Abraham, the two sons who came to Charleston, lived in New Jersey. After Noyes Burlew arrived in 1872 he was in the lumber business for a time, then spent several years as Revenue Collector, but resigned to establish a hardware store. He was appointed Adjutant General of West Virginia by both Governors Dawson and Glasscock, and was thereafter known as "General" Burlew. It was he who constructed, owned, and managed the famous Burlew Opera House, Charleston's first theatre, which, until 1919, when it was razed, stood on Capitol Street on the site of the present O. J. Morrison store building.

It was an unbelievably ornate three-story building, with towers, minarets, arched windows, roof balustrade, and all manner of embellishments, when such excrescences were considered the acme of architectural achievement. For all of the Burlew's inartistic exterior, its curtain went up on unexcelled "theatre" such as Charleston has never since witnessed. Here, on May 31, 1906, the indestructible and magnificent Sarah Bernhardt packed the house in her never-to-be-forgotten "Camille," and ten years later returned in three one-act plays, giving once more as a climax, the last act of "Camille." The exquisite ballerina, Anna Pavlowa, danced upon this stage; the fabulous and beloved Joseph Jefferson appeared in "Rip Van Winkle," followed by Helena Modjeska, Henrietta Crossman, John Drew, DeWolf Hopper, Otis Skinner, and many other actors of the theatre's golden days. "Ben Hur" thrilled the Burlew audience with horses galloping on treadmills in the sensational chariot race. It was in this theatre Charleston saw its first fifteen-minute eye-straining flicker film, "The Great Train Robbery," and later the first of the great spectacular productions — "The Birth of a Nation," and "Intolerance."

Still preserved by some of Charleston's residents are programs and souvenirs that bring back nostaglic memories of superb performances at the Old Burlew.

Kerr House

MacFarland House and the Rubys

OLD houses which have names of their own somehow acquire a distinction that goes well with their years, and they give one a pleasant feeling of things that endure. One of the most beautiful of Charleston's early homes is now well over a hundred years old, and yet repeated inquiries fail to reveal that any of its early owners saw fit to give it a name. The writer therefore must rather reluctantly refer to it as the MacFarland house—not that she resents Mr. MacFarland, who was doubtless a most estimable person, but she feels this fine old dwelling is worthy of an individual designation, and not merely to be noted as 1310 Kanawha Boulevard.

Facing the river, the house is placed far back in a deep, level lot. The long approach gives the right perspective to the impressive square brick building with its gray painted brick walls and enormous white columns extending from the ground level porch to the pointed roof line. Originally a second floor veranda, similar to that of the neighboring Rand house, extended the width of the house, but it was later removed, and replaced by a small bracket-supported balcony upon which opens a center door on the second floor. The entrance doorway is somewhat elaborate and is not placed under the balcony as one would expect, but opens into a hallway against the eastern wall. Around the heavy paneled door are reeded half columns decorated at the top with carved acanthus leaf design, and on each side and overhead, the small squares of original glass are replaced by leaded glass panels.

This and the Rand house, which stood next to it for a hundred years, were built at approximately the same time by Norris, one of the Whitteker brothers who were architects, stone and brick masons, carpenters, painters, and everything else essential to construction, and who erected a great number of the best of Charleston's century-old houses. If a Whitteker built it, then there was nothing more to be said—it was a good house.

William Whitteker, brother of Norris, had acquired the lot on January 1, 1834, from the Noyes brothers, Isaac and Bradford. Assuming he put his brother to work at once, the construction must have taken a year at least, so the year of its building would seem to be more nearly 1835 than 1831, which the writer has seen assigned to it again and again. In either case it was completed by December 19, 1836, as that is the date of the deed from William Whitteker to the first owner.

The purchaser was Henry Devol MacFarland (1808-1845), a Charleston resident, and half brother of James C. MacFarland (1792-1864), who was sixteen years his senior and a son of their father's first marriage. The latter died when the children of the second marriage were small, and responsibility fell early upon the shoulders of the older James, who in 1813, at the age of twenty-one, arrived in Charleston, determined to become a merchant. Without funds, he began industriously making nails by hand, and worked at it until he had accumulated enough money to purchase his first stock of merchandise. He had already impressed the villagers with his industry, and had acquired the valuable asset of "good will" when he opened the first mercantile establishment in Charleston, where his store stood on the river front below the courthouse.

 James MacFarland gained a reputation for fair dealing, and in a remarkably short time came to be recognized as one of the outstanding citizens of the village. Even as a young man he was regarded as of such high character and impeccable integrity that the townspeople felt their funds were more secure with him than in their own hands, and were constantly bringing their money and securities to him for safekeeping. It is even said when money became depreciated following the War of 1812, he issued notes of his own which were accepted and used as though they were government currency.

 All this trusteeship, while complimentary, may in time have become somewhat burdensome. At any rate James MacFarland was the moving factor in securing a bank for the community, and in 1832 a branch of the Bank of Virginia was opened in Charleston. There apparently was no thought of anyone other than Mr. MacFarland for president, and as a matter of course he continued to be re-elected annually so long as the bank existed, which was until two years before his death. In 1862, during the Civil War shelling of the town by Federal batteries on the south side of the river, the bank building, built of brick, with tall white columns, was struck and burned.

 James MacFarland was widely read, and while not a college man, possessed a strong and cultivated intellect. He wrote fluently, and for a period of over fifty years had made it a habit to set down the local happenings in a daily diary. Unfortunately this documentary record of Charleston's early history was lost in the bank conflagration. The bank had been a successful institution, and had declared an average dividend of fourteen per cent a year on the capital assigned to it.

Mr. MacFarland was not only a good banker but was actively interested in the upbuilding and development of the locality. Although averse to politics, he served in 1824 as Mayor of Charleston and as President of the town's Board of Trustees, and was several times elected a member of the House of Delegates. He was one of the founders of St. John's Episcopal Church, and was a vestryman for many years.

Mr. MacFarland was four times married, first in 1819 to Lethe, daughter of Major John Reynolds. His second wife was Dulce Chaddock; the third and fourth were Lucy W. Greenhow and Mrs. Maria Broome. Six children were born of these various marriages.

The James MacFarland home stood facing the river on a large tree-filled lot adjoining the manse of the Kanawha Presbyterian Church. The property extended to McFarland Street which was named for him, the first "a" of the name being omitted in the modern spelling.

The MacFarland family was of Scotch descent and had come from New England to Marietta, Ohio, in 1803. When James MacFarland arrived in Charleston the half brother, Henry, was a child, but by the time he was grown, James had a merchandising concern that was a successful business. Henry no doubt had come to Charleston as an associate, since he, too, was a merchant.

When Henry MacFarland purchased the newly completed brick house from Mr. Whitteker, he did so in anticipation of his approaching marriage to Julia Cook, which occurred a few days later on December 23, 1836. Soon afterward Mr. MacFarland brought his bride to their new home where they continued to live. They were not to have many years together, however, as his death occurred in 1845 while he was still a comparatively young man.

Littlepage Mansion

His widow remained in their home for a time, but her financial situation was such that it was necessary that she seek quarters elsewhere. Her brother-in-law, Major Lawrence Carr, came to her aid, and proffered the use of a house on the corner of Bradford and Washington streets, into which she and her two children, Anastine and Henry Devol, Jr.,* moved. She then opened a private school for girls.

The brick house on the Kanawha passed into other hands. Identified longer with the Ruby family than any other, it is still referred to as the Ruby house, although for the last twenty-five years there has been no association with that family.

John Christopher Ruby II was born in Ohio, son of John and Madeline Tilly Ruby, whose parents, also born there, were early settlers and farmers. The maternal grandmother of John C. Ruby II was a native of Lyons, France, the Tilly family having come to America about 1812 and joined the French settlement at Gallipolis.

John C. Ruby II came to Charleston when he was eighteen, and soon married Mary Frances Noyes, daughter of Harriet Oden Noyes and Bradford Noyes (1788-1850), wealthy salt-maker and merchant, and brother of Isaac Noyes.

The Rubys were the parents of five children, three daughters and two sons. The latter, John C. III and Bradford N. Ruby, followed their father in the grocery and real estate business under the firm name of Ruby Brothers, becoming financially substantial and owners of much residential property.

Just when or how the Ruby ownership of the MacFarland house originated is vague. There was an antenuptial contract in 1851 between Mary F. Noyes and

---
*Henry Devol MacFarland, Jr., was a member of the Kanawha Riflemen.

John C. Ruby II, by which certain property inherited by her from her father, Bradford Noyes, Sr., was transferred to William Rand, her trustee. Mr. Noyes and his brother, Isaac, had originally owned the land on which this house stood, and whether it came back into his possession and is the property mentioned, or some other, is not indicated. Dates given in various biographical sketches state that Mrs. Ruby was born in 1840 and John C. Ruby II in 1838. Such would make her eleven and her fiance thirteen at the time of their pre-marital agreement, which certainly seems rather a youthful age at which even to contemplate matrimony, much less to record such intentions in a formal document. The writer has attempted to clarify these seemingly incredible dates, but has found nothing additional to refute them. One thing appears unquestioned: In a court paper dated June 6, 1851, Mary F. Noyes refers to her husband, John Ruby, so the marriage had taken place prior to that date, and they were then owners and occupants of the MacFarland house.

John C. Ruby II was a member of the Kanawha Riflemen and entered the Confederate Army, serving under General McCausland and becoming a captain late in the war. His family had likely "refugeed to Dixie" with other of Charleston's Confederate families, as their house was taken over by Federal officers and used as a military hospital. Names of the soldiers who were quartered there were found scratched and cut in the plastered walls.

The highest point along the Charleston river front was the section between Morris and Bradford streets. When the frightful flood of 1861 inundated the Valley and the Kanawha rose to sixty feet, this house and its next door neighbor remained above water, a circumstance perhaps taken into consideration in selecting it for a hospital, although its location was not so safe in other respects. In range of Federal batteries on the south side of the river, it was struck by a cannon ball and the roof partly torn away.

In 1865, when the Confederate families returned to their Charleston homes, the Frazier Hansfords, relatives of the Rubys, who came to live in the house, found the soldier patients still in possession. The patients, however, moved out and established their hospital on the lawn in a tent under the trees, where they remained until their wounds were healed.

The house was occupied by various members of the Ruby family until 1922, when it was sold to Mr. J. B. Crowley. He undertook extensive improvements—the installation of electric lights and other modern conveniences, the addition of a sunroom on one side balanced by a portecochere on the opposite, interior paneling of first floor walls, and other alterations which have in no way detracted from the house—a statement one can seldom make as to modernization of old houses. To these have been added the happy combination of charming furnishings and harmonious colors created by the present occupant, Mrs. J. W. Hubbard, whose late husband purchased the house within the past few years.

Littlepage Mansion

AT a time when Charleston had emerged from a log cabin village straggling along the Kanawha, into a small town of many substantial brick buildings, its western boundary still terminated at Elk River. There a ferry took travelers across to the road that wound westward through wooded country along the base of the bluff extending to Kanawha Two Mile, the well-known creek along whose banks not many years before (1818) had been shot the last of the elk, once plentiful in this locality.

This area, originally within the boundary of the second of the two extensive Bullitt surveys, embraced all of the present West Charleston and was later owned by Major James Bream. After his death in 1842, the land passed to his wife, whose death occurred in 1845. It was not until after the death of Major Bream that a few farms were sold from the survey, and the first houses in West Charleston were erected upon them. One of these farms, purchased from Mrs. Bream by Dr. Spicer Patrick, was in the vicinity of the present Patrick Street bridge across the Kanawha near his home, "Forest Hill," which stood on the bluff above it.

In the fall of 1846 Dr. Patrick conveyed a part of his acreage lying on both sides of the turnpike near Two Mile Creek to Robert H. Thornton and his wife, Lucy Jane Thornton, the deed stating that it adjoined the land on which Thornton then resided, "and is the same land on which the party of the second part (Thornton) hath lately erected a stone house."

Little is known of the builder of the fine old house long known as the "Littlepage Mansion," as Mr. Thornton's ownership was very brief. The only scrap of identifying data obtained is certainly vague, and is that he was "a descendant of one of three brothers, who married three sisters named Gregory, who were cousins of George Washington"—which sounds like the childish jingle about "the house that Jack built."

Whoever this mysterious man may have been, he knew how a good house should be built, for this is one of the best in the Valley. He sold the property to Adam B. Littlepage on December 20, 1849. Since then it has been owned by members of the Littlepage family until within the past few years.

Its exterior unaltered—thanks, no doubt, to the deterring staunchness of the thick stone walls—in outward appearance, at least, it has withstood the changes that have shorn it of its gently sloping and tree-shaded grounds, and left it bleakly isolated in a veritable sea of concrete paving. No longer used as a dwelling, it is now the administration building for the surrounding community center of large brick housing units called "Littlepage Terrace."

The "Mansion" was somewhat of a show-place in its day. Unlike the few other houses west of Elk River, it alone was not built on the bluff high above the road, but in the bottom land. Perhaps the choice of location was governed by the difficulties which would have been encountered in handling heavy stone, had a site on the hillside been chosen.

More distant from Charleston than any of its neighbors, the "Mansion" was erected near the eastern bank of Two Mile Creek. Close to the public road (Route 21), the building was separated from it by a thick stone wall.

On the western side of the house the land sloped away through the orchard toward the creek, and in the rear and on the upper side were gardens, barns, and all the buildings necessary to plantation life. According to the date cut in one of the stone blocks of the outer wall, construction was in 1845.

Handsome and spacious, the proportions are good. Oblong in shape, the well-laid stone blocks of the walls rise to a steep roof above a full attic lighted by end windows. Pairs of stone chimneys in the two walls meant fireplaces in every room, a winter comfort not always considered essential for the sleeping rooms of a century ago. The small entrance portico shelters a lovely doorway, with side glass panels and circular fanlight above. Unusually good are the large windows, their upper sash having nine panes of glass, and the lower sash six. There are five windows across the second floor and two on each side of the portico. An early picture shows shutters on the lower windows.

The Kanawha pioneer of the Littlepage family was born in Greenbrier County, where his parents were early settlers in the Anthony's Creek region. Adam Littlepage I came to The Salines about 1840 and engaged in the salt business. He married Rebecca Todd Wood, born in Kanawha, who survived her husband many years, until 1898. Of their seven children, several died in infancy. Alexander became a physician, and Adam B. and Samuel D. were lawyers. A daughter, Rebecca, married Mr. A. M. Putney.

After his purchase of the stone house on Two Mile Creek, Mr. Littlepage removed from The Salines and established his household at the new location. He had accumulated a comfortable estate, but suffered severe business losses in the Civil War, many of which he claimed were unjust. In 1862, while attempting to substantiate his right to a valuable property, he died at Dublin, Virginia.

Except for nine hundred acres of land, little of his property remained. During the War, all of the buildings on the Littlepage estate, except the stone house, which was nearly indestructible, were burned by the soldiers. Dr. Patrick, the nearest neighbor, saw the smoke and flames, and, guessing the cause, gathered all the Negroes and farm workers he could summon, and hastened to give such assistance as was possible, but little was saved, as the log barn, cabins, and other wooden buildings burned readily.

It is said when the Confederate General, Henry A. Wise, requested use of the house as headquarters, Mrs. Littlepage, whose husband was absent from home, refused to vacate it. The irate General, in spite of his reputation for outspokenness, was apparently at a loss for words with which to cope with the situation, and leaving her in charge, retreated to the shelter of a tent under the trees.

The fields around the Littlepage house were camping ground for both Federal and Confederate armies in their various occupancies of the Valley, and until late years, grass-covered indentations of breastworks were still visible. A never-failing spring near Two Mile Creek, a well-known landmark that was of great value, supplied drinking water for both armies.

Adam Brown Littlepage II, one of the lawyer sons, was born in Charleston on April 14, 1859, and had a distinguished public life. He first began his practice in Indiana, but returned soon to Charleston, where he became absorbed in Democratic politics, shortly embarking on a career that first took him to the State Senate in

1906-10, and to the 62nd United States Congress in 1911-13. He was the defeated candidate for re-election to the 63rd, and was again successful as a member of the 64th and 65th Congresses. He died in 1921, soon after resuming his private law practice in Charleston.

Married in 1884, to Eva Collett, Congressman Littlepage and his wife had two children, S. Collett, Judge of the Criminal Court of Kanawha County at the time of his death, and Clara F.—Mrs. R. F. Irwin.

The Lovells and the Breams

AMONG outstanding citizens of early Charleston were members of the English families of Lovell and Bream. Joseph Lovell (who may have been Lord Lovell), husband of Lady Mary Shapton, lived but a few years after their marriage, leaving his widow with four small children: Lenora, who became the wife of the well-known Charleston pharmacist, Dr. Henry Rogers; Cassandra, who married a Mr. Lafong; Alfred, who died young, and Joseph Lovell, Jr., the Kanawha pioneer.

After the death of her husband, Mrs. Lovell married Major James Bream, a wealthy London merchant, and a genial, kindly, and generous person. In 1804 he brought his family to America, where they settled in Richmond, their home for the next fourteen years. Two children were born of Mary Lovell's second marriage: Alethia, who married Mr. Brigham, and Lavinia, who became the first wife of Dr. Spicer Patrick, one of Charleston's early physicians. Major Bream provided liberally for the education of his stepchildren, and in every way there appeared to exist the pleasant harmony and affection of a single congenial family group.

Joseph Lovell, Jr., who had been born in London on January 10, 1793, was eleven years old when he was brought to America. He received the latter part of his education in Virginia, where he studied law and received his license to practice. That accomplished, at the age of twenty-one he was ready to start on a trip westward to see where he should locate, and, incidentally, to look over lands for his stepfather, who contemplated making western real estate investments.

This young attorney possessed a brilliant and cultured mind, and was an eloquent and convincing speaker. Such qualities, coupled with ability and an attractive personality, insured his success. It is not surprising therefore that he was retained in a land suit so soon as he arrived at The Salines, his first stop after reaching the Valley in 1814. In the course of this employment it was necessary that he visit the courthouse in Charleston. Having inspected the little village at the mouth of Elk, he promptly decided his westward tour was at an end, and he need go no farther—this was the place where he would settle.

After Joseph had made inquiries and examined lands, he was ready with a favorable report of a desirable tract for his stepfather's consideration. Major Bream accordingly came to Charleston soon afterwards on an inspection trip, and ended by purchasing the property selected, which was nothing less than the Bullitt survey west of Elk River. Major Bream was well pleased with the region, and, filled with Joseph's enthusiastic insistence that he too come to Kanawha, departed for home determined to do so. Disposing of his property in Richmond, the Major, two years later, in 1818, returned with his wife and family to become permanent residents of the Valley. It was many years later, 1830, before Mrs. Bream apparently felt sufficiently Americanized to make application for citizenship.

Major Bream lived first at The Salines, near his stepson, where both were interested in salt production, Major Bream owning four wells. Religiously earnest, the Breams became members of the Presbyterian congregation then assembling in the Ruffner meeting house. A staunch Episcopalian, Mrs. Bream had been somewhat reluctant to leave her own denomination, but as there was no Episcopal church in The Salines, she finally yielded to the importunities of her husband that she become a member of the Presbyterian and, according to church records, did so in 1819. Having once made her decision, she stood by it, and did not transfer her membership, even after a church of her own denomination was established chiefly through the joint efforts of Mrs. Quarrier and herself. However, she contributed to it regularly. In 1832 Major Bream was elected an Elder in the Presbyterian church, and continued an active and valued member all his life.

At Mrs. Bream's death she left a bequest of $500 "to the Bishop of the Presbyterian Church in Charleston," but upon certain rigid terms and conditions. Since the Presbyterian church, unlike the Episcopalian, has no Bishop, it is said no minister has yet been willing to sign the receipt as such, nor to assume the obligations stipulated by Mrs. Bream.

The Breams later moved from The Salines to the Major's lands on the west side of Elk River, where the Bream home stood in the vicinity of the present Spring Street bridge, and there Major Bream later installed a ferry. Major Bream had acquired many properties other than the Bullitt survey, including valuable coal lands. When he died in 1842 he left the bulk of his very large estate to his wife, with smaller bequests divided equally among his children and his stepchildren. Mrs. Bream survived her husband only three years, dying in 1845. By her will all of their children shared equally in the estate.

The Bream cemetery was a plot of ground sixty-two

feet square, located in what is now the closely built residential section of Bigley Avenue, at a spot where a residence numbered 1008 now stands. The year after the death of her husband, Mrs. Bream conveyed this plot of ground to her son-in-law, Dr. Spicer Patrick, to be held in trust by him as a burial ground for the family and descendants of Major Bream.

As the years passed, it became necessary, in order to construct a street, to remove and re-inter the bodies in another cemetery. After this was done, the Bream heirs, in 1901, conveyed this lot, together with an adjoining area comprising several acres, to the "Southern" Presbyterian Church, with the provision it be used as a place of worship, and the congregation erect a church upon it within ten years. Such was done, and a church building stood on the site of the early burial ground. The property conveyed extended to present West Washington Street—three or more blocks. Now, facing this street, the successor of the first small church on Bigley Avenue has been erected. One of the largest, most active and influential churches of the city, it bears the name of its early benefactors and is called the Bream Memorial Presbyterian Church.

In 1818, the year in which the Breams arrived in Kanawha, their son, Joseph Lovell, was married by the Reverend Henry Ruffner to Miss Betty Washington Lewis. Born in 1796, she was a daughter of Ellen Hackley Pollard Lewis and Howell Lewis, and as a child had lived at Mount Vernon, during the time her father was secretary to his uncle, General George Washington. The parents of Howell Lewis were Betty Washington Lewis, only sister of George Washington, and Colonel Fielding Lewis, who, with their four sons, resided in Fredericksburg at "Kenmore," one of Virginia's most famed and beautiful historic homes, now open to the public.

Mrs. Lovell was a very attractive, and a very devout young woman, who was intensely interested in the Church. She, together with Mrs. Alexander Quarrier, was particularly outstanding in establishing the Episcopal church in Kanawha, and was especially mentioned in a two-volume work published in 1857 by Bishop William Meade, called *Old Churches, Ministers and Families of Virginia.*

Joseph Lovell had early joined the Virginia militia, having been recommended by the County Court and commissioned an Ensign by the Governor in 1815, the year after he arrived in Kanawha. He later attained the rank of Colonel of the 8th Regiment, 13th Brigade of the First Virginia Division, and thereafter was always referred to as "Colonel." It was a title that suited him, as he was a man to command respect either in military or civil life. Well liked and versatile, he engaged in various enterprises with equal success.

The legal profession at that time, however, was not a very lucrative pursuit, as lawyers all seemed to have at least one other business occupation—storekeeping and salt producing being the most favored. Joseph Lovell tried both. His two salt wells were on the south side of the river, but he lived on the north side, where his one-story double log house stood at Wilson's Hollow Branch, midway between Charleston and The Salines. Colonel and Mrs. Lovell had five children, all sons, the eldest of whom died in infancy. Richard Channing Moore (named for the second Bishop of Virginia in 1814, who was chiefly responsible for the revival of the Episcopal church in Virginia), the second son, was born in 1822 and married Mary Patrick, daughter of Dr. Spicer Patrick. Howell Lewis, born two years later, married Miss E. A. Beuhring, of Cabell County; Joseph, III, born 1827, married Sarah S. Nye, of Marietta, Ohio, and Fayette A., born 1830, the youngest son, married Sally Shrewsbury, of The Salines.

After some time the Lovells moved to Charleston, where Colonel Lovell built a story and a half brick house, the shell of which still stands. Located opposite the courthouse, on the northwest corner of Virginia and Alderson streets, it is said to have been built prior to "The Elms," its near neighbor, which was constructed in 1822. Long utilized as a store, with another floor above it added years ago, after a cyclone tore the roof away, there is now no suggestion that it was ever a dwelling, and nothing is left of the original building except portions of the brick side walls.

Colonel Lovell had a brief period of merchandising, and owned a store that stood on the river bank where the Union Building is now situated, but this he soon sold to James A. Lewis. With his particular gifts of leadership, his winning personality, and his ability to make an effective speech, it was inevitable that Colonel Lovell enter politics. Beginning as early as 1819, with his election to the Virginia House of Delegates, he continued to be re-elected repeatedly, and is said to have held every office to which he aspired. Not only that, but his influence was such that under his persuasive powers the county politics is said to have shifted from Jeffersonian to Whig, with Henry Clay as the salt-makers' idol. Colonel Lovell died in November, 1835, and was buried in the Bream cemetery near Elk River.

West Washington Street was for many years called Lovell Street. Today a shorter residential street bears the name of Lovell Drive. There is also a Bream Street.

Glenwood

PERHAPS no house in the Valley had a more delightful location at the time of its building in 1852 than did "Glenwood," the handsome house erected by Mr. James Madison Laidley. About a mile west of the mouth of Elk River, on the high bluff that extends westward to Two Mile Creek, it commanded a sweeping and magnificent view of lowlands, the Kanawha River and distant hills. At that time there were no disfiguring buildings to mar the landscape; no smokestacks of industrial plants and factories to soil the blue of the sky; no jarring sounds of passing trains and motor traffic, but only the beauty of the quiet river and the restful green of untouched woodland.

Although "Glenwood," today designated as 800 Orchard Street, is surrounded by neighboring residences and flanked by the impressive building of Stonewall Jackson High School, one of Charleston's most modern structures, it originally was a country estate that was no part of the little town of fifteen hundred people then grouped on the opposite side of Elk River.

Comprising an extensive acreage, bounded by the present streets of Delaware Avenue, Somerset Drive, and the Chandler Branch region of Edgewood hills, "Glenwood," prior to the Civil War, was next to the youngest of the five houses then existing in what is today West Charleston, of which group, it and the Littlepage house alone remain.

The first of the five was "Edgewood," the unpretentious

frame house built in 1848 by Major J. L. Carr. It was the one nearest to Elk River, standing on the bluff where the Woodrum homes are now located, near its present namesake, Edgewood Drive. On the property was a very fine lithia spring, whose water, bottled in huge demijohns, was for years sold on the streets of Charleston. Beyond "Edgewood" was "Glenwood"; next westward was the home of Mr. William Gillison, a magistrate known as "Squire Gillison," and a resident prior to 1840. A little farther on was "Forest Hill," the farm to which Dr. Spicer Patrick had removed in 1856 after selling his residence in town. The fifth and last house is the Littlepage place at Two Mile Creek, described elsewhere.

To reach the town of Charleston these neighbors followed the county road, now West Washington Street, along the foot of the bluff, and crossed Elk River by ferry until 1852, when a wire suspension bridge was erected. This bridge was not long enjoyed, however, as it was burned by General Lightburn during the Civil War.

The fertile acres of these farms largely supplied the needs of their owners, who required little from the merchants of the small community. However, the men rode to town more or less regularly to attend to business matters and to gather at the favorite meeting place—the Rogers Pharmacy. It served as a sort of men's club and information clearing house, where kindred souls could meet, exchange news, discuss national and local problems, and where they could always be sure of encountering friends and of being able to receive and deliver messages. The Rogers drug store had no coca-colas and messy soda fountains, and no cigarette smoking adolescents. Life was earnest in those days. Youth was brief, responsibility began early, and the men who lingered there were adult and serious-minded. The drug store was their daily newspaper, their weekly magazine, and their radio. Good talk was the attraction.

James Madison Laidley was one of the more recent members of the group. Formerly a resident of Parkersburg, where he had practiced law in the newly formed county of Wood, which he had represented several times in the Legislature, he had later removed to Charleston, where in 1850 he purchased from Mrs. Joseph Lovell* the three-hundred-and-sixty-six-acre tract of land which became the Glenwood estate.

The Laidley family was of Scotch ancestry, the name originally Laidlaw. Thomas, the American pioneer, arrived about 1774, and entered the army under General Washington, serving at Brandywine, Trenton, and elsewhere, in addition to commanding a gunboat on the Delaware. He married in Pennsylvania, settling first in Philadelphia and afterward moving to Monongalia County, Virginia, which he represented in the Legislature for two or more terms. His son, James Grant Laidley, born in Philadelphia in 1781, was educated for the bar, and had studied in Richmond under Chancellor George Wythe and others. There in 1806 he married Harriet B. Quarrier, daughter of Colonel Alexander and Elizabeth Dannenberry Quarrier,* the Scotch-English family who, five years later, moved to Charleston, where their home "Willow Bank" stood on the south side of Kanawha River opposite the courthouse.

When the War of 1812 commenced, James G. Laidley raised a volunteer company of riflemen and entered service as a captain under Generals Harrison and Leftwich in the Northwest. He participated in several battles and served throughout the war, but lived only a few years

---
*See "The Lovells and Breams."
*See "The Quarrier Family."

afterward. His three children were a little girl, who died in infancy; her twin brother, Alexander T. Laidley, who became an invaluable clerk of various courts and of different counties over a period of many years, serving much of the time in Charleston; and James Madison Laidley, the youngest child (1809-1896), who was only twelve years of age when his father died.

In 1840 James M. married Anna M. Beuhring at Cabell Courthouse, and they were the parents of ten children:

Frederick Alexander, b. 1841, m. Julia Rook (five children); Frances Amelia—unmarried; Harriet C., m. John D. Baines (one daughter); Mary Rowena—unmarried; James John, m. Josephine Wilson (children); Emma Louise, m. Henry Whitteker (two children); George Summers Laidley (prominent Kanawha County schoolman), m. (1) Cora Bradford (children), (2) Mary Byrd Fontaine (no children); Annie Virginia, m. James E. Johnston (two children); Madison Monroe, m. Frances Smith (four daughters); Juliette Shrewsbury, 1860, m. John Garnett Eskew (children).

Although Mr. Laidley followed the family propensity and became a lawyer, he also was a businessman, and after moving from Parkersburg to Charleston, became one of the Valley's wealthy salt manufacturers. No expense was spared in the construction of his well-built home. Engaging as his builder, William Preston, an English stonemason who had come to America soon after 1812, Mr. Laidley, immediately after his purchase, began erection of the house. Completed in 1852, it was named "Glenwood," from the near-by deep rock-strewn glen cut by a stream that cascaded from distant hills, today a paved street called Mathews Avenue.

It may have been the influence of his English builder

that accounts for the unusually heavy and somber wood trim of the interior, a feature distinctly more English than American. For, in spite of its generous hallway, its great rooms twenty feet square, the handsome paneled walnut doors and random-width pine flooring, the enormous windows that reach from eleven-inch baseboards almost to the twelve-foot ceiling and which are surrounded by ten-and-a-half-inch poplar casings stained yellow and finished in a grained effect—the chief beauty of "Glenwood" does not lie in its interior, but in the well-proportioned and altogether satisfying lines of its exterior. The structure has much dignity and distinction, and, happily, is still free from alterations which so frequently mar the good lines of early houses.

Square stone pillars whose capstones are cut into the shape of stars are still standing on each side of Park Avenue, which then marked the entrance driveway that led up the shaded slope to the door of "Glenwood." The house, built of bricks burned on the site, is tall and spacious. Placed well back in a deep and level lot, it was strongly and truly constructed, the outside walls of solid brick being eighteen inches thick, with the inner partition walls only four or five inches less. There is a carved dentil cornice across the front of the house, where the unusual roof line is broken and indented at intervals. The slope of the steep roof is longer toward the back where it covers wide double verandas.

The shuttered windows across the front and in the ends are topped by extended cornices supported by carved brackets, giving the house a decidedly formal atmosphere. This effect is further emphasized in the design of the small entrance portico, whose pointed roof is supported by pairs of graceful reeded columns, indicative of the Greek revival in architecture.

Having successfully executed this style in the dignified portico, an attempt was also made to carry the Greek idea indoors. The walls of the hallway were decorated with a design of Grecian columns painted gray-white in imitation of marble, and these were interspersed with panels of female figures about two-thirds life size. These wispy maidens, looking not exactly Grecian, don't seem very happy there, and apparently as time went on did not make the owners of the house feel very happy either, since a coat of paint later obliterated the somewhat dubious charms of all but two of the ladies.

On the grounds in the rear of the house stands one of the few substantially erected slave houses still existing in Charleston. Generally called "The Quarters," such buildings were for use of the house servants—log cabins ordinarily sufficing for the field workers. Constructed of brick, two stories in height, there are four rooms, with fireplaces in each, and a Dutch oven adjoining that of the kitchen on the first floor. An old settle, "hutch" table, chairs, and other pieces of simple furniture made by the slaves themselves are still in the rooms.

Mr. Laidley owned "Glenwood" but a few years, selling it in the summer of 1857 to the Honorable George W. Summers II, the man for whom Summers County was named, and who was one of Kanawha County's most illustrious and eminent citizens. His brother, Lewis, likewise attained prominence. Sons in a family of ten children, of whom George W. II, born 1804 (1868), was the youngest, and Lewis I, born 1778 (1846), was old enough to have been his father. Their parents were George Summers I and Anna Smith Radcliffe Summers, who had lived on a plantation near Alexandria, Virginia. In the winter of 1813 the family moved to Putnam County, and a short distance below Winfield built a log house called "Walnut Grove," which still exists. Near it is the burial ground where lie the older members of the Summers family.

The move to the Kanawha Valley was the result of a preliminary exploration trip, undertaken by the elder son, Lewis, at his father's request, who desired a firsthand report of the Kanawha region, its land, and conditions in general. The journey, described in a daily diary kept by the traveler, and titled "Lewis Summers' Journal of a Tour from Alexandria, Virginia, to Gallipolis, Ohio, in 1808," appeared in the Southern Historical magazine of February, 1892, and is a valued bit of West Virginiana.

After his journey, Lewis Summers I located in Gallipolis for two years, but after his father moved to the Kanawha Valley, he came also, residing in Charleston, where he led a busy life. A person of strong and vigorous intellect, he practiced law, and, along with many of the other professional men of the Valley, became interested in the salt industry. In addition, he was proprietor of the largest store at The Salines, at a time when that community was larger than Charleston. He took an active part in politics, repeatedly representing Kanawha in the General Assembly, and was a delegate and a most useful member in the Virginia Constitutional Convention of 1829. Lewis Summers was also a capable Judge, and for twenty-four years served in one or another of the western Virginia courts. He died, unmarried, at White Sulphur Springs in the summer of 1843.

His younger brother, George W. Summers II, attended Washington College at Lexington, then graduated at Ohio University, and after a year's legal study under the tutelage of Lewis, was admitted to the bar in 1827. A young man of exceptional ability, George Summers

He was well equipped for the important career that lay ahead of him. He not only had a keen mentality and was gifted with powers of oratory, but also possessed physical vigor and an impressive appearance.

His political debut came in 1830 with election to the House of Delegates in Richmond, and was followed by his re-election the following year, and in 1834 and 1835. This service led to his election to the United States House of Representatives in 1841, and again in 1843. He fought for protective tariff and won acclaim for his able speeches, particularly in 1850 as a member of the Virginia Convention, on the issue as to the basis of representation in the General Assembly, expressing the views of western Virginians against those of the Tidewater. He was a thorough Unionist, strongly opposed to slavery and loud in debate against it. In 1851 he became candidate for Governor under the new Constitution, but was defeated by those who shouted he was affiliated with the abolitionists. In May, 1852, he was elected Judge of the 18th Circuit, serving until 1858, when he resigned two years before the expiration of his term.

He was a member of the "Peace Conference" held in Washington in the spring of 1861 that sought futilely to find a means of averting the impending war. As a delegate to the Richmond convention of that year he made a strong speech against secession. Distressed at the inevitability of the conflict, and bitterly opposed to the stand his state had taken in voting for secession, Judge Summers withdrew from further public office, and for the few remaining years of his life, devoted himself entirely to his extensive legal practice and to supervision of his farm.

"Glenwood" grew to be a very modern establishment,

as the Summers family did not hesitate to adopt new ideas and improvements. It is said this was the first house in the county to install the magic innovation of "water works." Just what strange mechanical device was involved in this achievement one does not know, but it was operated from a cistern in the yard, and was quite complete—wooden bathtub and all! "Glenwood" also had one of the first telephones in the locality, but its usefulness at that period seems a little hard to visualize. No doubt, however, there was a certain satisfaction in grinding the crank, and thinking of possible brilliant conversations one might hold with the neighbors once they, too, had telephones.

Judge Summers and his family were safe at "Glenwood" during the war, as his well-known Union sentiments preserved his home from molestation, although he frequently stood on his lawn and watched shells fall on his property from batteries established on the hills behind his home.

Judge Summers had a small family. His wife, Amacetta Laidley, of Cabell County, daughter of John Laidley, and sister of the historian, W. S. Laidley, was very young at the time of their marriage in 1833. Of their several children, all died in infancy except two sons, George III and Lewis II, and only one of these survived his parents. This son, Lewis II, married Lucy A. Woodbridge in 1867. With the death of his mother in the same year, and that of his father occurring the following year, Lewis and his bride became master and mistress of "Glenwood," which still continues in family ownership, and is today the home of their son, Lewis Summers III, and his wife. Of their three other children, two are deceased, Amacetta Laidley and George W. IV, well-known journalist and local historical writer. A sister,

Elizabeth, married Russell G. Quarrier, and is a resident of Charleston.

Not the least of the charms of "Glenwood" are the delightful perennial, herb, and boxwood gardens planted and preserved by Misses Lucy and Elizabeth Quarrier, daughters of Mrs. Russell Quarrier. They also utilize the old slave house for recreational activities, one of which is weaving—a loom looking very much at home in this early setting, where the writer was shown a sheet, hand-woven from flax, with the date 1818 and the name "Summers" worked in one corner.

"Glenwood" yet contains numerous pieces of furniture brought to the house by Judge Summers in 1857, as well as a few pieces already there which he purchased from Mr. Laidley—two of these being a tall gilt pier glass mirror and the table over which it hung. There is a very handsome cherry dining table capable of seating twenty people, a tall secretary bookcase, floor clock, and piano; also chairs, beds, early Brussels carpet, and many other articles to delight the lover of antiques.

Hanging on the wall is a portrait of Lewis Summers I painted by an artist named Catlin while Mr. Summers was attending the Virginia Convention of 1829. In the same room is his work table, and underneath it his little canvas-covered trunk upon which are lettered his name and the address "Kanawha, Virginia." Another heirloom of Mr. Lewis' travels is a clever tubular box no larger around than a quarter, and only nine inches long, that is divided into separate sections to hold a quill pen, ink, and wafers with which to seal the letter.

Although the cheerful red brick of "Glenwood's" walls and the white of its woodwork have years ago been painted a dreary brown, they are softened by the ivy that clambers over the house, which, architecturally, has undergone no changes. "Glenwood," however, is much more than the rarest of all finds—an original example of the best in Charleston's early houses. It holds the unique position of having been part of the background of a surprisingly large number of interesting and exceptional people, whose lives have been outstanding in the Valley's early history, and who are all memorialized in the street names of Charleston: Bream, Lovell, Laidley, Summers, and Quarrier. And the name of the estate itself is perpetuated in Glenwood Avenue and also in Glenwood School.

Appendix

KANAWHA VALLEY

All of the territory of Virginia lying west of the Blue Ridge Mountains was taken from Orange County in 1738 and formed into the enormous county of Augusta and the smaller county of Frederick. From the southeastern area of this region the route of early westward migration led across the mountains to meet the Kanawha River, and to follow its valley to the Ohio River and beyond. By this route came the early settlers of the Kanawha Valley.

As time passed, western Augusta was partitioned into other counties, and they in turn were subdivided into still others. Greenbrier County, formed in 1777 from two of these, Montgomery and Botetourt, was large and productive, extending over many mountain ranges and bluegrass plateaus and throughout the entire length of Kanawha Valley. It was from this county and that of Montgomery that the county of "Kenhawa" was created in 1788. Beginning in the east of the Greenbrier County line on lofty Sewell Mountain, its boundaries extended westward to the Big Sandy River; on the north to the region of the Little Kanawha River, and on the south to the counties of Montgomery and Tazewell and the Kentucky state line.

The county is watered by several rivers, the largest being the important, navigable Great Kanawha, for which the county was named. It is formed thirty-nine miles east of Charleston by the union of New River, which rises in North Carolina, and the swift and narrow Gauley from West Virginia's northern mountains. Flowing through the county in a northwest direction for over ninety miles, the Kanawha empties into the Ohio at Point Pleasant, near the original northwestern boundary of the county.

The second largest river is the Elk, whose source is in the northern mountains of Randolph County. It flows into the Kanawha sixty miles above the Ohio, at Charleston, dividing the city into eastern and western sections.

Coal River, another tributary of the Kanawha, rising in the highlands of Raleigh and Wyoming counties, runs in a northwest direction for a hundred miles before it empties into the south side of the Kanawha, fourteen miles below Charleston. Before the Civil War, Coal River's tempestuous course was made navigable for thirty-seven miles from its mouth by a series of locks and dams, but they were obliterated by war and flood, few traces remaining. Today Coal River is a favorite stream for summer camps, and has several bathing beaches near its Upper and Lower Falls.

The crooked Pocataligo, smallest of the counties' rivers, flows in a southwest direction, reaching the north bank of the Kanawha five miles below Coal River.

After the turn of the nineteenth century the vast area of Kanawha County was greatly lessened, as other counties were formed from its territory, a process beginning in 1804 with Mason County, and continued in 1809, with Cabell, both taken entirely from Kanawha. Kanawha, together with other counties, also contributed of her lands toward the formation of the counties of Nicholas, Logan, Fayette, Jackson, Braxton, Boone, Gilmer, Putnam, Calhoun, Roane, Clay, and in 1867 to the last-formed county, Lincoln. Into these went much of her superior farming and grazing lands, as well as valuable minerals, timber, coal and iron resources. Thus, by 1876 Kanawha County had shrunk considerably, its eastern limit being then only twenty-eight miles above Charleston, its western limit fourteen miles below, with its greatest length forty-three miles, and its greatest width, thirty-seven.

Kanawha has the largest population of any county in the State, with Charleston, the State Capital, the largest city in the county. Crowded into the Kanawha and Elk valleys, Charleston's homes climb over the tops of the surrounding foothills and creep up the narrow hollows between them, while beyond its corporate limits, both to the east and west, lie hundreds of acres covered with the vast plants of the world's greatest chemical corporations. The once silent and verdant valley of the Great Kanawha, with its beauty untouched and its great resources undreamed of, is now fast becoming the Ruhr of America.

OFFICERS AND RANGERS WHO BUILT AND GARRISONED FORT LEE—APRIL 1788

Colonel George Clendenin
Captain William Clendenin
Lieutenant George Shaw
Ensign Francis Watkins
Sergeant Shadrack Harriman
Sergeant Reuben Slaughter

Privates

John Tollypurt
Samuel Dunbar
John Burns
Isaac Snedicer
William Miller
John Buckle
James Edgar
Levi Morris
Joseph Burwell
William Boggs
William Hyllard
Charles Young
Alexander Clendenin

Michael Newhouse
Robert Aaron
William Carroll
Thomas Shirkey
Nicholas Null
Archer Price
Benjamin Morris
William Morris
William Turrell
John Cavinder
Henry Morris
William George
John Moore

ORGANIZATION OF KANAWHA COUNTY
OCTOBER 5th AND 6th, 1789

Justices

Colonel Thomas Lewis
Francis Watkins
Charles McClung
Benjamin Strother
Captain William Clendenin

David Robinson
George Alderson
Leonard Morris
James Van Bibber
Robert Clendenin

Civil Officers

Sheriff_____Thomas Lewis
Deputy Sheriff_____John Lewis
Clerk_____William H. Cavendish
Deputy Clerk_____Francis Watkins
Surveyor_____Reuben Slaughter

Commissioners of Revenue

David Robinson   John Van Bibber   Benjamin Strother

Coroners_____William Droddy and William Rogers
Magistrate_____Abner Prior
Magistrate_____Joseph Woods

Military Officers

County Lieutenant_____George Clendenin
Colonel_____Thomas Lewis
Lieutenant Colonel_____Daniel Boone
Major_____William Clendenin
Captain_____Leonard Cooper
Captain_____John Morris
Lieutenant_____John Young
Lieutenant_____James Van Bibber
Ensign_____William Owens
Ensign_____Alexander Clendenin

By Act of the General Assembly December 19, 1794, "Charlestown" Established and the Following Trustees Appointed.

Reuben Slaughter

Andrew Donnally, Sr.
William Clendenin
John Morris, Sr.
Leonard Morris

George Alderson
Abraham Baker
John Young
William Morris

MORRIS FAMILY OUTLINE

The pioneer, William Morris, Sr., (I) (1722-1792), married Elizabeth Stipps (1729-1795).
Their children were:
(I) (Major) William Morris, Jr., (1746-1802), married Catherine Carroll 1768.

Major Morris was an officer in the Battle of Point Pleasant, and was wounded. A born leader of men. Appointed one of first trustees town of Charleston. Was also a Magistrate. The year after his father's death, 1793, served as a delegate to the General Assembly and for five sessions thereafter. Lived at Kelly's Creek and is buried under the small brick church later erected there, and first known as Virginia's Chapel. A bronze tablet is placed on the outer wall of the church in his memory. See "The White House Tavern" for further data.

Children:

(1) Jane (1770-1854)—married Major John Hansford in Lewisburg, 1787. He was born in Orange County, Virginia, 1765, died Kanawha, 1850 (see Hansford Houses for further data). Their children were: Herman; William, b. 1790; Sarah, b. 1792, m. Wm. Morris; Morris, b. 1794, m. Catherine Morris, went West but returned to Paint Creek; Felix G., b. 1795 (see Hansford Houses); John, b. 1798; Carrol, b. 1799; Charles, b. 1800; Alvah, b. 1803; Marshall, b. 1807 (see Marshall Hansford House); Gallatin, b. 1808; Melton, b. 1811, m. Mary, daughter of Andrew Parks, whose mother was a niece of General George Washington.

(2) Gabriel Morris, b. 1772—no data.

(3) William Morris (III), b. 1775. Inventor of important tool for deep drilling of salt wells, never patented. It is in use today in certain types of deep drilling. Married Polly Barnes. (Her mother, Mrs. Joseph Barnes, was a sister of James Rumsey of Shepherdstown, inventor of the steamboat. Rumsey's daughter Susan married a man named Fraley and after his death married Jacob Skiles and came to Kanawha to live. Skiles was a well-known pioneer who owned 40,000 acres on Kelly's Creek and 32,000 on Gauley and elsewhere. Moved later to Kentucky.) Their eight children were: Joseph Barnes, m. Sally Hughes; Catherine, m. Morris Hansford; Roxie, m. Joel Alexander; Janette; Cynthia, m. Wm. White; Wm. Morris (IV), m. Julia Mitchell; Maria, m. Norborne Thomas; Thomas Morris.

(4) Catherine, b. 1778. A woman of character and determination, much admired and very popular with young people.

Once decided to attend a social function on the north side of the Kanawha, but found no boat on her side, so taking the clothes she wished to wear, placed them in a sugar trough, and pushing it ahead of her, swam to the other side, and attended the party. She was very casual about it, and said she had done the same thing several times. Married Charles Venable (see "The White House Tavern") in 1800, and lived on the south side of the Kanawha opposite Charleston where Venable Branch enters the river. She left no children.

(5) Carrol Morris, b. 1779; m. _____. Their children were: Maria, m. John Hansford; Letitia, m. Norris Whitteker; Parthenia; Catherine, m. Dr. Sutherland; Michael; Carrol.

(6) John Morris, b. 1783; m. Polly Duke. Sold his place to Aaron Stockton and moved to Missouri.

(7) Cynthia Morris, b. 1792; m. Isaac Noyes, leading merchant and salt-maker. They lived adjoining the Venable home on the south side of the Kanawha. Lived to be quite elderly and were the ancestors of the Noyes, Smith, Rand, Arnold, Ruby, and other well-known families of the Kanawha Valley.

(II) Henry (1747-1824)—second son of Wm. Morris, Sr., married Mary Byrd of Bath County, Virginia, who with her sister had previously been captured by Indians and held captive for seven years until she was sixteen years old.

Henry Morris was a physical giant, a man of unusual and remarkable strength and agility, who could turn somersaults like a circus performer, kick a hat from a nine-foot pole, according to old legends, and knock out an adversary with one blow. He was the most noted pugilist in the early history of the county, and, meeting all comers, was champion of the heavyweights, year after year — the championship being decided at every Muster of the County Militia. A mighty hunter, and totally without fear, Mr. Morris, against the advice of his brothers, settled in 1791 on Peters Creek of Gauley River, with his only neighbors the Edward McClung and Conrad Young families. It was a rugged and remote section some miles farther east than the cabins of other members of the Morris family. John Young, son of Conrad, who later became a well-known scout and Kanawha pioneer, and Henry Morris had a successful season hunting and trapping, but the disaster feared by his relatives took its toll in the following year when two of the young Morris daughters, Betsey, b. 1778, and Margaret, b. 1780, were slain and scalped by the Indians not far from their father's cabin. Henry Morris realized too late his mistake in settling in so lonely a spot, and alarmed for the safety of the rest of his family, quickly abandoned the location and returned to the Kelly's Creek settlement. The tragedy grieved and embittered him, and vowing no Indian should ever again cross his path and live, he avenged the death of his daughters many times. He was in Battle of Point Pleasant. Mr. and Mrs. Morris had five other children: Sarah, m. Charles Young, 1793, of Kanawha; Polly, m. Jesse James of Bath County; John, b. 1783, m. Jane Brown, 1807; Catherine, 1787-1853, m. William Byrd of Bath County; Lean, m. Archy Price.

(III) Leonard Morris I, b. 1748—third son of William Morris, Sr. Came to Kanawha Valley in 1774. Perhaps the best known of the Morris family. A man of strong character and long life. Veteran of the Battle of Point Pleasant. Valued county officer and citizen. Lived first at the mouth of Slaughter's Creek on the south side of Kanawha River, later moving farther west to mouth of Lens Creek, eight miles above Charleston (Marmet). (See illustration.)

One of the first justices of the new county of Kanawha (1789), and later one of the first trustees of the town of Charleston. So few ministers were available in the sparsely settled valley that in 1804 the County Court designated two of its magistrates as authorized to perform marriages, Leonard Morris being one of them. Served as sheriff in 1798, and was often appointed to "view" the route for proposed roads, and to perform other public services.

Leonard Morris was married twice, the first time to Miss Margaret Price. The six children of this marriage were:

(1) John, went to Missouri.
(2) Meredith, went south.
(3) Mary, m. Lawrence Bryan in 1791.
(4) Sarah, b. in Donnally's Fort, 1775, m. (recorded) 1796 the famous scout and canoeman, Fleming Cobb(s), (parents of Hiram Cobb who won peach brandy canoe wager). See Cobb Homestead.
(5) Elizabeth Morris, m. Robert Lewis.
(6) Leonard, Jr., m. Ann Austin in 1805.

The second marriage of Leonard Morris, Sr., was to Margaret Lykens of Greenbrier County and their ten children were:

(7) Charles, (1790-1861), m. Lucinda Crockett, the parents of Leonard, b. 1819, lived Brownstown, Hamilton, Francis d. young, Andrew went Texas, Charles Jr., Margaret, Parthinia, John.
(8) Nancy Morris, daughter of Leonard, Sr., m. John Shrewsbury.
(9) Parthenia, m. J. B. Crockett.

(10) Joshua, m. _____ Jarrett.
(11) Hiram, unmarried.
(12) Peter, m. _____ Jarrett, daughter of Jonathan Jarrett.
(13) Andrew, unmarried.
(14) Cynthia, m. Samuel Hensley (see Hensley House).
(15) Madison, m. Nancy Spurlick.
(16) Dickinson (see "Harmony Hill"), m. Susan, daughter of James Morris, a son of Levi Morris.

(IV) Joshua, b. 1752, fourth son of Wm. Morris, Sr., (will recorded 1824). A reliable man of good judgment. Fought in Battle of Point Pleasant. Married Frances Simms of Virginia, and they were the parents of nine children:
  (1) William Morris (V), m. Sarah Maria Hansford, lived at Gauley Bridge near the Falls.
  (2) Edmund.
  (3) Henry.
  (4) Elizabeth.
  (5) Lucy, m. Mr. Chapman.
  (6) Nancy, m. John Harriman. (See Harriman House.)
  (7) Thomas.
  (8) Mary.
  (9) John (1794-1862), lived east of Milton in Cabell County. A wealthy stockman. Prominent. Frequently elected to the Legislature. At beginning of war went east with family and slaves, and his valuable home was burned during his absence with great loss to his estate. Married twice—first to Mary Everett and they had a daughter Eliza who married William Love. The second marriage was in 1819 to Mary Kinard and their children were: Charles K., m. Martha A. Kilgore; Albert A., unmarried; Capt. Joseph W., killed Civil War, m. Sarah A. Russell; Edna E., m. Addison T. Buffington; James R., m. Helen M. Russell; Mary S., m. first, Ira T. McConihay and second, John P. Sibrell.

(V) Levi (Levy) Morris (1753-1834). Fifth son of Wm. Morris, Sr., was in Battle of Point Pleasant. In settling the estate of their father, Leonard and John Morris, as Executors, deeded to Levi Morris, 100 acres on the south side of the Kanawha "where Levi Morris now lives"—1793. This location was near the present town of Montgomery, and he is considered the first settler. Married, first, Margaret Stark; second, Margaret (Peggy) Jarrett. Children:
  (1) Cynthia, m. L. Brannon, a hatter.
  (2) William.
  (3) Benjamin, m. Amanda Hamilton.
  (4) James, m. Sarah Shelton and their children were George,

d. young; Levi, went to North Carolina; Benjamin, m. Ann Montgomery; James D., m. Alice L. Hanmaker; Susan, m. Dickinson Morris (son of Leonard Morris, Susan's great uncle) (See "Harmony Hill"); Amanda, m. E. F. Flagg; Sarah, m. Wm. Hamilton; Ellen, m. Silas Custer; Eva, m. Dr. Mauser of Kentucky; Margaret, m. Joshua Harriman; Emma, m., first, Dr. Early; second, William Riggs (See "Old Riggs Place"); Mary, d. young. The other children of Levi Morris were:
(5) Frances, m. William Spurlock.
(6) G. W., m. Sarah Hamilton.
(7) Elizabeth, m. Levi Spurlock.
(8) Martha, m. Mr. Burgess.

(VI) Captain John Morris (1755-1818), sixth son of Wm. Morris, Sr. In Battle of Point Pleasant and with George Rogers Clark Expedition 1778-1779. Captain of Militia in the organization of Kanawha County, 1789. Also was appointed one of the first trustees of the town of Charleston, 1794. One of the best known of the Morris brothers. Highly regarded. Lived on south side of the Kanawha five miles above Charleston. Built a fort. Then lived at mouth of Campbell's Creek. Later moved to Cabell County. Very active in command of Rangers during border warfare. Married Margaret Droddy, the Droddy lands adjoining those of John Morris. Children: John Morris, Jr.; Edmund, first clerk of Cabell County; Levi; William; Thomas Asbury, who became a Bishop in the Methodist Church.

(VII) Carlos, Carrol, or Achilles, seventh son of Wm. Morris, Sr., b. 1760, m. Elizabeth Jarrett.

(VIII) Benjamin Morris (1770-1829), eighth son of Wm. Morris, Sr. In the settlement of his father's estate Benjamin Morris was deeded by the executors, who were his brothers Leonard and John, 135 acres of land on the southwest side of the Kanawha. This was no doubt a part of the tract below and including the site of Montgomery upon which Levi Morris was then living and which had been deeded to him in the settlement. There seems to have been a good deal of brotherly land "swapping" later. Benjamin built a brick house in 1824 on the north side of the river opposite these lands, but sold it to Levi and moved across on the south side to his lands there, which later became the Montgomery farm. Presumably Levi then shifted sides and moved across the river to live in the brick house on the north bank.

Benjamin Morris was a great hunter, and if the magnitude of the tales told of his prowess be even partly true, he would still be no mean shot by any standards. One such tale states that he killed 133 bears in one day.

Mr. Morris married Nancy Jarrett. The Jarrett family were early settlers on Muddy Creek in Greenbrier County, and as the Morris family lived on the same creek before coming to the Kanawha, the several Morris-Jarrett marriages likely resulted from this early acquaintanceship.

Children of Benjamin Morris were:
(1) Achilles, went to Mexico.
(2) Frances, m. Wm. Shelton, went west.
(3) Virginia, m. J. Kincaid of Ohio.
(4) Jane, m. Jacob Johnson.
(5) Celia, m. Captain John Harvey. Their son Morris Harvey became well known in West Virginia, where his name is perpetuated in that of Morris Harvey College in Charleston. Fanny, daughter of Captain Harvey, m. Captain Snelling C. Farley of steamboat fame.
(6) Eden, m. Miss Edgar of Greenbrier.
(7) Leah, m. Mr. Pardy.

(IX) Elizabeth Morris, b. 1772, ninth child and first daughter of Wm. Morris, Sr. Married Michael See who had come to the Kanawha with the Morris brothers and had helped them build Fort Morris. He had taken part in the Battle of Point Pleasant and he and his family were residing at Fort Randolph in the summer of 1792 when he was killed by Indians. The day of his death his wife gave birth to their son, William See. Elizabeth Morris See married (2nd) Thomas Cobb(s) in 1799.

(X) Frances, (Frankey or Fannie Morris), b. 1773, tenth child of Wm. Morris, Sr. Married John Jones (1755-1838) of Culpeper, Virginia, who first came to Valley with army of General Lewis. Wounded in Battle of Point Pleasant. In Revolutionary Army. After the war returned to Kanawha Valley. Took patents on 749 acres on Kanawha River, in 1797, 400 acres in Teays Valley, and for land on Paint Creek, where he lived and is buried at the present town of Pratt, which was his farm site. Children:
(1) Gabriel Jones.
(2) Nancy, m. Huddleston.
(3) Frances, m. Shelton.

WILL OF WILLIAM MORRIS, SR., THE FIRST TO BE RECORDED IN KANAWHA COUNTY 1792

In the name of, God, Amen. I William Morris Sen'r of the County of Kenhawa & Commonwealth of Va. Being Weak in body, but of perfect mind & memory And calling to mind the Mortality of Body And know that it is appointed for all Men once to die, do make & ordain This my Last Will & Testament. Firstly I will & bequeath my soul unto the hands of Almighty God the giver, And my body to the dust of the earth To be buried in a Christian Like & desent maner at the descretion of my executors hereafter named; Not doubting but at the General Resurrection they will again Reunite by the Almighty Power of God.

And as Touching such worldly Estate wherewith It has pleased God to bless me in this life do will and devise in the following manner & from That is to say I will & Bequeath to my Two sons, To wit, Levi and Benj, One hundred Acres Each of the Tract of Land whereon they now Live to include there present settlements which lands I do hereby will & decree that my Executors, hereafter named do convey a title in fee simple to them. And their heirs forever. And I do hereby also will & direct that my said Executors do in like manner convey in fee simple To my son William Morris & his heirs forever. The residue of the said tract of land above mentioned Which is his own property; Altho Included in a grant or patent Issued from the Register of Virginia in my name. I further will & devise that the whole Residue of my estate both real & personal be equally divided Amongst My Ten Children, to wit, William Henry Leonard Joshua, John Carlus Levi Benjamin Elizabeth & Frankey. To be them & their several Lawfull heirs freely & fully possessed & enjoyed Provided nevertheless that my Loving & Lawful wife Elizabeth Morris have all my movable Estate In her possession during her natural life at the termination of which said whole estate with the Increase thereof shall be divided as aforesaid. But if she my said wife Elizabeth should again Ingage herself in the Bonds of Wedlock with any person, then & on that condition It is my will & desire that my whole estate revert to my children or their Lawfull heirs agreeable to this my will & Testament, Prohibiting at all times my said Wife Elizabeth from selling or in any wise disposing of any of my aforesaid Estate. And lastly I do hereby constitute & appoint my Two sons, To wit, Leonard & John Morris Executors of this my last will & Testament; Hereby revoking, disallowing & dianulling all & every other Will & Testament by me in any wise Made in any manner or form whatever, Ratifying & Conforming this & no other to be my last will & testament. In Testimony Whereof I have hereunto set my hand & seal this 28th day of Feb. Anno Dominr 1792.

          his
       William M Morris
          mark.

FAMILY OF SAMUEL SHREWSBURY, SR. (1763—April 1, 1835), AND MARY PERRY (POLLY) DICKINSON (1768-1853), Daughter of Col. John Dickinson—Married, December, 1785
10 Children

(I) John Dickinson Shrewsbury (1786-1845), m. 1812 Nancy Jane Morris (1792-1835), dau. of Capt. Leonard Morris. Six children. Lived Charleston.
    (1) Charles Morris, b. 1814, m. (1) 1840, cousin Mary Morris, (2) 1872, Elizabeth Ralston.
    (2) Parthenia, m. 1840, Robert Filson Hudson. Five children.
    (3) Samuel M., d. 1861, m. Priscilla Warth. Five children. Settled Missouri.
    (4) Andrew M., unmarried.
    (5) Leonard M., unmarried. Went California as a "49er."
    (6) Margaret F., b. 1830, m. Dr. E. H. C. Bailey. Five children. Settled Missouri.

(II) Samuel Shrewsbury, Jr., 1789 (Bath County), unmarried.

(III) Martha Usher (Patsy) (Bath County), (1791-1874), m. 1816, Jacob Van Meter (1788-1874). Eight children. Moved Kentucky.

(IV) William Shrewsbury, (Bath County), 1794-1882, m. 1823, cousin Rhoda P. Shrewsbury of Bedford. Lived Charleston.

(V) Elizabeth Dabney (1796-1829), unmarried.

(VI) Joel, Jr. ("Little Joel"), (1798-1849), m. 1828, Fannie Burns Quarrier, dau. of Alexander Quarrier, Sr. Eight children. Lived Charleston.

(VII) Ann "Nancy" Lee, b. 1801, m. 1823 John Rogers, Jr. Nine children. Moved Cincinnati.

(VIII) Charles Lewis (1804-1872), m. Eleanor Woodburn, 1839. Lived Indiana.

(IX) Adam Dickinson, b. 1807, died at one year.

(X) Juliet, b. 1809, m. 1829 James Craik. Admitted to the bar. Then studied for ministry and was rector of St. John's Episcopal Church, Charleston, 1839-1844, when he removed to Kentucky. Eleven children.

FAMILY OF JOHN SHREWSBURY, SR., b.........., d. 1835, AND MARTHA USHER (PATSY) DICKINSON, Daughter of Col. John Dickinson—Married 1793. 3 Children.

(I) Samuel, Jr., "Good Sammy," m. 1827, Laura Angela Parks (1810-1885), dau. of Harriet Washington and Major Andrew Parks of Baltimore. Mrs. Parks was a daughter of Samuel Washington, brother of General George Washington.
Children of Samuel and Laura:
(1) Martha Dickinson, d. 1885, m. Nicholas Fitzhugh.
(2) Lawrence Washington.
(3) Andrew Parks.
(4) Harriet Washington, unmarried.
(5) Cornelia, m. E. S. Gans.
(6) Samuel.
(7) Henry Clay.
(8) Laura, the second wife of Nicholas Fitzhugh.

(II) Martha (Patsy), m. Joseph Darneal.
Children:
(1) Martha Dickinson, m. cousin William D. Shrewsbury, son of Joel, Sr.
(2) John Shrewsbury Darneal.

(III) John D. Shrewsbury, Jr., d. prior to June 30, 1831, m. cousin Julia B., daughter of Joel Shrewsbury, Sr.
Children:
(1) Martha Dickinson, m. Dr. Lawrence Augustine Washington, son of Lawrence A. Washington of Red House Shoals, Putnam County, who was a nephew of George Washington, his father, Samuel Washington of "Harewood," Jefferson County, being a full brother.
(2) Joel D.
(3) John Dickinson, Jr.
(4) Julian, referred to in will of John, Sr., as "my unfortunate grandson."

FAMILY OF JOEL SHREWSBURY, SR. (1778—March 19, 1859) AND SALLY DICKINSON, (1776-1842), Daughter of Joseph Dickinson of Bedford County—Married 1803. 8 Children.

(I) Julia B., b. 180__, m. (1) cousin John Shrewsbury, (2) James Turner.
(II) Elizabeth (1804-1843), m. General Lewis Ruffner, 1826.
(III) Caroline Winston, b. 1806, m. Alexander Washington Quarrier.

(IV) William D., (1808-1881), m. cousin Martha Darneal (1814-1875). 16 children.
(V) Samuel T., b. 1809, died at sixteen.
(VI) Sallie Lee (1812-1830), m. John D. Lewis (1800-1882), grandson of Col. John Dickinson of Bath County. One child, Joel S. Mr. Lewis was married four times, as follows:
(2) Ann Dickinson, dau. of Col. William Dickinson. 3 children: Sally J., m. Henry Clay Dickinson, bro. of John Q.; Charles C., m. Miss Elizabeth Wilson; Mary, m. John Quincy Dickinson, bro. of Henry C.
(3) Betty Darneal, dau. of Jacob Darneal. 2 children: Julia, m. James H. Beal of Mason County; Wm., m. Jennie G. Stanley.
(4) Mrs. Sally Spears—no children.
(VII) Dickinson, m. Mary McConihay.
(VIII) Eliza (1814-1898), m. Benjamin S. Smithers (1809-1881).

The will of Joel Shrewsbury, Sr., dated September 11, 1858, and probated March 22, 1859, three days after his death, is a characteristic and interesting document of fifteen pages, skillfully written by W. A. Quarrier. It shows a carefully considered and affectionate regard for his children. It also shows toward his numerous slaves a kindly thoughtfulness. Each is enumerated by name, and directions are given concerning their disposition among his descendants. He specified that certain ones should not be sold, but should have plots of ground for their own cultivation, and the executors were charged with seeing that none should come to want.

FAMILY OF COLONEL ANDREW DONNALLY, JR., (1778-1849) and MARGERY VAN BIBBER (1781-1850) MARRIED 1801. 13 CHILDREN.

These four died in infancy: Augustus, 1803; Charles, 1804; William Harrison, 1813-1814; Charles A., 1826-1828.

(I) Chloe (1805-1830), m. J. Henry Fry (1798-1863), great-grandson of Col. Joshua Fry who served in the Colonial Army in 1754. Two children:
   (1) Margery Jane, m. Alvin Goshorn—descendants are Harry Snyder (Charleston), Alvin Snyder (Washington, D. C.), Rear Admiral C. P. Snyder, U.S.N.
   (2) Philip Fry, m. Emily F. Reynolds—two children, Charles and Kate.

(II) Caroline (1807-1839), m. Col. John Lewis, grandson of Gen. Andrew Lewis, three sons, one daughter:
   (1) Andrew.
   (2) James.
   (3) John.
   (4) Margery, m., first, Edward Kenna by whom she had a son, Senator John E. Kenna and two daughters, and married, second, Richard Ashby, and had a son Walter Ashby.

(III) Van Bibber (1809-1882), d. in Buffalo, m. 1832, Mary B. Waggoner of Mason County. Ten children of whom eight reached maturity:
   (1) Ellen, m. Hamilton Morris, and had son Hamilton Morris, Jr., m. Margaret Bibby.
   (2) Andrew, m. Hannah English, five daughters:
      (a) Nina, m. Frank Cornwell.
      (b) Mary, m. T. A. Draper.
      (c) Anna, m. Forest Washington.
      (d) Julia, m. Herbert Wood.
      (e) Flora, m. Henry Brawley.
   (3) Cornelia, m. Henry Cushman.
   (4) Charles, m. Bertie Porter, three children, moved to Virginia.
   (5) Belle—unmarried.
   (6) Ada—unmarried.
   (7) Emma.
   (8) Wm. Boyd, b. 1851, m. Sally Ashton Cotton, 1881. Children:
      (a) Sadie, m. Lester L. Sheets, 3 children, Donnally, William, Dorothy.
      (b) John Cotton Donnally of Washington, D. C., m. Mary Annette Meyers and had Mary Annette and Henrietta Lee.

       (c) Boyd Donnally, m. Charlie Littlepage.
       (d) Henry F. Donnally, m. Erdena McGraw and had Sally Ashton and Henry Fitzhugh, Jr., who m. Ruth Turner and had Fitzhugh and Andrew Van Bibber.
       (e) Dorothy Donnally, m. Robert E. L. Ruffner.

(IV) Dryden Donnally (1811-1885), m. Mary R. Thomas. Nine children:
Following died young: Edward and Mary Rebecca.
Those unmarried were: Anna, Alma (?), Dryden, Jr.
Andrew lived in Idaho.
Fanny, m. James Crawford, had Emma, m. Ben Pine, Molly, m. John O'Shea;
Moses W., m. Molly Starke in 1887, four children: Moses S., m. Virginia Housekeeper and had son Moses S., Jr.
Edward T., m. Ercella Rhodes.
Willis Ward unmarried.
Mary, m. William T. Lively.

(V) Jane M. Donnally (1815-1892), m. Henry Fry who had been the husband of her deceased older sister Chloe. Four children:
    (1) James H. Fry, m. Julia Welch and had two sons, Henry Fry of Charleston and John Fry, unmarried.
    (2) Joseph L. Fry, m. Lila Follansbee, children: Frank, Joe, Cleveland, Darrow, Jane, and Virginia.
    (3) Mary Fry.
    (4) Sally Fry.

(VI) Andrew Franklin (1817-1883), m. Lucy Brown, three children to reach maturity.

(VII) John James (1820-1845), m. Catherine C. (Kitty) Morris in 1841 and had two daughters: Mary Virginia, m. Chas. C. Aleshire and had two sons died young; Lallah James, m. James S. Blackaller and had three children, Lavinia, Henry M., and Arthur.

(VIII) William (1822-____), m. Margaret Wood. Children:
    (1) James H., m. Anna Menager.
    (2) Edward W., m. Bessie Day and had son Edward J.
    (3) Lizzie, m. Monroe C. Snapp.
    (4) Wood, m. Mary Ruby and their daughter m. Charles Venable.
    (5) Wirt W., m. Lena Meadows and had son, Wirt W., Jr., who m. Dorothy Davis.
    (6) Nellie, m. C. A. Zirkle, two children: Howard, m. Edna McDaniel, and Ersythe, m. James Weimer.
    (7) Maude, m. A. B. Lewis and had Charles Pell Lewis who m. Marian Stine and W. Don Lewis who m. Vertna Harris.

(IX) Lewis Fry (1824-1895), m. first, in 1849 Eliza M. Reynolds (b. above Kanawha City (1830-1858)—two children:

(1) Carrie, m. Wm. E. Truslow and had
   (a) Lewis D.
   (b) Frances L., m. Norman S. Fitzhugh.
   (c) Wm. H., b. 1887, m. Hilda Shober.
   (d) Brown D., m. Clara Stine.
   (e) Harold G., m. Mabel Morton.
(2) Virginia Donnally, d. unmarried. Lewis Fry m., second, in 1859 Miriam Welch and had six children: Two died young, two died unmarried, and (5) Katharine, m. Magnus A. Tate and had dau. Miriam who m. Brue Maxon, (6) Amelia Smith Donnally, m. W. G. Hubbard.

FAMILY OF COL. ALEXANDER QUARRIER— THE KANAWHA PIONEER (1746-1827). Married

(1) Elizabeth Dannenberry (d. 1797), 1783.
Eight Children:

(1) Alexander Quarrier, 1783—d. infancy.
(2) Harriet—died infancy.
(3) Harriet B. (1787-1875), m. James G. Laidley (See "Glenwood").
(4) Eliza Washington, m., first, Samuel Dryden; second, John F. Faure (See "The Elms").
(5) Margaret Alexander, m., first, James Lynch; second, Robert Caldwell Woods.
(6) Helen Starke, m. John Eoff, M. D.
(7) Alexander Washington, m. Caroline Winston Shrewsbury.
(8) Betsy Dannenberry, m. Aaron Whitteker.

Married (2) Sally Burns (d. 1852), 1798.
Eight Children:

(9) William Burns, b. 1799, m. Mary A. L. Hudson.
(10) Frances—died infancy.
(11) Monroe, m. Elizabeth A. Wilson.
(12) James Young, m. Letetia B. Chilton.
(13) Gustavius Buchanan, m. Elizabeth R. Hudson.
(14) Archibald Alexander McRae, m. Mary H. Fitzhugh.
(15) Fannie Burns, m. Joel Shrewsbury, Jr., son of Samuel Shrewsbury, Sr.
(16) Virginia Southgate, m., first, John F. Snodgrass; second, Beverly Smith.

PARTIAL LIST OF PRE-CIVIL WAR SALT-MAKERS

1797—Elisha Brooks
1806—David Ruffner & Co.
1806—Tobias Ruffner
1815—Aaron Stockton
1818—William Tompkins
1820—William Dickinson
1820—Joel Shrewsbury

    Peter Grant
    Lewis Ruffner
    John Reynolds
    Luke Wilcox
    Lewis Summers
    Dr. John Cabell
    John & Samuel Shrewsbury
    Andrew Donnally
    A. Donnally & William Steele & Co.
    Donnally & Steele & P. Alexander
    A. Donnally & L. Morris
    A. Donnally & L. Welch
    A. Donnally & Charles Brown
    Joseph Lovell
    James Bream
    Isaac & Bradford Noyes
    Charles Venable
    Daniel Ruffner
    Andrew Parks
    John Warth
    L. & C. Morris
    William Whitteker
    Charles Reynolds
    Armstrong

James C. MacFarland

William R. Cox
John Anderson
James Hewitt
C. G. & C. Reynolds
Van B. Reynolds
Henry H. Wood
J. D. Lewis
John Welch
W. D. Shrewsbury
Moses Fuqua
Dr. R. E. Putney
George Warth
John Rogers
Stuart Robinson
R. C. M. Lovell
Dr. Spicer Patrick
J. H. Fry
Dr. Henry Rogers
Silas Ruffner
Jacob Darneal
W. C. Brooks
William Graham
John Clarkson
Dr. J. P. Hale
H. W. Goodwin
Charles Cox
David Clarkson
Gus Quarrier
Jesse Hudson
John Slack & James Ogborn
Dr. F. A. A. Cobbs
J. M. Laidley

Lewis Ruffner, Jr.
J. W. Oakes
William Dickinson, Jr.

KANAWHA RIFLEMEN

In Charleston on Kanawha Boulevard is a small public park, once the private cemetery of the Ruffner family. It contains a memorial to the Kanawha Riflemen, which bears the following roster of names:

THIS MEMORIAL
ERECTED
BY THE KANAWHA RIFLEMEN CHAPTER
UNITED DAUGHTERS OF THE CONFEDERACY
IN HONOR OF THE KANAWHA RIFLEMEN
FIRST ORGANIZATION OF THE COMPANY 1856

Captain _____George S. Patton
First Lieutenant _____Andrew Moore
Second Lieutenant _____Nicholas Fitzhugh
Third Lieutenant _____Henry D. Ruffner

SECOND ORGANIZATION 1858

Captain _____David L. Ruffner
First Lieutenant _____Richard Q. Laidley
Second Lieutenant _____Gay Carr
Third Lieutenant _____John P. Donaldson

THIRD ORGANIZATION 1861

Captain _____Richard Q. Laidley
First Lieutenant _____John P. Donaldson
Second Lieutenant _____Henry W. Rand
Third Lieutenant _____Alanson Arnold

NON-COMMISSIONED OFFICERS AND PRIVATES

Arnold, E. S.
Barton, Norman
Blaine, Charles
Boswell, Martin
Brodt, J. T.
Bradford, Henry
Brooks, W. B.
Broun, Thos. L.
Broun, Jo. M.
Brown, Siline
Cabell, H. Clay
Caldwell, William
Carr, Gay
Carr, John O.
Chambers, John

Chewning, Charles
Clarkson, A. Q.
Cook, Walton
Cox, Frank
Cushman, William
Doddridge, J. E., Jr.
Doddridge, Philip
DeGruyter, M. F.
Fry, James H., Jr.
Grant, Thos. T.
Hale, John P.
Hansford, Carroll M.
Hare, Robert
Hopkins, _____
Lewis, James F.

Lewis, Joel S.
Lewis, John
McQueen, Archibald
McFarland, Henry D.
McMullen, John
McClelland, Robert
Malone, William
Mathews, John
Miller, Samuel A.
Miller, H.
Noyes, Benjamin
Noyes, Frank
Noyes, James B.
Noyes, James B., Jr.
Noyes, William

Noyes, John
Parks, Cecil
Parks, Bushrod
Patrick, A. S. Dr.
Patrick, John
Quarrier, Joel S.
Quarrier, William A.
Quarrier, Monroe
Rand, Noyes
Read, Fred M.
Reynolds, Fenton M.
Reynolds, William
Roberts, Thomas
Ruby, Edward

Ruby, John C.
Rundle, John
Ruffner, David L.
Ruffner, Daniel, Jr.
Ruffner, Joel, Jr.
Ruffner, Meridith P.
Ruffner, Andrew L.
Shrewsbury, Andrew
Shrewsbury, Joel
Spessard, Jacob
Smith, Isaac Noyes
Smith, Thomas
Singleton, Albert
Snyder, W. B.
Smithers, David

Summers, William S.
Summers, Geo. W., Jr.
Swann, John S.
Swann, Thomas B.
Teays, Stephen T.
Thompson, Cameron L.
Thompson, Thornton
Turner, Benjamin F.
Watkins, Joseph F.
Wehrle, Meinhart
Welch, George L.
Welch, Levi
Welch, James
Wilson, Henry
Wilson, W. A.

Dedicated to those who served in the Confederate Army—1861-1865

CHARLESTON STREETS NAMED FOR EARLY KANAWHA RESIDENTS

Alderson	Fife	Reynolds
Bradford	Goshorn	Ruffner Avenue
Brooks	Hansford	Summers
Bream	Hale	Stockton
Baines	Laidley	Smith
Brown	Lewis	Slack
Carr	Littlepage Avenue	Sentz
Clendenin	Lovell Drive	Simms
Dryden	Morris	Shrewsbury
Dunbar	McFarland	Truslow
Dickinson	Noyes Avenue	Venable
Donnally	Rand	Whitteker (Whittaker)
Estill	Patrick St. & Bridge	Welch
Fry	Quarrier	Young

STREETS WITH EARLY ASSOCIATIONAL MEANING

Greenbrier—Kanawha's parent county.

Bullitt—owner of first surveys of Charleston area.

Kanawha (Street) Boulevard—named for the river.

Washington—George Washington was a large landowner in Kanawha Valley.

Daniel Boone Drive—name of First Lieutenant Colonel of Kanawha County.

"Edgewood" Drive—name of Major Carr's home in vicinity.

"Glenwood" Avenue—name of Laidley-Summers Estate.

"Beechwood" Avenue—later name of Dr. Patrick's former home, "Forest Hill."

Bibliography

BOOKS

AMBLER, CHARLES H. *West Virginia, the Mountain State* (1940).
ATKINSON, GEORGE W. *History of Kanawha County from its Organization in 1789 until the Present Time (1876).*
ATKINSON, GEORGE W. *Bench and Bar of West Virginia* (1919).
Biographical Dictionary of the American Congress.
CALLAHAN, JAMES MORTON. *Semi-Centennial History of West Virginia* (1913).
COOK, ROY B. *The Annals of Fort Lee* (1935).
COOK, ROY B. *Washington's Western Lands* (1930).
DAYTON, RUTH WOODS. *Greenbrier Pioneers and Their Homes* (1942).
Dictionary of American Biography, Various Volumes.
GALLAHER, D. C. *Genealogical Notes of the Miller-Quarrier-Shrewsbury-Dickinson Families* (1917).
HALE, JOHN P. *History of the Great Kanawha Valley,* Vol. 1 (1891).
HALE, JOHN P. *Trans-Allegheny Pioneers.*
HARDESTY, H. H. *Historical and Geographical Encyclopedia* (1884).
HOWE, GENERAL HENRY. *Historical Collections of Virginia* (1845).
JOHNSTON, DAVID E. *History of the Middle New River Settlement* (1906).
KENNY, HAMILL. *West Virginia Place Names* (1945).
KENTON, EDNA. *Simon Kenton, His Life and Period 1755-1836* (1930).
KING, EDWARD. *The Great South* (1875).
LAIDLEY, W. S. *History of Charleston and Kanawha County* (1911).
LEWIS, VIRGIL A. *History of West Virginia* (1889).
LEWIS, VIRGIL A. *First Biennial Report of Department of Archives & History* (1906).
LEWIS, VIRGIL A. *Second Biennial Report of Department of Archives & History* (1908).
LEWIS, VIRGIL A. *Third Biennial Report of Department of Archives & History* (1911).
LEWIS, VIRGIL A. *Life and Times of Anne Bailey* (1891).
LEWIS, VIRGIL A. *Handbook of West Virginia.*
LEWIS, VIRGIL A. *History and Government of West Virginia* (1896).
MEADE, BISHOP WILLIAM. *Old Churches, Ministers and Families of Virginia* (1857).
MILLER, THOMAS C. AND MAXWELL, HU. *History of West Virginia and its People,* Vols. 2 and 3 (1913).

National Cyclopedia of American Biography—various volumes.
PARKMAN, FRANCES. *Montcalm & Wolf*, Vol. 1 (1901).
PORTER, SARAH HARVEY. *Life and Times of Anne Royall* (1909).
ROYALL, ANNE. *Sketches of History, Life and Manners in the United States* (1826).
Shepherd Supplement to Hening Statutes at Large (Virginia) Vol. 1.
STRICKLER, HARRY M. *Forerunners* (1925).
SUMMERS, FESTUS P. *The Baltimore & Ohio in the Civil War* (1939).
THWAITES AND KELLOGG. *Dunmore's War* (1905).
Virginia State Papers, Calendar Of, Vol. 1.
WADDELL, JAMES A. *Annals of Augusta County 1726-1872* (1902).
WASHINGTON, BOOKER T. *Up From Slavery*.
West Virginia Geological Survey, Vol. 8 (1937).
WHITE, STEWART EDWARD. *Daniel Boone, Wilderness Scout* (1926).
WITHERS, ALEXANDER S. *Chronicles of Border Warfare* (1831).

PAMPHLETS, NEWSPAPER AND MAGAZINE ARTICLES

"A Genealogical Table and History of the Quarrier Family in America," By a Descendant (1890).
AMBLER, C. H. "The Diary of John D. Sutton, 1770-1839; and Kanawha County Land Grants, Sept. 20, 1791—May 11, 1797," *West Virginia History Magazine* (April, 1943).
CARPENTER, CHARLES. "Early Maps of West Virginia Territory," *West Virginia Review* (December, 1931).
"Bridge Across mouth of Elk Proposed," *Charleston Daily Mail*, (August 29, 1937).
COLE, JOHN L. "How First Settler Defied Dangers of Old Gauley."
COOK, ROY B. "Annals of Pharmacy in West Virginia" (1946).
Court Records, Kanawha County—Deeds, Wills, Marriages, etc.
CRAWFORD, E. T., JR. "Salt—Pioneer, Chemical Industry of Kanawha Valley," *West Virginia Review*, (March, April, May, 1936).
EDWARDS, W. H. "Reminiscences of Alva Hansford of Kanawha County, 1884," *West Virginia History Magazine*.
ESKEW, GARNETT L. "Drilling Club Turned to War," *Charleston Gazette* (May 21, 1922).
ESKEW, GARNETT L. "Only Five Homes on West Side in 1861," *Charleston Gazette* (1922).
FRANKLIN, ROBERT S. "Ruffner Lineage of Mary Roger Ruffner Payne" (1938).
HOGE, MARY RHINEHART. "Salt on the Frontier" (Thesis, 1931).
HALE, J. P. "Historical and Descriptive Sketch of the Great Kanawha," *West Virginia History Magazine* (April, 1901).
HEDRICK, CHARLES. "History of Ruffner Family of Kanawha" (1884).

"History of the Presbyterian Congregation and other Churches of 'Kenhawa,' 1804-1900," (1930).

HULL, FORREST. "Kid Glove Soldier," *Tracks*, C. & O. RR. Magazine (November, 1944).

JEFFERIES, THOMAS G. "Memorable Events in the Life of Charleston" (1939).

JOHNSTON, ROSS B. "West Virginians in the Revolution," *West Virginia History Magazine* (April, 1944).

LAIDLEY, W. S. "Colonel Joseph Lovell," *West Virginia History Magazine*, (1904-05).

"Memorial of the Manufacturers of Salt in the County of Kanawha, Virginia, against Repeal of the Duty on Imported Salt" (1828).

"Monument Erected in Memory Kanawha Riflemen," *Charleston Gazette* (June, 1922).

RUFFNER, DR. WM. HENRY. "The Ruffners," *West Virginia History Magazine* (April, 1901).

RUFFNER, REV. HENRY, (President of Washington College). "Notes of a Tour from Virginia to Tennessee in the months of July and August 1838," *Southern Literary Messenger* (January, 1839).

"Salt Seeker Drilled First Oil Well on Continent," *Charleston Gazette* (May 21, 1922).

STUTLER, BOYD B. "Anne Royall, a Militant Free Lance," *West Virginia Review* (November, 1931).

SUMMERS, GEORGE W. "Boat Works Once Top City Industry."

SUMMERS, GEORGE W. "Valley's Oldest Presbyterian Church Plans Centennial."

SUMMERS, GEORGE W. "Pages From the Past" (1935).

SUMMERS, GEORGE W. "Kanawha Street Home. Believed oldest in the City," undated clipping, *Charleston Daily Mail*.

SUMMERS, LEWIS. "Journal of a Tour from Alexandria, Virginia, to Gallipolis, Ohio, 1808," *Southern Historical Magazine*, Vol. 1 (February, 1892).

INDEX OF PERSONS

A

Adams, Charles Lee—188
Adams, John Quincy—171
Adams, Mrs. John Quincy—171
Alderson, George—47, 67, 68, 69
Alderson, John—222
Alexander, Leonora Caroline Ruffner—115
Alexander, William A.—115
Arbuckle, Captain Matthew—29, 212
Archer, William—166
Audubon, John J.—58, 106

B

Bailey, Anne (Hennis)—38-45, 78, 174
Bailey, John—40
Baines, Harriet Laidley—278
Baines, John D.—278
Baker, Abraham—69
Banks, Henry—21, 31, 32
Barnum, Phineas Taylor—47
Barton, General Seth—190
Batts, Captain Thomas—2, 3
Bennett, Dr. Jesse—67
Benton, Thomas H.—188
Bernhardt, Sarah—256
Boone, Chloe Van Bibber—54, 215
Boone, Daniel—9, 13, 21, 48, 50-58, 98, 106, 215
Boone, Daniel Morgan—51, 57
Boone, Israel—51
Boone, James—51
Boone, Jemima—51
Boone, Jesse—50, 51, 54, 55, 57, 215
Boone, Lavinia—51
Boone, Nathan—51, 56, 57
Boone, Rebecca (Bryan)—51, 56, 57
Boone, Susannah—51
Boreman, Governor Arthur—254
Bream, Major James—226, 233, 264, 269-272
Bream, Lavinia V. M.—226, 264
Breckenridge, John C.—188
Brennen, Mrs. Dennis (Eleanor Baillie)—89
Brigham, Alethia Bream—269

Brooke, Robert—70
Brooks, Elisha—122, 124
Brooks, Frederick—71
Broun, Thomas—245
Brown, Benjamin B.—223, 224
Brown, Miss Ceres—223
Brown, Charles—25, 220, 250
Brown, Mrs. Fayette A. Lovell (Shrewsbury)—224
Brown, Judge James H.—223
Brown, James F.—224
Brown, Rev. James M.—200
Brown, Miss Jean—223
Brown, Rev. John C.—183
Brown, Louise M. Beuhring—224
Brown, Mary—183
Bullitt, Cuthbert—32
Bullitt, Thomas—12, 18, 32
Burlew, Abraham—255
Burlew, Elizabeth Rand—255
Burlew, Noyes S.—255
Burns, Robert—239
Buster, Claudius—220
Butler, Colonel James—164

C

Cabell, C. A.—205
Cabell, Hewitt—205
Cabell, John D.—127
Cabell, John J.—125
Cabell, Lavinia Wood—205
Calvert, C.—195
Calvert, Drusilla Oakes—195
Calvert, Eliza Oakes—195
Calvert, F.—195
Caperton, Captain—40
Carr, Major James L.—183, 276
Carr, Sallie Cook—183
Carroll, Joseph—40, 76
Carson, Kit—51
Cavendish, William—47
Chilton, Samuel—221
Christy, Lawrence—205
Clark, General George Rogers—12, 20, 213
Clay, Henry—106, 149, 188, 274
Clendenin, Alexander—31, 48, 67, 99
Clendenin, Charles—31, 69, 134

313

Clendenin, Colonel George—21, 31-37, 41, 46-49, 55, 56, 60, 61, 66-70, 81, 99, 122, 123, 137, 138, 190, 213, 235
Clendenin, Jemimah—33
Clendenin, Mary Ellen—31
Clendenin, Robert—31, 47
Clendenin, William—31, 33, 35, 43, 47, 48, 67-70, 75, 99, 100, 139
Cobb (Cobbs), Fleming—59-65, 67
Cobb, Fleming, Jr.—65
Cobb, Hiram—62
Cobb, Jane Dickinson—155
Cobb, Mrs. Philena—249
Coleman, Almira Anderson—196
Coleman, Bradford—91
Coleman, Kathleen Veazey—91
Coleman, Captain N. B.—196
Comstock, Dr. Lucius—115
Cook, Dr. Roy Bird—76
Cooper, Leonard—44, 48
Cornstalk, Chief—210, 211, 213
Couch, Rachel Brown—181
Cowan, (Gardner) Ann Malvina—164, 166, 167
Cox, Elizabeth Wood—205
Cox, William R., Jr.—205
Craik, George Washington—244
Craik, James—150, 243, 244
Craik, Dr. James—244
Craik, Juliet Shrewsbury—244
Craik, Maria D. Tucker—244
Craik, Marianne Ewell—244
Crocker, Mr. and Mrs. W. T. L.—80
Crossman, Henrietta—256
Crowley, J. B.—263
Cunningham, Charles—203, 205
Cunningham, Emily Hogue—203, 205, 218

D

D'Aberdiel, M.—187
Davis, Jefferson—153
Davis, Thomas—60
Dawson, Governor Wm. M. O.—255
De Bienville, Captain Celoron—4, 5, 10
De la Galissoniere, Marquis—4
DerStraten, Baron von—188
Destronde, J.—187
Dickinson, Adam—141
Dickinson, Charles C.—131, 133
Dickinson, Elizabeth Woolbridge—151
Dickinson, Folby Candler—151
Dickinson, Henry C.—132, 155
Dickinson, Colonel John—97, 121, 141-145, 147
Dickinson, John L.—133, 152, 155

Dickinson, John Quincy—132, 133, 155, 253
Dickinson, Joseph—145, 151
Dickinson, Margaret C. Gray—155
Dickinson, Mary Margaret D. Lewis—155
Dickinson, Pleasant—151
Dickinson, Mrs. Sally Lewis—205
Dickinson, Sally Jane Lewis—155
Dickinson, William—131, 132, 150-153, 157, 159
Dickinson, William, II—132, 153, 154, 155, 159
Dinwiddie, Governor—7
Doddridge, Joseph—235
Doddridge, Phillip—89, 234
Doddridge, Miss Margaretta—234
Doddridge, Sally Hansford—89
Donnally, Colonel Andrew, Sr.—21, 46, 50, 67, 69, 75, 191, 209, 210, 212, 213, 214, 220, 239
Donnally, Colonel Andrew, Jr.—50, 203, 205, 214, 215, 217
Donnally, Elizabeth—214
Donnally, Jane McCreery—209
Donnally, Lewis Fry—193
Donnally, Margaret Wood—205
Donnally, Margery Van Bibber—50, 215
Donnally, Miriam Welch—193
Donnally, Nancy—214
Donnally, William—205
Doyle, Ann Electa Putney—207
Doyle, Samuel—207
Draper, Mrs. John—118, 119
Drew, John—256
Droddy, William—47
Dryden, John—223
Dryden, Samuel—223
Dunbar, Judge—247
Dunbar, Matthew—220
Dunmore, Lord (Governor)—12, 51
Duvall, John P.—195

E

Early, Mrs. B. H.—79
Echols, General—255
Ellis, Richard, Jr.—207
Eskew, John Garnett—278
Eskew, Juliette Laidley—278
Ewell, Sarah Ball—244

F

Faure, Eliza W. Quarrier (Dryden)—223
Faure, John Francis—223
Fife, Thomas—226
Fitzhugh, Nicholas—199, 245

Foster, Mrs. James (Emma Doddridge)—234
Frazer, Mr. and Mrs. Herndon V.—84
Frazer, Roland C.—84
Friend, Thomas—229
Fry, Ann Jane Wilson—143
Fry, James H.—193
Fry, Judge Joseph L.—143
Fry, Julia Welch—193

G

Gallaher, D. C.—229
Gardner, Charles—160
Gardner, Mary Reynolds—160
Gardner, Newton—168, 169
Gillison, William—276
Glasscock, Governor William E.—255
Goshorn, George—217, 221
Graham, Edward—134, 136
Gramm, Lavinia Patrick—226
Gramm, Major William—226
Grant, Jesse R.—177
Grant, Captain Noah—176
Grant, Peter—177
Grant, General Ulysses S.—160, 177, 180, 181, 253
Grant, Mrs. Ulysses S.—253
Grey, Lord—237
Grosscup, Nan Nash—108

H

Hale, James—76
Hale, Dr. John P.—71, 72, 121
Hanna, Samuel—85
Hansford, Annie Noyes—89
Hansford, Felix G.—87-90
Hansford, Frazier—263
Hansford, James—89
Hansford, Jane Morris—86
Hansford, Major John—86, 87
Hansford, Louella Hamilton—89
Hansford, Dr. Marshall—90, 91
Hansford, Mary Parks—89
Hansford, Milton—89
Hansford, Morris—85
Hansford, Sarah Herndon Frazer—88
Harbeth, Lord—188
Harriman, John—75, 76, 220
Harriman, Nancy Morris—76
Harriman, Shadrack—33, 75
Harriman, Susanna Pryor—75, 76
Harris, F. G.—196
Harris, Lulu Oakes—196
Harrison, General—277

Harrison, President William H.—160
Harvey, Celia Morris—81
Harvey, Captain John—81
Harvey, Morris—81
Hayes, President Rutherford B.—241
Hedrick, "Camellia"—193, 194
Hedrick, Charles—193
Henderson, Sally Donnally—214
Henderson, Samuel—214
Henry, Patrick—210
Hensley, Cynthia Morris—25
Hensley, Samuel—25
Hensley, William—167
Hobson, Philadelphia Hansford—89
Hobson, William—89
Hogue, Andrew B.—205, 247
Holt, J. A. B.—91
Holt, Verna Veazey—91
Hopper, DeWolf—256
Houston, Samuel—106
Hubbard, Anastasia M.—194
Hubbard, Mrs. J. W.—263
Huddleston, Daniel—56, 98
Huddleston, Paddy—56, 97, 98
Hudson, Jesse—220
Huling, Bettie Wood—205
Huling, J. H.—205

I

Ingles, Thomas—121
Ingles, Mrs. William—118-121
Irwin, Mrs. R. F. (Clara F.)—268

J

Jackson, President Andrew—106, 188
Jefferies, Thomas E.—72
Jefferson, Joseph—256
Jefferson, Thomas—18, 210, 213, 239
Johnson, John—188
Johnston, Annie Virginia Laidley—278
Johnston, James E.—278
Jones, John—73, 74, 252

K

Kay, Mrs. John F.—234
Keenan, Patrick—167
Keith, Admiral—237
Kelly, Walter—16
Kenna, Edward—191
Kenna, Senator John S.—191
Kenna, Marjorie Lewis—191
Kenton, Simon—9-13, 51
King, Rufus—188

L

Lafayette, General—165, 170
Lafong, Cassandra Lovell—269
Laidley, Alexander T.—278
Laidley, Anna Beuhring—278
Laidley, Cora Bradford—278
Laidley, Frances Amelia—278
Laidley, Frances Smith—278
Laidley, Frederick Alexander—278
Laidley, George S.—278
Laidley, Harriet Quarrier—277
Laidley, James Grant—238, 277
Laidley, James John—278
Laidley, James Madison—238, 275, 277, 278, 280, 284
Laidley, John—283
Laidley, Josephine Wilson—278
Laidley, Julia Rook—278
Laidley, Madison Monroe—278
Laidley, Mary Byrd Fontaine—278
Laidley, Mary Rowena—278
Laidley, Richard Q.—247
Laidley, Thomas—277
Laidley, W. S.—199, 283
Laird, Dr. William—94
La Salle—2
Lee, Henry—35
Lee, General Robert E.—35, 242
Leftwich, General—277
Levi, Mordecai—72
Levi, Noyes Rand (Plus)—72
Lewis, General Andrew—12, 14, 17, 48, 74, 93, 121
Lewis, Ann Dickinson—155
Lewis, Betty Washington—272
Lewis, Colonel Charles—143
Lewis, Lieutenant Charles—143, 155
Lewis, Charles Cameron, Sr.—71, 143, 155
Lewis, Ellen Hackley Pollard—272
Lewis, Colonel Fielding—272
Lewis, Howell—272
Lewis, James A.—252, 274
Lewis, Jane Dickinson—142
Lewis, John D.—143, 155, 157
Lewis, Colonel Samuel—18, 212
Lewis, Thomas—47, 48, 70
Lightburn, General—112, 276
Lincoln, President Abraham—161
Littlepage, Adam—266
Littlepage, Adam B.—207, 265, 266, 267
Littlepage, Alexander—266
Littlepage, Eva Collett—268
Littlepage, Rebecca Todd Wood—266, 267
Littlepage, S. Collett—268
Littlepage, Samuel D.—266

Loring, General—112
Lovell, Alfred—269
Lovell, Betty Washington Lewis—272, 273, 277
Lovell, E. A. Beuhring—274
Lovell, Fayette A.—274
Lovell, Howell Lewis—273
Lovell, Joseph—125, 220, 226, 233, 269
Lovell, Colonel Joseph, Jr.—233, 269, 270, 272, 273, 274
Lovell, Joseph III—274
Lovell, Mary Patrick—226, 273
Lovell, Lady Mary Shapton (Bream)—233, 269, 270, 271, 272
Lovell, Richard Channing Moore—226, 273
Lovell, Sally Shrewsbury—274
Lovell, Sarah Nye—274

M

MacFarland, Anastine, 261
MacFarland, Dulce Chaddock—260
MacFarland, Henry Devol—253, 257, 258, 260
MacFarland, Henry Devol, Jr.—261
MacFarland, James C.—190, 220, 221, 222, 251, 257-260
MacFarland, Julia Cook—260
MacFarland, Lethe Reynolds—260
MacFarland, Lucy W. Greenhow—260
MacFarland, Mrs. Maria Broome—260
Madison, President James—239
Mandt, Mrs. William F.—110
Mann, Mrs. Moses—39
Marmet, Edwin—25
Marmet, William—25
Marshall, Chief Justice John—35, 205, 226, 239
Matics, Mrs. C. H.—77
Matthews, Thomas—220
McCausland, General—262
McClung, Augustus—108
McClung, Charles—47
McCreery, John—209
McCue, Rev. John—40
McElhenney, Rev.—197
McKee, Captain William—29, 210, 211
McKinley, President William—241
Meade, Bishop William—240, 273
Meigs, Mrs. John—70
Middleton, Bettie Hansford—89
Middleton, James—89
Milburn (Melburn), David—76, 220
Miller, Helen Quarrier—229
Miller, Samuel A.—229

Modjeska, Helena—256
Monroe, President James—239
Montgomery, Major Henry—78, 93, 94
Montgomery, James—93
Montgomery, Michael—94
Montgomery, Nancy Keeney—93
Moore, Andrew—245
Morris, Achilles (Carrol)—15
Morris, Ann Montgomery—94
Morris, Benjamin—15, 19, 79, 81, 82, 94
Morris, Carrol—252
Morris, Dickinson—74, 79, 83, 84, 85
Morris, Elizabeth—15
Morris, Fenton—76
Morris, Frances—15, 74
Morris, Hansford—85
Morris, Henry—15, 19, 81
Morris, James—79, 83
Morris, John—15, 16, 17, 19, 48, 69, 185, 186
Morris, Joshua—15, 19, 76
Morris, Leonard—15-19, 23, 24, 25, 47, 63, 69, 83, 212
Morris, Levi—15, 78, 79, 81, 82, 83, 94
Morris, Mary (Polly)—186
Morris, Nancy Jarrett—81
Morris, Sarah (Sally)—63
Morris, Sarah Hansford—76
Morris, Susan—79, 83
Morris, William, Sr.—14, 15, 16, 19-23, 69, 74, 76, 78, 81, 86, 182, 185, 186, 220
Morris, William, Jr.—15, 16, 18, 19, 22, 81, 126, 182, 252, 254

N

Nash, James H.—108
Nelson, Mrs. Jessie—150
Newport, Mary (Butler)—163-165
Newport, William—163
Newton, Thomas—159
North, Mrs. C. O.—117
Norton, Frances N. Putney—207
Norton, Moses—207
Noyes, Bradford—71, 125, 248, 249, 250, 252, 253, 258, 261, 262
Noyes, Charles—249
Noyes, Cynthia Morris—254
Noyes, Franklin—249
Noyes, Rev. James—248
Noyes, James—253
Noyes, Harriet Oden—261
Noyes, Isaac—71, 125, 248, 249, 250, 252, 253, 258, 261, 262
Noyes, Mary F.—261

O

Oakes, Allen—195
Oakes, Almira—196
Oakes, Drusilla Drown—195
Oakes, Ebenezer—195
Oakes, Ebenezer II—195, 196
Oakes, Ebenezer III—196
Oakes, Frances—196
Oakes, Ira—195
Oakes, James W.—195
Oakes, John C.—195
Oakes, Leonidas—195
Oakes, Lucy Parks Coleman—195, 196
Oakes, N. B.—196
Oakes, Thomas—195
Oakes, Willard L.—196
O'Keefe, Mrs. John—110
Osburn, Bishop—188
Owens, William—48

P

Parks, Andrew—89, 220
Patrick, Dr. Alfred S.—226
Patrick, George—226
Patrick, George H.—128
Patrick, Harvie—226
Patrick, Jacob—225
Patrick, James B.—226
Patrick, John—226
Patrick, Lavinia V. M. (Bream)—115, 225, 226, 269
Patrick, Sarah Spicer—225
Patrick, Dr. Spicer—115, 200, 205, 221, 225, 226, 227, 264, 267, 269, 272, 273, 276
Patrick, Susie—226
Patrick, Virginia Harvie—205, 226
Patrick, William—226
Patton, Ellen R. Tompkins—184
Patton, Captain George S.—244
Patton, General George S.—244
Patton, George Smith, Jr. (II)—245, 246, 247
Patton, Colonel Oliver A.—184
Patton, Susan Glasell—245
Pavlowa, Anna—256
Peelere, Felix—188
Perry, Lady Mary—142
Pointer, Dick—212, 213
Porter, Sarah Harvey—163
Preston, William—278
Price, William—27
Pryor, John—213
Pryor, William—75
Pryor, William II—76
Putney, Alethia Todd—206, 207
Putney, Alexander Moseley—207

Putney, Ann Ruffner—206, 207
Putney, David H.—207
Putney, Ellis—206
Putney, Mrs. Ellis—206
Putney, Dr. James—206
Putney, Julia Bedell—207
Putney, Lewis—207
Putney, Mary E. Reed—206
Putney, Rebecca Littlepage—207, 266
Putney, Dr. Richard Ellis—206, 207

Q

Quarrier, Alexander—220, 223, 229, 237-240, 249, 252, 277
Quarrier, Caroline Shrewsbury—229
Quarrier, Elizabeth—284
Quarrier, Elizabeth Dannenberry—238, 273, 277
Quarrier, Elizabeth Summers—284
Quarrier, James Y.—221
Quarrier, Joel—252
Quarrier, Lucy—284
Quarrier, Margaret Alexander—237
Quarrier, Russell G.—284
Quarrier, Sally Burns—239, 240
Quarrier, William A.—229

R

Radcliff, Stephen—125
Rand, Anne Norvell—255
Rand, Christopher—254
Rand, Ella Noyes—253, 254
Rand, Isaac Noyes—255
Rand, Jacob—254
Rand, Lucy Jackson—254
Rand, Nancy McArthur Pines—254
Rand, William—253, 254, 255, 262
Randolph, Edmund—36
Reed, Isaac—243, 245
Reese, Joel—11
Reynolds, Bettie Burns—160
Reynolds, Major John—125, 166, 168, 215, 222, 239, 260
Reynolds, Robert F.—159, 160
Reynolds, Van B.—220
Riggs, Emma Morris—79
Riggs, William—79
Robertson, Nancy Dickinson—151
Robinson, David—47
Robinson, Rev. Stuart—201
Rogers, Dr. Henry—115, 221, 233, 269
Rogers, Mrs. Henry—226, 233
Rogers, J. H.—234, 235
Rogers, James A.—235
Rogers, John, Jr.—149
Rogers, Leonora Lovell—115, 233, 269
Rogers, Nancy Shrewsbury—149
Rogers, William—47

Royall, Anne—129, 130, 161-175
Royall, Major William—165, 166, 167, 170, 173
Ruby, Bradford N.—261
Ruby, John—261
Ruby, John C. II—261, 262
Ruby, John C. III—261
Ruby, Madeline Tilly—261
Ruby, Mary Frances Noyes—261, 262
Ruffner, Abraham—100
Ruffner, Anastien W.—108
Ruffner, Andrew—107
Ruffner, Andrew L.—108
Ruffner, Anna Hedrick—107
Ruffner, Anne—101, 191
Ruffner, Anne Brumbach—100, 123
Ruffner, Anne Heistand—96
Ruffner, Augustus—107, 114, 115, 117
Ruffner, Benjamin Franklin—127
Ruffner, Catherine—107
Ruffner, Catherine Daggs—100
Ruffner, Colonel Charles—107, 125
Ruffner, Daniel—100, 101, 103, 106, 107, 110, 114, 125, 220
Ruffner, Daniel, Jr.—107
Ruffner, Colonel David—71, 100, 101, 102, 105, 122, 123, 125, 126, 127, 143, 191, 197, 199, 200, 201, 206, 220
Ruffner, David C.—107
Ruffner, Diana S. Mayre—107, 110
Ruffner, Eliza Hadassah—108
Ruffner, Elizabeth Painter—100, 106
Ruffner, Elizabeth Singleton—100, 106
Ruffner, Elizabeth V. Wilson—107
Ruffner, Ellen McFarland—107, 108
Ruffner, Esther—100
Ruffner, Dr. Henry—126, 172, 197, 198, 200, 272
Ruffner, Colonel Henry Daniel—115, 117, 226, 245
Ruffner, Isaac—127
Ruffner, James—107, 108
Ruffner, Colonel Joel—107, 110, 111, 114
Ruffner, Joseph—70, 71, 96-101, 103, 107, 110, 121, 122, 123, 137, 142
Ruffner, Joseph, Jr.—100, 101, 122, 123, 126
Ruffner, Leonard—125
Ruffner, General Lewis—123, 127, 157, 200, 220
Ruffner, Margaret—100
Ruffner, Martha Morton—107, 108
Ruffner, Martha Ross—100

Ruffner, Mary—108
Ruffner, Mary A. Jackson—107
Ruffner, Mary Elizabeth Rogers—107, 115
Ruffner, Mary Muzzleman—100
Ruffner, Mary Steinman—95
Ruffner, Meredith P.—108
Ruffner, Peter—95, 96
Ruffner, Sally Patrick—226
Ruffner, Samuel—100
Ruffner, Sarah Alethea Patrick—115
Ruffner, Silas R.—108, 127
Ruffner, Tobias—100, 101, 108, 122, 123, 127
Ruffner, Walter—107
Ruffner, William St. J. E.—107

S

Salley, John Peter—3
See, Michael—17
Shaw, George—33
Shawnessy, T. O.—188
Shepherd, Mr. and Mrs. Walton, Jr.—230
Shields, L. D.—188
Shrewsbury, Charles L.—149
Shrewsbury, Elizabeth (Betsy) Dabney—144
Shrewsbury, John, Sr.—125, 144, 145, 146, 149, 150, 154, 157
Shrewsbury, John, Jr.—147, 149
Shrewsbury, John D.—125, 150
Shrewsbury, Joel, Sr.—131, 132, 144, 145, 149, 150, 151, 153, 154, 156, 157, 159, 195, 220
Shrewsbury, Joel, Jr.—149
Shrewsbury, Laura Angela Parks—146
Shrewsbury, Martha Usher Dickinson—142
Shrewsbury, Mary Perry Dickinson—142, 149, 150
Shrewsbury, Rev. Nathan—144
Shrewsbury, Sally Dickinson—145, 151
Shrewsbury, Samuel, Sr.—125, 142, 144-147, 149, 150, 154, 156, 157, 159, 244
Shrewsbury, William—149, 154, 194, 224
Skinner, Otis—256
Slack, John—220
Slaughter, Elizabeth—25
Slaughter, Goodrich—193, 214, 215
Slaughter, Hannah—193
Slaughter, Mary Donnally (Polly)—25, 214
Slaughter, Reuben—25, 33, 47, 67, 214

Sloughton, J. E. M.—107
Sloughton, Virginia Ruffner—107
Smith, Amelia Welch—193
Smith, Benjamin H.—220
Smith, Colonel B. H.—254
Smith, John B.—193
Smith, John S. F.—89, 91
Smith, Martha Jane Hansford—89, 91
Smith, Mattie B.—91
Smith, Roxalana Noyes—254
Stalnaker, T. B.—235
Stanley, Mrs. I. J.—206
Starkes, John—220
Staton, James—220
Steele, John—47
Steele, Colonel Robert M.—226
Stephenson, George—240
Stipps, Elizabeth—15
Stockton, Aaron—91, 94, 125, 176, 185, 186
Stockton, Elizabeth Tompkins—186
Strader, George—10
Stratton, Edna Dickinson—151
Strickler, Abraham—95, 96
Strickler, Benjamin—96
Strickler, Jacob—96
Strother, Benjamin—47
Stuart, Colonel John—212
Summers, Amacetta Laidley—283
Summers, Anna Smith Radcliffe—280
Summers, George—280
Summers, George W., II—280-284
Summers, George III—283
Summers, George IV—283
Summers, Lewis—137, 138, 229, 280, 281, 284
Summers, Lewis II—283
Summers, Lewis III—283
Summers, Lucy A. Woodbridge—283
Swann, Thomas B.—253
Swann, Mrs. Thomas B.—180
Swinburn, Ralph—240

T

Tackett, Hannah—37
Tackett, Lewis—37, 67, 68
Tarleton, General—145
Taylor, Mrs. D. W.—76
Taylor, Phineas—47
Thayer, James—207
Thayer, Otis—241
Thayer, Susan Eve Putney—207
Thompson, William H.—188
Thornton, Lucy Jane—264
Thornton, Robert H.—264, 265
Tompkins, Beverly—184
Tompkins, Charles C.—184

319

Tompkins, Ellen Carr—183
Tompkins, Henry Preston—184, 187, 188
Tompkins, John Grant—184, 189
Tompkins, Rachel Maria Grant—176
Tompkins, (Brown), Virginia—181, 183
Tompkins, William—149, 176, 177, 179, 180, 181
Tompkins, Mrs. William, Jr.—179, 180, 181
Tompkins, Captain William H.—183, 184, 186
Traytree, G. F. J.—188
Trotter, Mary (Cooper)—44
Trotter, Richard—39
Trotter, William—39, 44
Truslow, John A.—71
Tucker, Captain John—244
Turner, John P.—220, 221

U

Upton, Thomas—59, 60, 62
Upton, Thomas, Jr.—60
Usher, William—142

V

Van Bibber, James—47, 48
Van Bibber, Captain John—47, 215
Van Bibber, Matthias—57
Veazey, Edward—92
Veazey, Eliza Stockton—91
Veazey, James A.—91
Veazey, Louis A.—92
Veazey, Marguerite Beirne—91
Veazey, Maude C. Perry—92
Veazey, Oscar A.—91
Veazey, Victor S.—91
Venable, Catherine Morris (Kitty)—185
Venable, Charles—185

W

Wade, Benjamin H.—188
Walker, Ezra—243
Walker, Dr. Thomas—6
Ward, Colonel—13
Washington, Booker T.—118, 200
Washington, George—7, 18, 19, 37, 46, 50, 89, 147, 161, 165, 235, 238, 244, 265, 272, 277
Washington, Dr. Lawrence Augustine—147
Washington, Mary Ball—244
Watkins, Francis—33, 47
Wayne, General Anthony—13
Welch, Alexander—66, 190

Welch, Camillia—193
Welch, Caroline Donnally Kenna—191
Welch, Catherine G. Slaughter—193
Welch, Cornelia H.—190
Welch, Eliza—190
Welch, George—190
Welch, George Lewis—190
Welch, James—190
Welch, John—190, 191
Welch, John S.—193
Welch, Julia McFarland—190
Welch, Levi—190-194, 220
Welch, Lolla V.—193
Whitteker, Aaron—221, 228, 249-252
Whitteker, Betsy Quarrier—249
Whitteker, Emma Louise Laidley—278
Whitteker, Henry—278
Whitteker, Leticia Morris—252
Whitteker, Levi—249
Whitteker, Norris S.—249, 251, 253, 258
Whitteker, Thomas—249
Whitteker, William—249-253, 258, 260
Wilcox, Luke—25, 26
Williams, Garner—27
Wilson, Elizabeth Ruffner—107
Wilson, Governor E. W.—229
Wilson, Colonel James—71, 123, 143
Wilson, Captain John—214, 220
Wilson, Katherine Donnally—214
Wilson, Nathaniel V.—107
Winkler, Mary Dickinson—155
Winthrop, Rev. Edward—188
Wise, General Henry A.—246, 267
Wood, Major Abraham—2
Wood, Ann Ruffner Reynolds—203, 205
Wood, Colonel Henry Hewett—203, 205
Wood, Dr. John—12
Wood, Rebecca Littlepage—207, 207
Wood, William—250
Wood(s), Eve Ruffner—100
Wood(s), Nehemiah—100
Wyatt, Mathew P.—85
Wythe, Chancellor George—239, 277

Y

Yeager, John—10, 11
Young, John—17, 48, 60, 62, 67, 68, 69, 76

www.ingramcontent.com/pod-product-compliance
Lightning Source LLC
Chambersburg PA
CBHW071950220426
43662CB00009B/1069